MW01596283

PERFORMANCE-DRIVEN IT MANAGEMENT
Five Practical Steps to Business Success

Ira S. Sachs

GOVERNMENT INSTITUTES

An imprint of
THE SCARECROW PRESS, INC.
Lanham • Toronto • Plymouth, UK
2011

Government Institutes

Published by Government Institutes
An imprint of The Scarecrow Press, Inc.
A wholly owned subsidary of The Rowman & Littlefield Publishing Group, Inc.
4501 Forbes Boulevard, Suite 200, Lanham, Maryland 20706
http://www.govinstpress.com

Estover Road, Plymouth PL6 7PY, United Kingdom

Contents

Figures and Tables

Figures

Tables

Note to the Reader

THIS BOOK INCLUDES SELECTIVE TEXT and illustrative materials published by a wide range of federal agencies and other organizations. These materials are in the public domain, but accreditation has been given in the text and in the reference section. I contributed to a number of these documents.

Introduction

Why This Book Is Needed

There is no such thing as an IT project in isolation from its business change program. (*Getting IT Right for Government*, Intellect, June 2000)

- Despite organizations implementing numerous best practices, information technology (IT) implementations remain risky and can often have questionable business value propositions.
- An improved IT management approach is needed based on understanding and maintaining the business value proposition from concept through to implementation.

LARGE IT PROGRAMS are inevitably fraught with risks that often result in cost and schedule overruns, lack of functionality, less-than-envisioned business impact, and—at times—outright program failure. These results have plagued large IT acquisitions and modernization programs for decades despite the use of more structured acquisition processes, advanced program and project management techniques (such as earned value analysis), process improvement programs (such as Capability Maturity Model Integration [CMMI]), and advances in the technology underlying systems development. On a separate track, many large public-sector organizations have initiated enterprise architecture (EA) and performance management programs. Unfortunately, however, these EA-related initiatives have had little impact beyond meeting statutory requirements.

Clearly, these approaches are not adequately mitigating program risk, and a fresh approach is needed. This book proposes a new integrated approach to program and project management called performance-driven management (PDM). This approach has two key elements. First, it focuses on developing a strategically aligned business case and IT architecture that supports the desired business-performance outcomes. Second, it uses this business case and validation of this business case to manage system implementation and benefits realization. For example, if a key business outcome is to support business activities that require 24-7 system usage, then system availability and redundancy are identified as critical elements for achieving this outcome. In response, architecture is developed to enable highly reliable, 24-7 availability. Then, systems producing this business outcome are designed, developed, and implemented and performance improvements measured and verified.

This book will demonstrate how PDM can reduce IT program risk by increasing the likelihood that systems will deliver the desired business outcomes. Unlike more traditional methods—which often lose sight of the program goals (the "forest") within the complexity of detailed requirements, design, and testing (the "trees")—this approach provides a crucial connection between business outcomes, systems development, and benefits realization. It can help keep IT investments bounded and can help identify risks early in a project when mitigating actions are cheaper and easier to implement. In addition, this book will describe—in practical terms—how these two key elements and their supporting methodologies can be integrated with program and project management for rapid results.

The Current State of IT Investments and Organizational Challenges

Many best practices in IT have been implemented in recent years, with minimal results in terms of reducing project risk. These include:

- Enterprise Architecture (EA)—can guide and constrain IT projects to optimize enterprise value.
- Earned Value Management (EVM)—is an integrated management control system for assessing, understanding, and quantifying what a contractor or field activity is achieving with program dollars. It can identify when projects are overrunning cost and schedule.
- IT Dashboards—highlight current project issues but are not proactive.
- Capability Maturity Model Integration (CMMI)—can improve process discipline but cannot fix a poorly conceived project.

02OR- C- 5-21

Performance Driven IT Management:
Sku: 4KVIIL000FIE

LikeNew

Ship To
Jennifer Roberts
5630 Huckleberry Dr
Bryantown, MD 20617

Order Details
Order ID	111-6679455-1694657
Order Date	3/16/2016 7:16:05 PM
Shipping Service	Standard
Buyers Name	Jennifer Roberts

Madison Book Sellers strives to have e
and every customer 100% satisfied wi
their purchase. If for any reason you a
not 100% satisfied please email us a
mlyons@rowman.com with your
concerns.

If we need to make something right, \
will, Guaranteed!

- Asset Management—provides data on current IT hardware and software—"as is" architecture—at a detailed level.
- Service-Oriented Architecture (SOA)—can hide the complexity of a project, and it is challenging to implement at the enterprise level.
- Agile Development—provides flexibility for unknown or changing requirements and generally applies only to the development phase. It has to be carefully managed.

Despite adopting these practices, IT implementations remain risky and often have questionable business value propositions before the project even starts. The bottom line is that many of these approaches do not give project managers the tools needed, and it is easy to veer off course. That is why a new approach is needed and why PDM can be the answer.

Both the government's and the private sector's records on effective investments and oversight over the last decade have hardly been stellar. However, the problems are particularly evident in the federal government, where projects are large and complex, which is why these projects are the focus of this book.

High Failure Rate of IT Projects

IT Projects are generally high risk, as much of delivery is intangible, difficult to specify; therefore, it is difficult to ensure that a given investment will deliver the desired business results.

While all IT projects have risks, the purpose of the PDM approach is to proactively identify them in order to resolve them to ensure project success. Major risks, which can often lead to failure, come from many quarters and include:

- Lack of executive support
- Lack of user involvement
- Lack of clear business objectives and business outcomes
- Lack of proven technologies
- Lack of experienced project managers
- Lack of focus—looking at too broad a picture rather than focusing on essentials

Over the years, there have been some stunning IT project failures. In the 1990s, the Federal Aviation Administration (FAA) set up a development team to work on replacing the air traffic control system. They came up with the

Advanced Automation System—six years late—and were still trying to iron out the many bugs ten years later. Eventually, the software was considered too unreliable. The project failed because the people working on it did not have the right skill sets, and the project management did not have the right expertise and investment-related focus on desired business outcomes to lead them.

IT Project Studies

Many reports that have reviewed major IT projects around the world have come to similar conclusions regarding the high risk of IT projects. Some of these are referenced below to show the scale of the problem. The alarming thing is that little has changed, and in many cases, the same mistakes are still being made.

CHAOS Report

In 1986, Alfred Spector, president of Transarc Corporation, coauthored a paper comparing bridge building to software development. The premise: bridges are normally built on time, on budget, and do not fall down. On the other hand, software never comes in on time or on budget. In addition, it always breaks down. (Nevertheless, bridge building did not always have such a stellar record. Many bridge-building projects overshot their estimates, time frames, and some even fell down.)

One of the biggest reasons bridges come in on time, on budget, and do not fall down is the extreme detail of design. The design is frozen, and the contractor has little flexibility in changing the specifications. Therefore, a more flexible model must be used. This could be and has been used as a rationale for development failure.

But there is another difference between software failures and bridge failures, besides 3,000 years of experience. When a bridge falls down, it is investigated, and a report is written on the cause of the failure. This is not so in the computer industry, where failures are covered up, ignored, and/or rationalized. As a result, we keep making the same mistakes over and over again.

It was on this premise that the Standish Group compiled the *CHAOS Report* in 1995 to find out the main reasons why many IT projects were flawed and failed. The *CHAOS Report* found that the main reasons that projects were impaired and ultimately cancelled was because of:

- Incomplete requirements
- Lack of user involvement

The report was based on a survey of 365 IT managers from companies of various sizes and in various economic sectors. Other reasons for failure included:

- Lack of resources
- Unrealistic expectations
- Lack of executive support
- Changing requirements and specifications
- Lack of planning
- Didn't need it any longer
- Lack of IT management
- Technology illiteracy

> Note: Unrealistic expectations are one of the major reasons for project failure and why our new approach is needed. It is essential to understand not only the benefits that will be achieved but also how they will be realized in advance.

According to their survey, only 28,000 application development projects met the criteria for success—completed on time, on budget, and with all features and functions originally specified.

In *Extreme CHAOS 2001*, the Standish Group found that researchers and project managers are learning how to become more successful at IT project management. Results showed that 78,000 U.S. projects were successful—28 percent of all those surveyed. However, 23 percent failed, and 49 percent were "challenged." Standish categorizes projects into three resolution types:

- Successful: The project is completed on time and on budget, with all features and functions originally specified.
- Challenged: The project is completed and operational, but over budget, late, and with fewer features and functions than initially specified.
- Failed: The project is canceled before completion or never implemented.

The reasons for the increase in successful projects varied. The average cost of a project had been more than cut in half. Better tools had been created to monitor and control progress, and more highly skilled project managers were using improved management processes. The fact that there were processes was significant in itself.

The original CHAOS study identified 10 success factors. Standish updated the CHAOS 10 for 2000. Although no project required all 10 factors to be successful, the more factors present in the project strategy, the higher the confidence level.

TABLE I.1
Recipe for Success: CHAOS 10

Confidence Level	Success Factors
Executive support	18
User involvement	16
Experienced project manager	14
Clear business objectives	12
Minimized scope	10
Standard software infrastructure	8
Firm basic requirements	6
Formal methodology	6
Reliable estimates	5
Other criteria	5

Each factor has been weighted according to its influence on project success—the more points, the lower the project risk.

1. Executive support: Traditionally, executive support occupied the number 2 spot; however, it is now the number 1 factor in project failure. Executive support influences a project's process and progress. Lack of executive input can jeopardize a project.
2. User involvement: Lack of user involvement traditionally has been the number 1 reason for project failure. Conversely, it has been the leading contributor to project success. Even when delivered on time and on budget, a project can fail if it doesn't meet user needs or expectations. However, this year, user involvement has moved to the number 2 position. Despite how that may sound, user involvement hasn't decreased in importance; it's just that IT professionals have, in effect, solved this major problem.

> Note: Executive support and user involvement are critical. Without them, you can only guess at what is needed. If you have executive support and user involvement—and you must—you will know exactly what has to be done and why. The benefits will be clearly defined and understood and can be managed at every stage of project implementation.

3. Experienced project manager: 97 percent of successful projects have an experienced project manager at the helm.
4. Clear business objectives: Although there is clear evidence that experienced project managers increase success rates, the lack of clear business

objectives is still a main reason for project failure and the primary reason for writing this book.

> Note: Without clear business objectives, it is difficult to obtain executive support, user involvement, minimized scope, firm basic requirements, and reliable estimates (numbers 1, 2, 5, 7, and 9 in this list). This vividly illustrates how important having clear business objectives is and how dependent it is on all the other factors in this list and vice versa. The project can only succeed if there are clear business objectives from the outset. Once these have been determined and agreed upon, the project manager can ensure they are always kept in sharp focus. Achieving business objectives must always be one of the strongest drivers throughout implementation.

5. Minimized scope: Wrapping up the top five is minimized scope. Time is the enemy of all projects, and since scope affects time, or project duration, they are linked. Clearly then, minimizing scope increases a project's chances of success. Minimized scope has replaced small milestones. While these two factors are similar, the act of minimizing scope leads to greater success than does creating small milestones. Concentrating on the top five will result in 70 success points.

6. Standard software infrastructure: Requirements are in a state of constant flux, but infrastructure needs stability. The Standish Group's research shows that 70 percent of application code is infrastructure. Some of this code is unique to the application; nonetheless, much of this code could be purchased from an infrastructure vendor.

   By using standard infrastructure, the application development team can concentrate on business rules rather than on technology. Many application development projects fail not in stand-alone application development but in existing application integration. Standard infrastructures can shortcut application integration.

7. Firm basic requirements: The word "basic" refers to base-level requirements. Creating minimal, obtainable base requirements and then developing those features will reduce the effect of change. Delivering minimal features allows users and executive sponsors to see quick results. As a result, project managers are better prepared to articulate the needs and priorities of the next project phase.

> Note: If the business benefits are clearly understood, there is a higher likelihood that the project requirements will be better specified.

8. Formal methodology: This provides a realistic picture of the project and resources committed to it. And it results in steps and procedures the team can reproduce and reuse. It also enables the team to maximize consistency. Formal methodology incorporates lessons learned into active projects. The process encourages "go" or "no go" decision checkpoints. It also helps the project team proceed with a higher level of confidence or halt or alter steps to fit changing requirements. CHAOS research shows that 46 percent of successful projects use a formal project management methodology, compared with 30 percent of challenged and failed projects. So this factor should increase success rates by about 16 percent.

9. Reliable estimates: Systematic project estimating must be approached realistically because estimating is difficult, and there are organizational pressures to reduce estimates to fit tight budgets. Then, add to that the complexity of redeveloping, purchasing, and integrating components into existing and packaged applications and outside services. IT managers must use all their collective knowledge and experience to come up with estimates that reflect the true effort required and stand by them during organizational reviews.

    Recognizing this challenge, the Government Accountability Office (GAO) has developed a detailed cost estimating guide (GAO-09-3SP). According to the GAO, the ability to generate reliable cost estimates is a critical function, necessary to support the Office of Management and Budget's (OMB) capital programming process. Without this ability, agencies are at risk of experiencing cost overruns, missed deadlines, and performance shortfalls—all recurring problems that our program assessments too often reveal. Furthermore, cost increases often mean that the government cannot fund as many programs as intended or deliver them when promised.

10. Other criteria: In last place is a collection of other factors. These factors include small milestones, proper planning, competent staff, and ownership. In the past, each of these factors was given its own category.

The CHAOS 10 success factors continue to be valuable for assessing project potential. While nothing can guarantee project success, adhering to the CHAOS 10 will increase your odds of putting together a winning project.

The OASIG Study (1995)

The study was undertaken by members of OASIG, a U.K. government Department of Trade and Industry (DTI)–supported special interest group (SIG) concerned with the organizational aspects of IT.

Substantial interviews were conducted with 45 leading researchers and consultants in the United Kingdom. Collectively these "experts" drew on over 900 years of professional work in this field and on findings from a total sample of approximately 14,000 user organizations. Between them, these experts have researched and consulted in all the major sectors of U.K. economic activity, working with a wide array of users and suppliers and with all forms of IT. The main reasons why systems fail to meet their objectives are:

- Lack of attention to the human and organizational aspects of IT
- Poor project management
- Poor articulation of user requirements
- Inadequate attention to business needs and goals
- Failure to involve users appropriately

In general, IT failures are rarely considered as purely technical. The integration and mutual influence of organization and IT is emphasized throughout the OASIG study.

In May 2007, the chief information officer of the U.K. Department for Works and Pensions reported that 7 in 10 government IT projects in the United Kingdom had failed.

Speaking at a government IT summit, Joe Harley said, "Today, only 30 percent of government IT projects and programs are successful. We want 90 percent by 2010/2011. We want to achieve a 20 percent overall reduction on IT spend in government, including reducing the total cost of a government laptop by 40 percent in the same timescale."

"The criteria for success of a project included whether it was delivered on time, to cost, and to the quality promised," Harley said. While private-sector IT projects had a similar failure rate, government IT projects needed to be more efficient both in terms of cost and delivery.

"The government spends £14 billion ($20 billion) per year on IT in the United Kingdom. It's not sustainable as a government to continue to spend at these levels. We need to up the quality while reducing the spend," Harley added.

The Bull Survey

In 1998, the French computer manufacturer and systems integrator, Bull, requested an independent research company, Spikes Cavell, to conduct a survey in the United Kingdom to identify the major causes of IT project failure in the finance sector.

A total of 203 telephone interviews were conducted with IT and project managers from the finance, utilities, manufacturing, business services, telecoms, and

IT service sectors in the United Kingdom. All the managers interviewed had previously taken the lead in integrating large systems within organizations in the *Times* Best 100 Companies. The main success criteria identified were:

- Meeting milestones (51 percent)
- Maintaining the required quality levels (32 percent)
- Meeting the budget (31 percent)

The survey revealed that the major causes of project failure during the life cycle of the project are a breakdown in communications (57 percent), a lack of planning (39 percent), and poor quality control (35 percent).

> Note: Lack of planning includes lack of a well-defined business case and benefits realization plan, which are emphasized as key elements of success in the PDM approach.

The KPMG Canada Survey (1997)

In April 1997, KPMG Canada sent a survey questionnaire focusing on IT project-management issues to Canada's leading 1,450 public- and private-sector organizations. The main purpose was to outline the reasons behind the failure of IT projects. The main causes of project failure that were identified were:

- Poor project planning: Specifically, inadequate risk management and a weak project plan. Risk management becomes more important as the organization gets bigger, so larger organizations need to pay more attention to this area.
- Weak business case: The need for the system should be justified in ways that relate directly to the organization's business needs.

> Note: A strong business case is the cornerstone of the PDM approach.

- Lack of top management involvement and support: This often dooms the project to failure before it starts. Securing buy-in from the top, often by a strong business case backed up with a realistic project plan, is an essential step.

Additional findings were:

- Projects fail more often because of schedule overruns than budget overruns.
- Many projects fail because they use new or unproven technology.
- Poor estimates or weak definitions of requirements at the project-planning stage also contribute to project failure.
- Projects can run into trouble due to the vendors' inabilities to meet commitments.
- Sixty percent of the failed projects were planned to take less than one year to complete.

The following section describes specific projects that have faced the challenges described in the studies above.

Case Studies

The Farm Program Modernization (MIDAS)

According to a 2008 GAO report (GAO-08-657), the U.S. Department of Agriculture (USDA) has experienced significant problems with its IT systems that support the delivery of benefits programs to farmers. In October 2006, these systems began experiencing considerable delays while attempting to process a large number of transactions, and by January 2007, the systems became inoperable for one month. In response to these issues, the USDA developed a near-term stabilization plan and long-term plans to modernize its delivery of these programs.

The USDA's near-term plan to stabilize the agency's farm program delivery systems focused on technical issues, such as expanding telecommunication capacity and acquiring a means for disaster backup and recovery; however, it did not address key managerial issues, such as the department's inconsistent tracking of users' reported problems with the system. Additionally, the USDA did not have system performance goals or dedicated staff to analyze and use system performance data, and the stabilization plan did not address these issues. Moreover, the plan did not clearly define the roles and responsibilities for the organizations involved in the stabilization effort in order to ensure proper accountability. While department officials indicated that they planned to address system performance management issues in a future version of the stabilization plan, they did not yet have plans to enable the USDA to consistently track users' reported problems and to clarify roles and responsibilities. As a result, the USDA could not be assured that its stabilization efforts would enable the department to reliably deliver farm benefit programs to its customers. Regarding the USDA's proposed long-term investment known as

MIDAS—Modernize and Innovate the Delivery of Agricultural Systems—officials had plans under way to obtain the necessary information for assessing the capability of products to integrate existing systems. However, business requirements were not used as a basis for the department's life-cycle cost estimate of $455 million for the modernization initiative. Instead, the estimate was based primarily on the cost estimate for another unrelated USDA IT investment. Similarly, the department had not adequately assessed its schedule estimate. According to department officials, they committed to accelerating the implementation of MIDAS from 10 years to 2 years in order to more quickly deliver a long-term solution to problems the department is experiencing with its existing program's delivery systems. However, business requirements were not considered when developing this schedule estimate. As a result, it was uncertain whether the department would be able to deliver the modernization initiative within the cost and schedule time frames it had proposed.

Field Data Collection Automation (FDCA)

The FDCA program is intended to provide automation support for the 2010 Census field data collection operations. The program includes the development of handheld computers for identifying and correcting addresses for all known living quarters in the United States (known as address canvassing) and the systems, equipment, and infrastructure that field staff will use to collect data. The FDCA handheld computers were originally to be used for other census field operations, such as following up with nonrespondents through personal interviews. However, in April 2008, due to problems identified during testing and cost overruns and schedule slippages in the FDCA program, the secretary of commerce announced a redesign of the 2010 Census, and rebaselined FDCA in October 2008. As a result, FDCA's life-cycle costs have increased from an estimated $596 million to $801 million, a $205 million increase. Furthermore, the responsibility for the design, development, and testing of IT systems for other key field operations was moved from the FDCA contractor to the Census Bureau.

The Integrated Deepwater System

This is a 25-year, $24 billion major acquisition program to recapitalize the U.S. Coast Guard's aging fleet of boats, airplanes, and helicopters, ensuring that all work together through a modern, capable communications system. This initiative is designed to enhance maritime domain awareness and enable the Coast Guard to meet its post–September 11 mission requirements. The program is composed of 15 major acquisition projects, including the Common Operational Picture (COP) program.

Deepwater COP is to provide relevant, real-time operational intelligence and surveillance data to human capital managers, allowing them to direct and monitor all assigned forces and first responders. This is expected to allow commanders to distribute critical information to federal, state, and local agencies quickly, reduce duplication, enable earlier alerting, and enhance maritime awareness.

The program's master schedule contained weaknesses, such as a large number of concurrent tasks and activities without resources assigned. Officials were aware of some, but not all, of the weaknesses in the schedule and had controls in place to mitigate the weakness they were aware of.

The Veterans Health Information Systems and Technology Architecture– Foundations Modernization (VistA-FM)

The program addresses the need to transition the Veterans Affairs electronic medical record system to a new architecture. According to the department, the current system is costly and difficult to maintain and does not integrate well with newer software packages. VistA-FM is designed to provide a new architectural framework as well as additional standardization and common services components. This is intended to eliminate redundancies in coding and support interoperability among applications. Ultimately, the new architecture will lay the foundation for a new generation of computer systems in support of caring for America's veterans. During the course of review, the department's chief information officer suspended multiple components of the VistA-FM program until a new development plan could be put in place. This action was taken as part of a new department-wide initiative to identify troubled IT projects and improve their execution.

Federal Bureau of Investigation's Trilogy Project

For several years, the FBI's IT systems were considered archaic and inadequate for efficiently and effectively investigating criminal and other cases. Initiated in mid-2001, Trilogy—the FBI's largest IT upgrade to date—was intended to modernize the FBI's IT infrastructure and systems and provide needed applications to help FBI agents, analysts, and others do their jobs. The Trilogy project consisted of two primary efforts—upgrades to the FBI's IT infrastructure and development of an investigative application system to more efficiently access case files, which became known as the Virtual Case File (VCF) system.

> Note: The development of an investigative application system was the key benefit to be realized, and, as you can see below, because of poorly defined and slowly evolving design requirements, which became the drivers for this project, this key benefit was not achieved through Trilogy. However, had the process described in this book been followed using enterprise architecture along with an understanding of a benefits realization plan, that objective could more likely have been realized.

The FBI entered into an interagency agreement with the General Services Administration (GSA), which served as the contracting agency to acquire the services of two primary contractors to carry out the Trilogy project. Dyn-Corp—now Computer Services Corporation (CSC)—was responsible for the IT infrastructure upgrade, while Science Applications International Corporation (SAIC) was responsible for development of the VCF system. In addition, the FBI contracted with Mitretek to assist in the administration and oversight of the project.

Although the original scheduled completion date for the overall Trilogy project was June 2004, after September 11, 2001, the FBI instituted an accelerated deployment plan. The targeted completion date for the portion of Trilogy related to the FBI's IT infrastructure was accelerated from May 2004 to July 2002. However, after several delays, the upgrade was completed in April 2004, only a month before the "preaccelerated" due date.

While the scheduled completion date for the VCF system was originally June 2004, the due date for the first VCF deliverable was accelerated to December 2003. However, in July 2004, the VCF portion of the Trilogy project was scaled back after the completion of the first phase of the project was determined to be infeasible and cost prohibitive as originally envisioned. The scaled-back VCF effort was recast as a pilot that ended in March 2005 and was to be used by the FBI to help develop requirements for a successor information-management system initiative, referred to as Sentinel. The overall cost of the Trilogy project, originally estimated at approximately $380 million, ultimately escalated to approximately $537 million.

The Department of Justice Office of Inspector General has reported on numerous issues that contributed to the cost increases and delays, including poorly defined and slowly evolving design requirements, contracting weaknesses, unrealistic task scheduling, and lack of management continuity and oversight for tracking and overseeing costs effectively

GAO Assessment on Trilogy

The GAO earlier reported on weaknesses in the FBI's IT systems development and management capabilities, including contractor oversight. The

FBI's review and approval process for Trilogy contractor invoices, which was carried out by a review team consisting of officials from the FBI, the GSA, and Mitretek, did not provide an adequate basis for verifying that goods and services billed were actually received by the FBI or that payments were for allowable costs. This occurred in part because responsibility for the review and approval of invoices was not clearly defined or documented. In addition, contractor invoices frequently lacked detailed information required by the contracts and other additional information that would be needed to facilitate an adequate review process. Despite this, invoices were paid without requesting additional supporting documentation necessary to determine the validity of the charges. These weaknesses in the review and approval process made the FBI highly vulnerable to payment of unallowable or questionable contractor costs.

> Note: While invoice review is an important part of the accounting and oversight process, it is not a major focus of this book—which is the need to focus on and implement functionality and realize benefits.

The FBI's Trilogy IT project spanned four years, and the reported costs exceeded $500 million. The GAO review disclosed that there were serious internal control weaknesses in the process used by the FBI and the GSA to approve contractor charges related to Trilogy, which made up the majority of the total reported project cost. While the review focused specifically on the Trilogy program, the significance of the issues identified during our (GOA's) review may indicate more systemic contract and financial management problems at the FBI and the GSA, in particular when using cost-reimbursable-type contracts and interagency contracting vehicles. These weaknesses resulted in the payment of millions of dollars of questionable contractor costs, which may have unnecessarily increased the overall cost of the project.

U.S. Federal Government—Overall Assessment

In testimony before the Senate Subcommittee on Federal Financial Management, Government Information, Federal Services, and International Security (part of the Senate Committee on Homeland Security and Governmental Affairs), on April 28, 2009, the GAO said management and oversight of projects totaling billions of dollars needed more attention.

David A. Powner, director of information technology management issues at the GAO, said billions of taxpayer dollars are spent on federal IT projects each year. Given the size of these investments and their significance to the health, economy, and security of the nation, it is important that the OMB and federal agencies are providing adequate oversight and ensuring transparency of these programs. Appropriate oversight and transparency will help ensure that programs are delivered on time, within budget, and with the promised capabilities.

The OMB has made progress implementing several initiatives aimed at improving oversight and transparency of federal IT investments, and more initiatives are planned but as the GAO previously reported and recommended, more attention needs to be placed on improving these initiatives. For example, the OMB's management watch list identified poorly planned projects, and the office also identified and listed high-risk projects failing to meet one of four performance evaluation criteria. The OMB took steps to improve the identification of the poorly planned and performing projects by, for example, issuing a central list of management watch list projects and publicly disclosing these projects' deficiencies. With regard to the high-risk list, the OMB clarified the project criteria and started publicly releasing aggregate lists of high-risk projects on its website in September 2006. However, more needs to be done by both the OMB and the agencies to address recommendations the GAO has previously made, such as identifying and publicizing performance shortfalls on high-risk projects. Additionally, the future of the management watch list and high-risk list is uncertain because OMB officials stated that they have not decided if the agency plans to continue to use these lists.

As another step aimed at increasing oversight of agencies' IT investments, the OMB required agencies to provide investment justifications for major IT projects to demonstrate both to agency management and to the OMB that the projects are well planned. However, the GAO raised concerns about the accuracy and reliability of the information agencies used to comply with this requirement and recommended changes to the reporting process. In response, the OMB required agencies to disclose weaknesses in their information. The OMB also required the use of EVM, an approach to project management that can provide insight into project status, warning of schedule delays and cost overruns, and unbiased estimates of total costs.

However, the GAO identified weaknesses in agencies' use of this management tool. For example, the FAA was using EVM to manage IT acquisition programs, but not all programs ensured that their earned value data were reliable. The GAO made a number of recommendations to federal agencies to clarify and expand their EVM policies and strengthen their oversight processes at the program level. Until agencies expand and enforce their EVM policies, it will be difficult for them to optimize the effectiveness of this management tool.

Building on successes and looking for more efficient and comprehensive ways to bolster oversight and transparency of the federal IT budget will help ensure that federal IT dollars are wisely spent and agency mission performance is enhanced. Accordingly, the OMB needs to decide if it is going to continue to use its management watch list and high-risk list, or similar tools. If the OMB decides not to use these tools, it should promptly implement other appropriate mechanisms to help oversee IT investments.

Over the past four years, the OMB testified on hundreds of projects, totaling billions of dollars, that they had placed on the management watch list. For example, in 2008, the OMB determined that 352 projects—totaling about $23.4 billion—were poorly planned. According to the OMB's evaluation of the Exhibit 300s, investments were placed on the watch list primarily because of weaknesses in the way they addressed (1) cost, schedule, and performance; (2) security; (3) privacy; and (4) acquisition strategy.

In their analysis of the high-risk projects in June 2008, they found that of the 472 IT projects that were categorized as high risk, at least 87 had performance shortfalls—collectively totaling about $4.8 billion in funding requested for fiscal year 2009. Agencies reported cost and schedule variances that exceeded 10 percent as the most common shortfall.

To improve the identification and oversight of the high-risk projects, the OMB recommended, among other things, that a structured, consistent process be established to update the list of high-risk projects on a regular basis, including identifying new projects and removing previous ones to ensure that the list is current and complete. The OMB also recommended that a single aggregate list of high-risk projects and their deficiencies be developed and used to report to Congress the progress made in correcting high-risk problems, actions under way, and further actions that may be needed.

As another step aimed at increasing oversight of agencies' IT investments, the OMB—in response to the Clinger-Cohen Act and other statutes—required agencies to prepare investment justifications for major IT projects, referred to as the Exhibit 300. The Exhibit 300 is a reporting mechanism intended to enable an agency to demonstrate to its own management, as well as to the OMB, that a major project is well planned in that it has employed the disciplines of good project management, developed a strong business case for the investment, and met other administration priorities in defining the cost, schedule, and performance goals proposed for the investment.

> Note: The importance of developing a strong business case and performance goals have been stressed by the OMB and are consistent with our PDM approach.

TABLE I.2
Risk Elements—Construction versus IT Projects

Risk Element	Construction Project	IT Project
Scope	Explicitly defined by architectural drawings and specifications, late significant changes unlikely	Defined by requirements that can be unclear, incomplete, and late significant changes often occur.
Cost	Cost estimates based on historical experience, high level of precision in estimate accuracy	Cost estimates challenging since all projects are different and estimating based on common criteria (i.e., function points) is not generally done. Low level of precision in estimate accuracy.
Schedule	Schedule estimates based on historical experience, high level of precision in estimate accuracy	Scheduling estimates challenging since all projects are different and estimating based on common criteria is not generally done. Low level of precision in estimate accuracy.
Functionality	Clearly defined by architectural drawings, generally understood by project workforce and customers	Defined by requirements and use cases (generally not in business case where it should be), subject to variation in interpretation, not always clearly understood by project workforce.

IT projects are inherently more complex than other types of projects because the results are often, to some degree, intangible. Benefits are often difficult to measure and quantify, as opposed to, say, a construction project. Construction projects have been done for thousands of years (vs. about 50 years for IT projects), and the techniques and results are well known to both the builders and customers. Table I. 2 describes these differences.

Guidance and Legislation to Date

This section traces the legislation and regulations that have been introduced over the last several decades to address IT project issues. In many ways, the history of federal IT projects over the last 20 years has been like that of a patient in hospital. Sometimes, by adapting the new regulations and introducing changes, the patient has made significant improvements, sometimes the patient has actually gotten worse, and in extreme cases, the patient has died. Very rarely, has the patient completely recovered. Various "attempted cures" are listed in this section—most of which highlight an ailing patient desperately in need of help.

Chief Financial Officer and Federal Financial Reform Act of 1990

The Chief Financial Officer and Federal Financial Reform Act of 1990, or CFO Act, signed into law by President George H. W. Bush on November 15, 1990, is a United States federal law intended to improve the government's financial management, outlining standards of financial performance and disclosure. Among other measures, the OMB was given greater authority over federal financial management. For each of 24 federal departments and agencies, the position of chief financial officer was created. In accordance with the CFO Act, each agency or department vests its financial management functions in its chief financial officer. This was one of the first acts to begin to recognize the need for performance measures—specifically for financial results.

Government Performance and Results Act (GPRA)

The act is a public bipartisan law passed by Congress in 1993 (Public Law 103-62) to improve stewardship in the federal government by linking resources and management decisions with program performance. The law requires federal programs to do the following:

- Develop strategic plans that specify what will be accomplished over a three- to five-year period
- Annually set performance targets related to the strategic plan
- Annually report the degree to which the targets set in the previous year were met
- Regularly conduct evaluations of programs and use those results to explain successes and failures based on performance data

The GPRA is one of a series of laws designed to improve government management. It requires agencies to engage in management tasks such as setting goals, measuring results, and reporting progress. In order to comply with the GPRA, agencies produce strategic and performance plans and conduct gap analyses of projects. Agencies are required to develop five-year strategic plans, which must contain a mission statement for the agency, and long-term, results-oriented goals covering each of the agencies' major functions. Agencies are required to prepare annual performance plans that establish the performance goals for the applicable fiscal year, a description of how these goals are to be met, and a description of how these performance goals can be verified. Finally, agencies must prepare annual performance reports that review the agency's success or failure in meeting its targeted performance goals.

The National Performance Review (NPR), of March 1993, defined strategic planning as "a continuous and systematic process where the guiding members of an organization make decisions about its future, develop the necessary procedures and operations to achieve that future, and determine how success is to be measured." One of the benefits of strategic planning, as established in the tenets of the GPRA, is that it can be an opportunity to unify the management, employees, stakeholders, and customers through a common understanding of where the organization is going, how everyone involved can work to that common purpose, and how progress and levels of success will be measured.

For many successful organizations, the "voice of the customer" drives operations and charts the course for the future. Companies, as well as federal, state, and local governments, have begun focusing on customers as one of the key drivers in planning for the future. When the "voice of the customer" becomes an integral part of organizational strategies, the organization becomes what is termed a "customer-driven" organization. A customer-driven organization is "one that maintains a focus on the needs and expectations, both spoken and unspoken, of customers, both present and future, in the creation and/or improvement of the product or service provided."

Clinger-Cohen Act (CCA)

The Clinger-Cohen Act was implemented to ensure that agencies improve the initial capital planning process (business case) for large acquisitions to develop realistic cost, schedule, and performance goals that are tied directly to agency strategic mission goals within available budget resources. It also encourages the use of performance- and results-based management of these initiatives. The Federal Acquisition Streamlining Act requires that IT initiatives be tied to mission and strategic goals; have cost, schedule, and performance goals; and achieve, on average, 90 percent of these goals. The CCA specifically states: "The head of each executive agency shall design and implement in the executive agency a process for maximizing the value and assessing and managing the risk of the information technology acquisitions of the executive agency," and

The process shall:

1. provide for the selection of information technology investments to be made by the executive agency, the management of such investments, and the evaluation of the results of such investments;
2. be integrated with the processes for making budget, financial, and program management decisions within the executive agency;
3. establish minimum criteria to be applied in considering whether to undertake a particular investment in information systems, criteria related to the quantitatively expressed projected net risk adjusted return on investment

and specific quantitative and qualitative criteria for comparing and prioritizing alternative information systems investment projects;
4. provide for identifying information systems investments that would result
in shared benefits or costs for other Federal agencies of State or local governments;
5. require identification of quantifiable measurements for determining the
net benefits and risks of a proposed investment; and,
6. provide the means for senior management to obtain timely information
regarding the progress of an investment, including a system of milestones
for measuring progress, on an independently verifiable basis, in terms of
cost, capability of the system to meet specified requirements, timeliness,
and quality."

Note: The federal government has made enormous efforts to comply with the
CCA, and including enterprise architecture. This subject is addressed in greater
detail further on.

President's Management Agenda (PMA)

The PMA of 2001, outlines the Bush administration's strategic initiatives
for improving the management of the government. The purpose of the PMA
is to help federal agencies adopt disciplines that ensure their focus on results is
effective and lasting. There are five government-wide, interrelated initiatives
that apply to federal agencies and ten program specific initiatives. The five key
government-wide areas are:

- Strategic management of human capital: This involves establishing processes to ensure the right person is in the right job, at the right time, and
is performing at the expected level.
- Competitive sourcing: Competitive sourcing is a tool to assist organizations benchmark against other like-organizations or service providers, to
challenge the way your own organization conducts business. Competitive
sourcing leverages competition to enhance business results.
- Improved financial performance: This is ensuring the ability to account
for the taxpayer's money and giving managers timely and accurate
program-cost information to make informed management decisions and
to control costs.
- Expanded electronic government: This is ensuring that the significant investment in IT improves the government's ability to serve citizens and programs are delivered on time, on budget, and meet all security requirements.

- Budget and performance integration: This enhances the government's ability to evaluate competing demands for federal dollars by equipping decision makers with better information on the results of individual programs.

The PMA was launched in 2001 as a strategy for improving the management and performance of the federal government. The focus is on areas where deficiencies were the most apparent and where the government could deliver concrete, measurable results. The five government-wide initiatives are all performance-related; however, the budget and performance integration (BPI) initiative is specific to how performance is managed.

Each governmental agency will leverage the PMA and develop its strategic guidance based on its overall mission. Alignment of the governmental agency strategy with the PMA is critical to the success of that agency. Strategies and performance measurement alike cascade throughout an organization and, more importantly, roll up, which is why it is imperative the efforts are aligned. Reports in 2004 indicated that the habits and disciplines of the federal department and agencies are also fundamentally changing as a result of this initiative.

E-Government Act of 2002

The stated purpose of this act, enacted on December 17, 2002, was to improve the management and promotion of electronic government services and processes by establishing a federal chief information officer within the Office of Management and Budget and establishing a framework of measures that require using Internet-based IT to improve citizen access to government information and services and for other purposes. The main provisions are:

- To provide effective leadership of federal government efforts to develop and promote electronic government services and processes by establishing an administrator of a new Office of Electronic Government within the Office of Management and Budget
- To promote use of the Internet and other information technologies to provide increased opportunities for citizen participation in government
- To promote interagency collaboration in providing electronic government services, where this collaboration would improve the service to citizens by integrating related functions, and in the use of internal electronic government processes, where this collaboration would improve the efficiency and effectiveness of the processes
- To improve the ability of the government to achieve agency missions and program performance goals

- To promote the use of the Internet and emerging technologies within and across government agencies to provide citizen-centric government information and services
- To reduce costs and burdens for businesses and other government entities
- To promote better-informed decision making by policy makers
- To promote access to high quality government information and services across multiple channels
- To make the federal government more transparent and accountable
- To transform agency operations by utilizing, where appropriate, best practices from public- and private-sector organizations
- To provide enhanced access to government information and services in a manner consistent with laws regarding protection of personal privacy, national security, records retention, access for persons with disabilities, and other relevant laws

Federal Guidance Calls for Using EVM to Improve IT Management

In Federal Acquisitions Regulation M-05-23, dated August 4, 2005, the OMB required the following actions:

- Establishing and validating performance measurement baselines with clear cost, schedule, and performance goals
- Managing and measuring projects to within 10 percent of baseline goals through use of an EVMs compliant with the guidelines in ANSI/EIA STD-748 or, for steady-state projects, perform operational analyses
- Assigning to each project a qualified project manager
- Avoiding duplication by leveraging interagency and government-wide investments to support common missions or other common requirements
- Developing agency policies no later than December 31, 2005
- Including EVMs in contracts
- Performing reviews to ensure the EVMs meet established requirements
- Ensuring performance goals are appropriate

Specifically, this guidance directs agencies to (1) develop comprehensive policies to ensure that their major IT investments are using EVM to plan and manage development; (2) include a provision and clause in major acquisition contracts or agency in-house project charters directing the use of an EVM system that is compliant with the American National Standards Institute (ANSI) standard; (3) provide documentation demonstrating that the contractor's or agency's in-house EVM system complies with the national standard; (4) conduct periodic surveillance reviews; and (5) conduct integrated baseline reviews on individual programs to finalize their cost, schedule, and performance goals.

Without meaningful and coherent cost and schedule information, program managers can have a distorted view of a program's status and risks. EVM is a project management approach that, if implemented appropriately, provides objective reports of project status, produces early warning signs of impending schedule delays and cost overruns, and provides unbiased estimates of a program's total costs.

> Note: EVM focuses primarily on cost and schedules and is a useful tool for ensuring that work on hand is done to budget and on time, but it has no direct connection with benefit realization, which is the focus of this book. By the time a project is appearing to be in trouble in an EVM system, the project is already in trouble (could be for multiple reasons); the "horse is already out of the barn." The focus of the approach in this book is to be proactive so projects do not reach the troubled state.

What EVM Does

Differences in these values are measured in both cost and schedule variances. Cost variances compare the value of the completed work (i.e., the earned value) with the actual cost of the work performed. For example, if a contractor completed $5 million worth of work and the work actually cost $6.7 million, there would be a negative $1.7 million cost variance. Schedule variances are also measured in dollars, but they compare the earned value of the completed work with the value of the work that was expected to be completed. For example, if a contractor completed $5 million worth of work at the end of the month but was budgeted to complete $10 million worth of work, there would be a negative $5 million schedule variance. Positive variances indicate that activities are costing less or are completed ahead of schedule. Negative variances indicate activities are costing more or are falling behind schedule. These cost and schedule variances can then be used in estimating the cost and time needed to complete the program.

Without knowing the planned cost of completed work and work in progress (i.e., the earned value), it is difficult to determine a program's true status. Earned value allows for this key information, which provides an objective view of program status and is necessary for understanding the health of a program. As a result, EVM can alert program managers to potential problems sooner than using expenditures alone, thereby reducing the chance and magnitude of cost overruns and schedule slippages. However, EVM only uncovers project issues after they have occurred, not proactively.

EVM Effectiveness to Date per GAO

The GAO's analysis of 16 investments shows that agencies are using EVM to manage their system acquisitions; however, the extent of implementation varies. Specifically, for 13 of the 16 investments, key practices necessary for sound EVM execution had not been implemented. For example, the project schedules for these investments contained issues—such as the improper sequencing of key activities—that undermine the quality of their performance baselines. This inconsistent application of EVM exists in part because of the weaknesses contained in agencies' policies, combined with a lack of enforcement of policies already in place. Until key EVM practices are fully implemented, these investments face an increased risk that managers cannot effectively optimize EVM as a management tool.

Furthermore, earned value data trends of these investments indicate that most are currently experiencing shortfalls against cost and schedule targets. The total life-cycle costs of these programs have increased by about $2 billion. Based on the GAO's analysis of current performance trends, 11 programs will likely incur cost overruns that will total about $1 billion at contract completion—in particular, 2 of these programs account for about 80 percent of this projection. As such, the GAO estimates the total cost overrun to be about $3 billion at program completion. However, with timely and effective management action, it is possible to reverse negative trends so that the projected cost overruns may be reduced.

In reviewing agencies' implementation of the OMB's EVM guidance, the GAO identified weaknesses with policies and implementation at several major federal departments. Examples included the following:

- The Department of the Treasury had an EVM policy that clearly defined criteria for which programs were to use the management tool. However, this policy did not require and enforce EVM training for personnel with investment oversight and program management responsibilities, nor did it adequately address key elements for ensuring reliability of earned value data—including program EVM compliance with the national standard.
- The FAA was using EVM to manage IT acquisition programs, but not all programs were ensuring that their earned value data were reliable. One program did not adequately validate contractor performance data. The GAO found anomalies in which the contractor reported spending funds without accomplishing work and others in which the contractor reported accomplishing work while crediting funds to the government.

Building on the OMB's requirements, in March 2009, a guide on best practices for estimating and managing program costs was issued. This highlights the policies and practices adopted by leading organizations to implement an effective EVM program. Specifically, it identifies the need for organizational policies that establish clear criteria for which programs are required to use EVM, specify compliance with the ANSI standard, require a standard product-oriented structure for defining work products, require integrated baseline reviews, provide for specialized training, establish criteria and conditions for rebaselining programs, and require an ongoing surveillance function. In addition, it identified key practices that individual programs can use to ensure that they establish a sound EVM system, that the earned value data are reliable, and that the data are used to support decision making.

Rebaselining

At times, management may conclude that the remaining budget and schedule targets for completing a program (including the contract) are significantly insufficient and that the current baseline is no longer valid for realistic performance measurement. An agency's rebaselining criteria should define acceptable reasons for rebaselining and require programs to (1) explain why the current plan is no longer feasible and what measures will be implemented to prevent recurrence, and (2) develop a realistic cost and schedule estimate for remaining work that has been validated and spread over time to the new plan.

> Note: This is key to effective implementation of PDM. If a project is significantly off track for meeting its business case objectives, rebaselining is required.

Since the 1960s, landmark legislation, such as the Chief Financial Officer (CFO) Act, the Government Performance Results Act (GPRA), the National Partnership for Reinventing Government (NPR), the Government Management Reform Act, and the Clinger-Cohen Act (CCA) collectively have set the tone for financial reform and refocused the federal government on the use of performance measurement. Each piece of legislation provided guidance on how to improve the management aspect of the government's performance and how to institutionalize performance measurement "as a way of doing business." The CFO Act and the GPRA, respectively, focused on improving financial management and establishing strategic plans and annual performance plans.

Obama Administration Initiatives

In the *Memorandum on Transparency and Open Government*, issued on January 21, 2009, President Obama instructed the director of the OMB to issue the Open Government Directive. Responding to that instruction, the OMB issued its directive on December 8, 2009. It directs executive departments and agencies to take specific actions to implement the principles of transparency, participation, and collaboration set forth in the president's memorandum.

The three principles of transparency, participation, and collaboration form the cornerstone of an open government. Transparency promotes accountability by providing the public with information about what the government is doing. Participation allows members of the public to contribute ideas and expertise so that their government can make policies with the benefit of information that is widely dispersed in society. Collaboration improves the effectiveness of government by encouraging partnerships and cooperation within the federal government, across levels of government, and between the government and private institutions.

The Open Government Directive establishes deadlines for action. But because of the presumption of openness that the president has endorsed, agencies are encouraged to advance their open government initiatives well ahead of those deadlines.

As part of the open government initiative, federal departments have also been urged to exchange information and best practices and to contribute to the federal dashboard, which is designed to help them assess the effectiveness of government IT spending—and make this information available to the public. Departments are also being encouraged to review their data center policies and consider the economics of switching to cloud computing. It must be stressed, however, that while all these initiatives and directives are commendable, they are generally budget focused. The aim of this book is purely performance focused because the critical objective is the performance improvements and measurable benefits achieved. More information on this memorandum is given in step 2.

On December 9, 2010, the Obama administration released the 25 Point Implementation Plan to Reform Federal Information Technology Management, which contains commendable points, but still lacks a performance/investment focus.

Congress Acts

Congress took note, and in May 2010, the Senate approved the Information Technology Investment Oversight Enhancement and Waste Prevention Act of 2009. Coauthored by Senators Tom Carper (D-DE) and Susan Collins (R-ME), the act seeks to better monitor the approximate $80 billion that federal agencies spend every year on IT.

The bill is in response to a series of hearings held by Senator Carper as chairman of the Subcommittee on Federal Financial Management, Government Information, Federal Services, and International Security, which examined federal agencies' management of costly, high-risk IT investments. The hearings discovered severe failings, including a costly malfunction of handheld data collection devices used by census workers. The data collection devices did not perform as promised, resulting in an additional $1 billion to revert the 2010 Census follow-up to a paper-based system.

At the request of Senators Carper and Collins, the GAO conducted an investigation into the IT investments made by federal agencies. The GAO released its report in October 2009 and identified 11 mismanaged IT investments made by federal agencies that will likely cost taxpayers $3 billion more than the original price tag. For example, the National Aeronautics and Space Administration's James Webb Space Telescope and the Department of Veterans Affairs Health Information System Modernization will collectively overrun their original budgets by $798.7 million.

"At a time when our country is facing record deficits it is simply unacceptable that federal agencies continue to waste billions of dollars by mismanaging information technology investments," said Carper. "Information technology is critical to ensuring that our government runs well in an increasingly digital age but it's clear that federal agencies are dropping the ball when it comes to deploying the right technology in a timely and cost-effective manner. We can do better and frankly we must. This legislation will provide the planning and oversight needed to reduce waste and improve the federal government's information technology operations."

"The increased level of oversight that would be provided in this bill is welcomed news for every taxpayer in America," said Senator Collins, ranking member of the full Senate Homeland Security and Governmental Affairs Committee. "We have invested tens of billions of dollars in the federal government's IT infrastructure, and, given the digital age that we are living in, such investments will only increase in the future. This bill would address systemic weaknesses through transparency and oversight that would help end ballooning costs associated with poorly planned projects, prevent costly delays when critical IT projects lag behind, and ensure that promised capabilities are realized. The bottom line: This bill would help protect the investments that taxpayers have made and improve the overall IT operations of the federal government."

The bill would address many of these IT waste problems by requiring federal agencies to conduct an independent cost estimate for projects prone to mismanagement and by giving the OMB the ability to send in a team of highly qualified experts to prevent project costs from spiraling out of control. The bill also would require agencies to alert Congress when an IT investment significantly exceeds the expected cost estimate and mandates that the project undergo a rigorous analysis to get it back on track. Now that the legislation has been passed by the Senate, it likely will be referred to the House Oversight and Government Reform Committee for approval.

On June 16, the House passed the Government Efficiency, Effectiveness, and Performance Improvement Act of 2010 (H.R. 2142), which would require agencies to set high-value goals and make public quarterly assessments on how they've met those goals. "My bill will help reduce the deficit by rooting out government waste," says Congressman Henry Cuellar (D-TX), author of the bill, in a release. "With this bill, Congress can make more informed decisions as we fund federal agencies and their programs. Better information yields better results, and these reports will help us invest in what works and fix what doesn't." There is no Senate companion bill.

Introduction to the Five-Step Process

The various initiatives detailed above have not solved the IT project problems, and serious challenges still remain. Reviewing the case studies, it is clear that many IT projects are doomed to failure from the outset. That is why a new approach is needed.

- Business value, as measured by improved business performance after implementation, is the singular connecting thread from concept through system development, implementation, and operations.
- The business case is key to determining the business benefits (as measured by performance improvements) to be obtained for the resources and time invested on a given project (business value proposition).

Performance-Driven Management is a systematic approach to IT project risk mitigation through an ongoing process of establishing strategic performance objectives; developing an accurate business case, validating projected performance improvements at key checkpoints during project implementation to ensure a project is on track; measuring performance to validate that the business case has been fulfilled; collecting, analyzing, reviewing, and reporting performance data; and using that data to drive further performance improvement.

- Each separate step in a project life cycle provides an opportunity for a project to veer from the business value proposition that the approved project was based on.
- Validating the business value proposition at key points across the life cycle will confirm that a project is on track or suggest corrective action. That is what the five-step process is all about.

> Note: The PDM approach is well suited to both private- and public-sector organizations, and all concepts in this book apply to both. This book focuses, to a degree, on the U.S. federal government because projects in the federal government are generally larger and more complex than most private-sector projects, taxpayer funds are at stake, numerous laws and executive orders have been promulgated to address IT project issues (with limited success), and large federal projects often underdeliver or fail publically.

The Five-Step Process

Each step takes you through a highly disciplined process that is necessary to help ensure that IT programs and projects will be successful. PDM, however, is a continuous process—not a one-shot proposition. It is practiced throughout the five-step process, and each step builds on the other to ensure continual focus and eventual success. Organizational experience in the five-step process will improve organizational risk mitigation over time across multiple projects.

As you work through the steps, you will note that while they follow a logical progression, some of the steps, especially steps 1 and 2, are interrelated, with common factors that have to be considered both in regard to that particular step and how it impacts on other steps. The detailed step-by-step chart below illustrates this. You can see from the chart that developing an actionable strategy in step 1 cannot be done in isolation. It must be considered alongside how to improve business performance, which is part of step 2, and funding is, of course, something that is of critical importance to the success of all five steps. The process involves:

- Developing the overall strategy
- Developing an accurate business case focused on accurate cost estimation and benefits realization and setting up the ability to measure benefits to ensure the project effectively and viably meets business goals (if it does not, revise or rethink the strategy)

- Selecting the appropriate implementation strategy and choosing the appropriate resources to implement it
- Checking ongoing cost of implementation and likely benefits realization to ensure the project remains on time and within budget and continuing to validate that the strategy and its implementation continue to meet business goals
- Measuring the achieved benefits to ensure the right results have been achieved

Step 1: Develop an Actionable Business and IT Strategy

Developing an effective actionable IT strategy is probably the single most important role of an organization's chief executive officer. This may surprise those of you who thought this was the sole responsibility of the chief information officer. However, there needs to be a quantum leap beyond IT to consider the business as a whole—because it impacts every part of the organization.

The second is implementing and sustaining it. The strategy is not just about IT, it must incorporate the organization's business plan, its long-term goals, and its visions for the future. A strategy is then developed that leverages technology in the most effective and efficient way in order to meet these goals and objectives.

It is more important to focus on capability improvement; although, cost reduction should be another major benefit. The overriding goal is to improve business performance—ideally to make it better, faster, and cheaper and, in the private sector, more profitable.

Step 1 must consider the internal business drivers. What are the user needs? Does the workforce—the human capital—have the necessary skills, knowledge, training, and awareness to effectively implement needed changes? Does management have the ability and resolve to see it through? Are processes and costs ineffective and need change?

You must also consider all the external business drivers. You must not only consider the needs of your customers but also you must take into account all external business drivers—what do they expect of you, and how can you exceed their expectations? How are these needs likely to change in the next few years, and how will these changes be accommodated? Are there any external constraints that might prevent you from implementing your strategy or interfere with it? Are you in compliance with federal/agency guidelines and directives? Has an adequate budget been set aside to allow the project to be satisfactorily implemented? Are there new laws and guidelines to be implemented? What other external factors might impact on your plans?

With all this information in hand, a detailed strategy can then be developed. The result is a definitive business strategy with IT enablement clearly identified.

Step 2: Define Business Performance Targets—Overall and for Specific Investments

The next step establishes your business performance targets. Too many IT projects focus on getting the latest, the best, and the fastest, which can turn out to be a colossal waste of money, if there are no measurable benefits around cost and business processes. Until you know what your performance needs are, you cannot correctly identify the best solution for you and the customers you serve. The definition of performance targets allows you to measure benefits against defined, quantitative criteria and simulate process and projects to validate benefits realization and mitigate risk.

This step necessarily requires an understanding of business performance cause and effect with respect to the organization's IT projects and investments.

Step 3: Invest for Results

The focus of step 3 is the development of the business case for a change or operations initiative. The business case is the foundation of an organization's choice to invest scarce resources to achieve a specific business objective. The estimation of costs, benefits, and risks is paramount to making an investment decision. Once the investment is selected, it is up to the implementation project to implement the investment in a manner that preserves the parameters of the business case. Hence, the PDM approach is one of continually assessing a project against its business case to ensure that the parameters are being met; otherwise, the project is no longer implementing according to the business case it was based on. After a business case is complete, that investment must compete against other proposed investments for funding. The ranking of investments by effective return on investment (ROI) (financial ROI plus nonfinancial factors) is a process used by organizations to rank and select investments—usually investments with the higher ROIs are selected until funds run out, leaving the lower ROIs unfunded.

Finally, selected investments are integrated with ongoing investments to create an evolving transition plan, by which new capabilities are implemented and business performance improved. You can see that step 3 utilizes the outputs from all the activities carried out in steps 1 and 2.

Step 4: Achieving Investment Results

The focus of this step is to revalidate the business case and to constantly monitor the project's progress to ensure that the expected ROI is being achieved. This is done during key project checkpoints.

With unlimited funds, one can, of course, build pretty much anything, but good governance requires that the project is not just necessary, but there has to be an acceptable return on the cost of implementing it. An acceptable ROI is always important, especially when tax dollars are involved. Execution of this step helps ensure that an investment is on track with its business case and allows for proactive adjustments to projects that are beginning to veer off track. This step is a key differentiator of the PDM approach, assessing projects against the business case as opposed to narrow process assessments to proactively mitigate risk.

This is all part of the process of validating the project by demonstrating that it is viable, cost-effective, and will lead to enhanced performance. Benefits in the form of better performance, however, cannot be realized until implementation has been completed. There may be incremental benefits along the way, but the full potential cannot be realized and, therefore, cannot be fully realized, until the project has been completed and all stages implemented.

The assessment analysis continuously predicts project performance against its ability to implement the business case. Ultimately, the benefits will be realized after implementation, hopefully along the lines of the business case—small differences between the business case analysis and actual results can be used as a basis for lessons learned.

Step 5: Realize the Benefits and Close the Strategy Loop

The final step validates everything you have done. Using measures, you can compare your results against your target values to show that you have achieved what you set out to do.

Hopefully the project has been delivered on time and within the budget and you are able to demonstrate performance improvements, as spelled out in step 2, through accepted measurement techniques.

This step also effectively closes the strategy loop and allows the results to be fed back into the next round of strategic planning. However, no project can be treated in isolation. During the course of this project, you will have learned many lessons that could benefit future projects. These should be written down, documented as best practices, and shared. By feeding all the information learned—both good and bad—back into the process, you close the loop on this project and pave the groundwork for the next successful project.

Benefits of the PDM Approach

PDM has many benefits, including:

1. The most important one is that it reduces the risk that a program or project will spend large sums of money over a period of time and not produce the planned results.
2. It provides a structured approach to focusing on strategic performance objectives. In other words, performance-driven management focuses on the achievement of results, not on the number of activities.
3. It provides a mechanism for accurately reporting performance to upper management and stakeholders. Performance-driven management takes the guess work out of, "How are we doing?" Because all work is planned and done in accordance with the strategic performance objectives, the end result is an accurate picture of individual, program, and organizational performance.
4. It brings all "interested" parties into the planning and evaluation of business performance. Performance-based management brings customers, stakeholders, employees (i.e., those who do and/or are most familiar with the work), and management together to plan strategies and goals and to evaluate results. It is the antithesis of the "command and control" style of management of the past. The key word is *involvement*. Performance-based management involves those who should be involved in the process.
5. It provides a mechanism for linking performance and budget expenditures. At the beginning of the cycle, performance-driven management provides a framework for showing what goals will be accomplished and what resources will be necessary to accomplish those goals. At the end of the cycle, it shows what was actually accomplished and what resources actually were used to achieve those results. Thus, performance-based management takes the uncertainty out of budget allocations and provides an effective accounting for dollars spent.
6. It provides an excellent framework for accountability. Performance-driven management ensures accountability for results.
7. It brings together organizational responsibility for performance improvement. In the performance-based management process, performance improvement becomes a joint responsibility between the organization and its stakeholders/customers or between the individual and his or her management. This "jointness" assures input from both sides and increases involvement in the process, ownership of results, and accountability for performance.

The following graphics provide an overview and detail on the five-step PDM process.

Each step will be discussed in detail in this book.

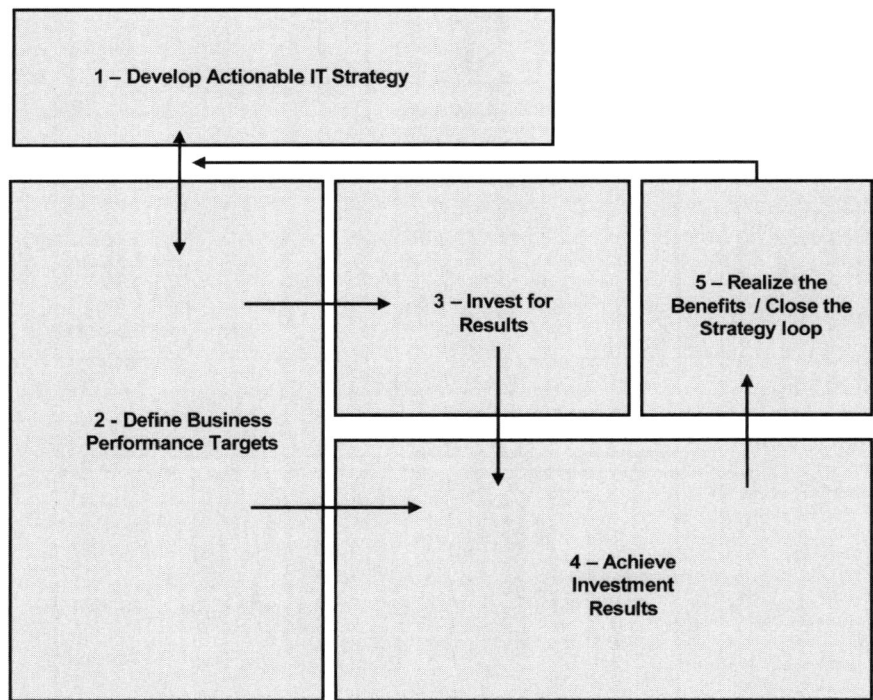

FIGURE I.1
High Level Overview of Five-Step Approach

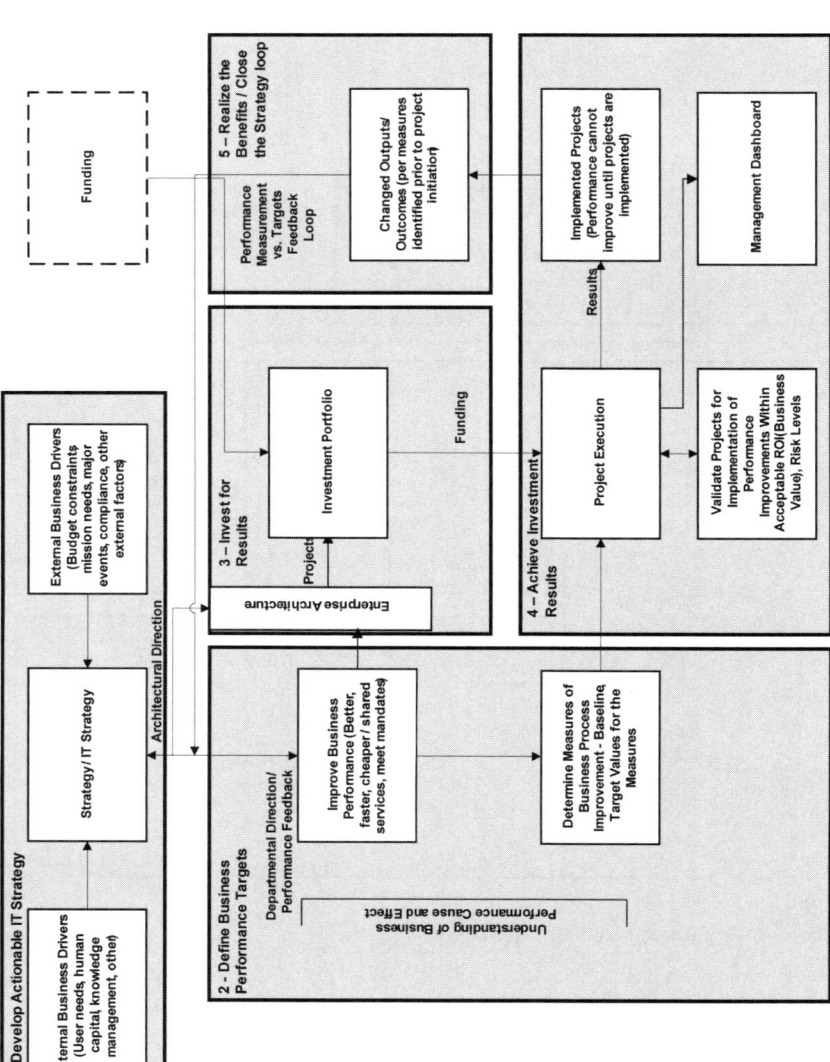

FIGURE I.2
Overview of Five-Step Approach

1

Developing Actionable Business Strategy

- Determine internal business drivers
- Determine external business drivers
- Develop your business strategy

Overview

Setting Strategic Directions

THE PIVOTAL POINT in the strategic management process is the point at which strategic direction (i.e., the organization's goals, objectives, and strategies by which it plans to achieve its vision, mission, and values) is set. It is at this point that an organization's knowledge and insights about its past, present, and future converge, and a path is chosen around which the organization will align its activities and its resources.

Without strategic direction, an organization risks both internal misalignment and the likelihood that it will fail to respond to the vagaries of a changing world. Regardless of the structure of the planning process, its timing, or its participants, guidance from the highest levels plays a central role in ensuring success. Nowhere is the voice of the customer more important to heed than in the direction-setting process.

In order to establish a performance-driven approach, you must define the organizational mission and strategic performance objectives. This is the *strategic planning phase* of performance-driven management (PDM).

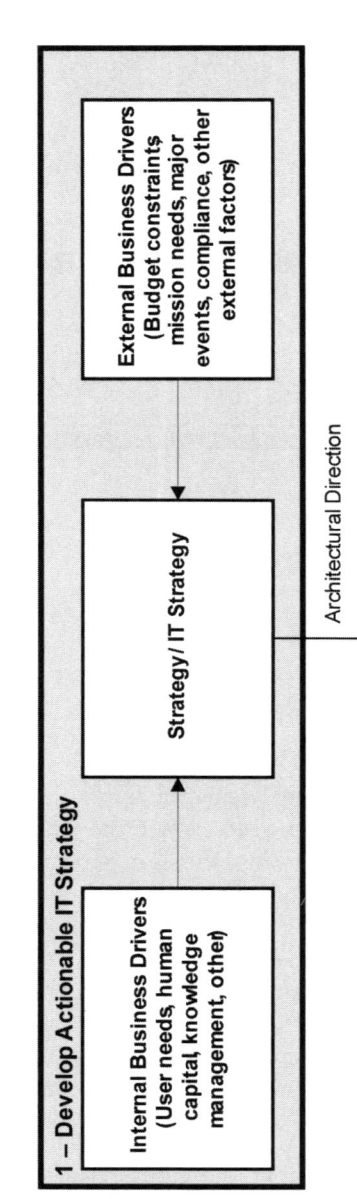

1 – Develop Actionable IT Strategy

Internal Business Drivers
(User needs, human capital, knowledge management, other)

Strategy / IT Strategy

External Business Drivers
(Budget constraints mission needs, major events, compliance, other external factors)

Architectural Direction

FIGURE 1.1
Overview of Step 1

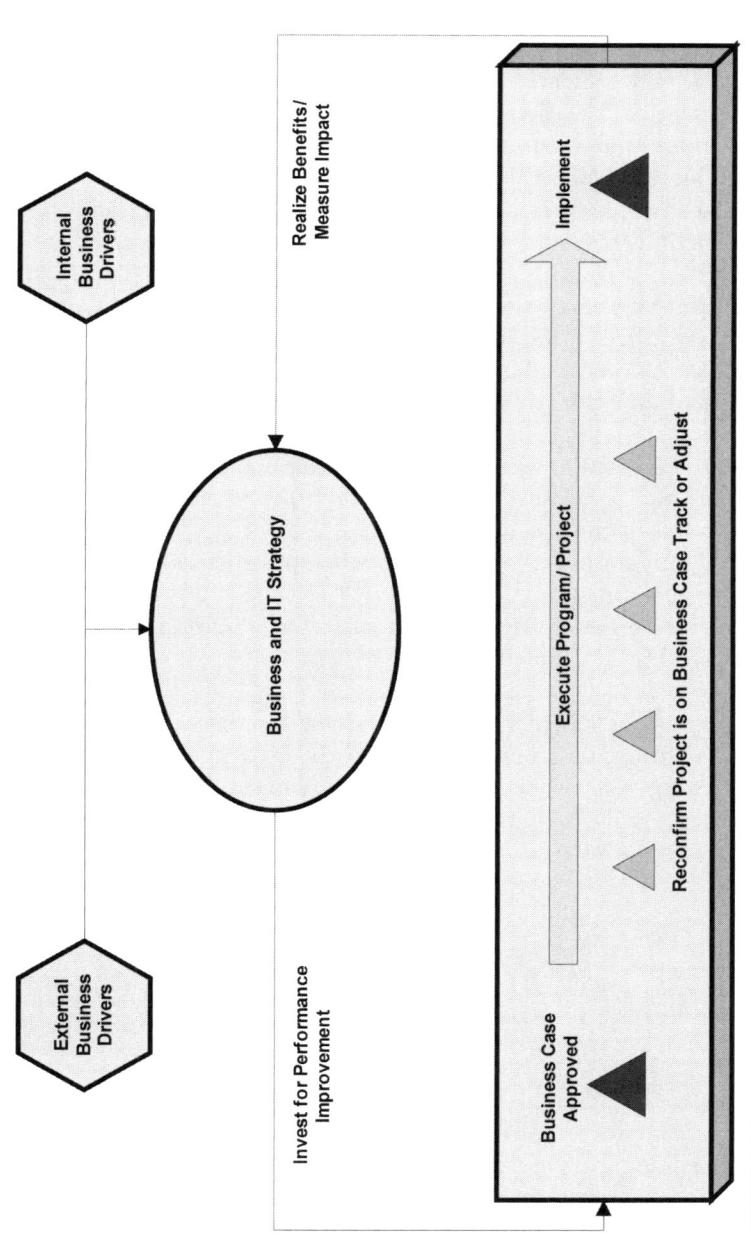

FIGURE 1.2
Performance-Driven Management Overview

Figure 1.2 illustrates the strategy dimension of the PDM process, the importance of each element, and the dependency and relationship of the elements to each other. Strategic planning is central to the PDM approach. All elements have to be validated and implemented for the project to be successful and the expected benefits realized.

Organizations of all kinds appear to have decided that maintaining an internal focus on excellence will not provide them with the advantage they need to succeed; a strategic direction must be set. Components integral to setting strategic direction are:

- A mission statement that identifies the purpose for which the organization is organized or the function that is now carried out in the business world (see "About the Mission Statement" below)
- A vision of the future business environment and the organization within it
- A values statement of the organization's code of ethics or the values it espouses related to teamwork, quality, and protection of the environment and community in which it operates
- Assumptions about the business environmental drivers that are expected to exist in the future
- Business strategies or broad statements of how objectives are to be accomplished (e.g., a growth strategy)

Developing an actionable, effective business strategy means visioning a more effective future for an organization by identifying goals and approaches to reach those goals. This visioning should involve all stakeholders—both internal and external—and make sure that everyone is on the same page from the outset.

> Note: This section describes an enterprise-wide business strategy for IT enablement, concepts that will be used throughout this book. That strategy drives transformation, brought about by investment, and performance measures assess the effectiveness of the strategic transformation efforts.

The key goals in doing this are to ensure operational requirements are met leading to performance improvements—and to focus on costs from the outset so that money is not only spent on what is required but also the value of every dollar spent is maximized and return on investment is achieved.

Simply getting everyone involved is not enough, even though that in itself can be a challenge for a variety of reasons, including lack of buy-in, protecting personal fiefdoms, and unwillingness to share information.

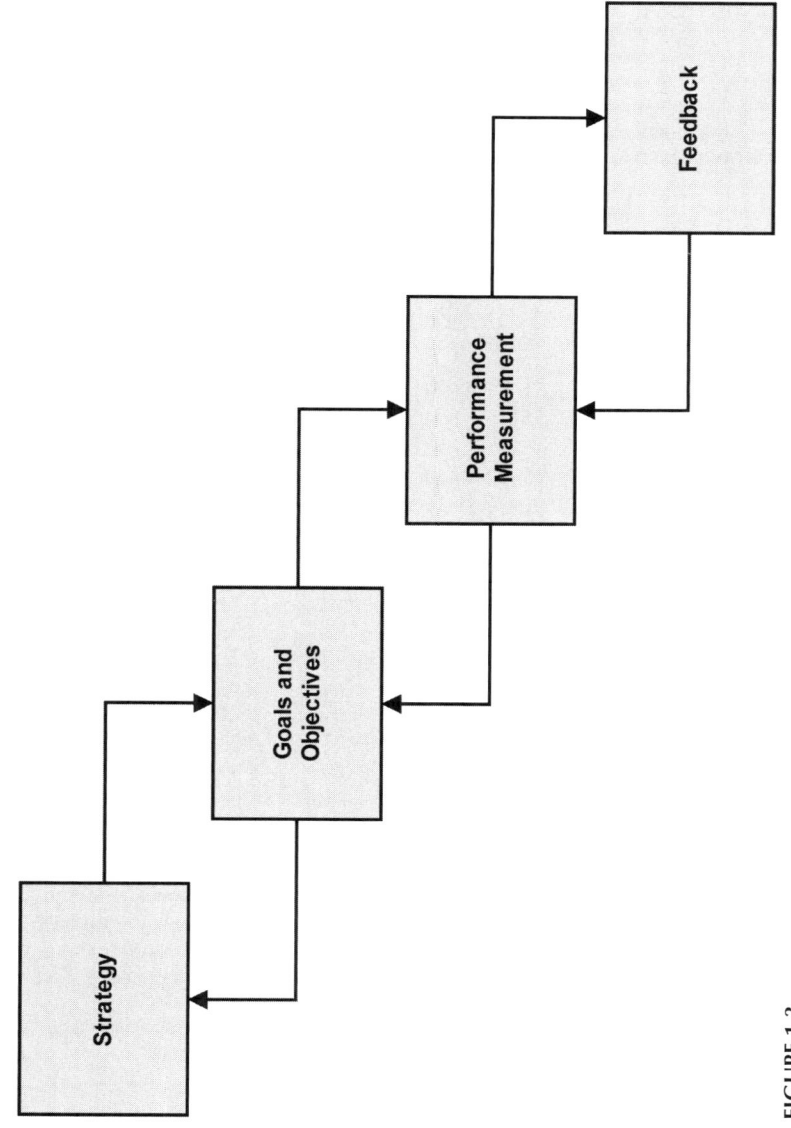

FIGURE 1.3
Strategy/Feedback Loop

It is also important to remember that step 1 is only concerned with developing the strategy. When you have developed a strategy, you have to apply measurements to see if it going to be successful and achieve the anticipated benefits. However, measurement is step 2, so we are getting ahead of ourselves.

Strategic Planning Approach

The following table is the recommended approach to strategic planning.

TABLE 1.1
Strategic Planning Approach

Step	Benefits	Effect on the Transformation Program
Define business drivers	Identifies business drivers and reason(s) for change	Identifies program champions and develops the foundation for organizational buy-in.
Architect and align strategies	Aligns transformation program goals with the organization's business strategy	Ensures early alignment of the initiative with the existing organizational strategy and capabilities
Develop vision	Identifies the key business drivers, organizational goals, and performance measures	Reduces the risk of initiating transformation programs without clearly defined performance measures
Current state understanding	Provides a clear map of the existing processes and identifies potential areas for improvement	Identifies root causes and reasons behind process bottlenecks early and the key features of future state processes
Future state design	Defines the renewed processes and identifies required organizational assets needed to enable continuous improvement	Confirms the vision and develops the foundation for developing the implementation road map
Roadmap development	Defines in detail the future state implementation road map, such as critical milestones and early wins	Reduces program management risks and identifies required steps to accomplish key milestones

The following briefly describes the steps above.

Define Business Drivers

Successful organizations recognize that strategic plans must be based on accurate, timely, and complete information. Current and future customer requirements and environmental factors are the driving force behind the creation of strategic direction for the best-in-class organizations.

The gathering of external and internal data for the purpose of strategic planning is generally known as *environmental scanning* (i.e., the 360-degree gathering and analysis of information from a variety of sources on such matters as customers' needs and expectations, technology developments, marketplace dynamics, demographics, politics, and societal trends). Many organizational planners see this information as the key to the planning process.

Environmental scanning begins by: first identifying potential sources of data that can impact business operations, both from outside and inside the organization; gathering the data; and analyzing the data to provide insight into customers, the industry, the organization, and its future. Best-in-class organizations gather external and internal data continuously and use that data as input to all facets of the planning process.

The external environmental scan consists of an assessment of the outside world in which the organization will operate over the planning horizon. The internal environmental scan consists of an organization looking inward, assessing its own strengths and weaknesses.

John F. Rockart of MIT's Sloan School of Management categorized drivers as follows:

- Industry—these factors result from specific industry characteristics. These are the things that the organization must do to remain competitive.
- Environmental—these factors result from macro-environmental influences on an organization. Things like the business climate, the economy, competitors, and technological advancements are included in this category.
- Strategic—these factors result from the specific competitive strategy chosen by the organization. This is the way in which the companies choose to position themselves, market themselves, whether they are high volume, low cost or low volume, high cost producers, and so forth.
- Temporal—these factors result from the organization's internal forces. Specific barriers, challenges, directions, and influences will determine these critical success factors.

Internal Drivers

Internal drivers are all those factors that affect the organization's operating environment—both positive and negative, strengths and weaknesses—from within the organization. For instance, a positive internal factor could be a strong, dynamic management, while a negative factor might be a shortage of trained IT staff or rapid employee turnover.

These drivers are often the result of department- and organization-level goals and objectives. In addition, drivers can include discussions with other organizations working toward common goals. These internal drivers include:

- Organization's existing priorities
- Staff/stakeholders
- Limited resources and increasing demands
- Inspector general (IG) audits/lack of compliance issues
- Human resource issues and management
- Business process issues

External Drivers

External drivers include everything that might have an impact on the project that is outside the organization. The most important of these are the customers and end users, but external factors must also take into account all legislation and regulations that have to be complied with, as well as political, social, technical, and environmental environments. Each of these external factors can add complexity and needs to be identified and addressed. Compiling a list of all external drivers requires input from many different departments to ensure that all are taken into consideration. These external drivers can include:

- Presidential initiatives and directives
- Legislative requirements
- Disclosure requirements
- Office of Management and Budget (OMB) guidance
- Government Accounting Office (GOA) reports
- Citizens
- Public opinion
- Customers/stakeholders
- Competitors—existing and potential
- Suppliers
- Prime contractors and subcontractors

- Evolving technologies and opportunities those technologies can provide
- Increasing sophistication of security threats
- Increasing appearance of mass collaboration
- Increasing use of the Internet as context for problem solving

Architect and Align Strategies

Effective planning requires a structured, cohesive process. There are several key issues to be addressed when developing the strategic plan and aligning strategies:

- Who is the strategic planning process owner, and how much commitment is there to strategic planning?
- Who will execute the planning process in the organization?
- How will customers and other stakeholders be represented in the planning process?
- What are the strategic planning and business planning horizons?
- What information is needed for a successful planning process, and who will be responsible for developing and managing it?
- What are the expected outcomes or results to be achieved?
- How do we define success, and how will we know when we get there?
- Who is going to be responsible for deployment and performance, and who will help and in what ways?
- What resources (e.g., money, people, or other inputs) exist to enable the process?

There are many different and correct answers to these questions, and the right ones will be dictated by the realities of the individual situation. In other words, there is no single set of right answers on how to prepare and plan to develop and deploy an organization's strategic planning process. However, these are the types of questions that must be asked and answered in the context of the organization. Taken together, they will dictate the structure and alignment of a successful strategic planning process.

Develop Vision

Vision statements (like organizations) tend to stand for long periods of time, but they should be examined and debated periodically. A whole hierarchy of missions and visions exists in a large organization, and each level derives its vision from the vision of the parent. It is important for the planning team to be certain they are "performing" the right vision and mission.

The vision statement serves to clarify the purpose of the organization for people both within and outside. In addition to clarifying the purpose, it should serve to narrow and focus, as well as to inspire and motivate. It should be debated and reduced to the essence—100 words is one "rule of thumb"—that tells *why* we do *what*, for *whom*, and *how* in an easy, understandable way. It should describe what products or services are provided to what customers (products) or clients (services) or sponsors and what activities or kind of work we do to provide these products or services. When developing a vision statement, consider the following questions to facilitate group discussion:

- Will it be clear to everyone within and outside the organization?
- Does it tell what our job is, what needs we are trying to fill, for whom, how?
- Is it clear who we regard as our customers—not only who they are but also who they should be?
- Is our primary focus or strategic thrust clear? Does it reflect our distinctive competence?
- Does it reflect our core values, philosophy, and beliefs? Will it energize, motivate, and stimulate our organization?
- Is it concise enough for people to remember the main points?

Once the vision statement is defined, strategic planning can continue, always working back to the vision as "true north."

Current State Understanding

The next step is to see where we are today in regard to that vision. The current state understanding (some call it situational analysis) is done by gathering facts and analyzing trends that give an objective picture of where the organization stands in the "world" of this business and the external and internal pressures and factors likely to affect the future and achievement of the general goals and objectives. Also, it shows how the organization is performing today.

Staff specialists and key subordinate managers can gather and analyze much of this information. For major corporations, the analysis of the business climate, marketplace, competition, and so forth can get very detailed and voluminous. And for the major programs and activities, the data collection could likewise easily exceed the capacity of the planning team to digest and assess it. The team will want to focus on information that may impact on the choice of long-term objectives, particularly looking at the organization's stakeholders, key performance indicators, and trends that represent opportunities or threats, internal weaknesses/strengths, and planning assumptions.

In business or corporate strategic planning, the term *benchmarking*—as a method of assessing performance—usually entails an external comparison with competitors and is done as part of the current state understanding step. Just as effectively, however, the term can be applied internally. As such, benchmarking emphasizes continual improvement. Most organizations need to benchmark themselves, that is, with past best performance, striving over the long haul to carry out each of their missions efficiently and effectively. Continual performance improvement must be based on honest appraisal of strengths and weaknesses together with participation of all their people. Additionally, other organizations providing the same or similar products and services can be assessed for comparison purposes.

Future State Design

The discussion of drivers and current state will generate a lot of discussion. In developing strategies, we finally get to the point of the process, that of coming up with the directions we want to move toward now and in the future to reach our long-term strategic objectives. The future state design provides a basis for courses of action that will lead in the direction we must move to reach an objective or to overcome some obstacle. We can, of course, set courses of action (strategies) without thinking in any depth about objectives. We often do so both personally and professionally. We buy something we want and then think of reasons to justify the purchase. Many of us have encountered orphan programs or projects whose objectives are not well understood or accepted by all. Careful strategy development is critical to achieving an organization's goals and objectives.

The difference between strategies and action plans is mostly in detail. The basic concern of both is getting on with the mission. The strategy lays out the direction, and the road map addresses detailed questions of resources and timing. Both deal with the achievement of desirable goals and strategic objectives. The strategy will be an enduring course of action (like a policy) that will be a guide (with annual refresh) for many years and not just a single project or program that will be carried out in the next year or so.

Road Map Development

Once the strategy has been defined and the future state described, the final element is to determine how to get there. This is done through development and execution of a strategic and investment road map. The road map should include specific investments and projects, time-phased milestones, and performance metrics. Another key element is to document how the various projects relate to each other—what are the dependencies and key interactions? Additionally, it is critical to determine, at a high level, what benefits are anticipated to be realized and when. These high-level benefit realization requirements will then filter down into the individual project business cases (see step 3).

Case Study Examples

Department of Labor

Strategic planning is performed in varying ways in different organizations, generally executing the steps outlined above. As an example, see below the strategic planning process employed for IT strategy development taken from the Department of Labor's *IT Strategic Plan 2005–2009*:

1. Establish a structured, inclusive, and collaborative process with each agency, bureau, and office of the department.
2. Examine and evaluate the current mission and vision of the department and the alignment and performance of agency programs.
3. Consult with key stakeholders: IT managers, agency heads, and staff.
4. Scan the external environment: federal legislation, presidential directives, CIO (Chief Information Officer) Council recommendations, OMB guidelines, other departments of the U.S. government.
5. Consider and weight the strategic external factors.
6. Scan the internal environment: catalog all agency-level programs, and associate these programs with specific IT needs.
7. Consider and weight the strategic internal factors.
8. Consider all strategic factors in light of the current department situation.
9. Review and revise as necessary the IT Program's mission, vision, and objectives.
10. Generate and evaluate strategy alternatives and strategic program initiatives.
11. Select and recommend best strategy and best strategy program initiatives that align with the department's mission and vision, the agency program needs, and the external stakeholder requirements.
12. Implement strategies and define, launch, and direct IT initiatives: understand and define the skills, resources, and processes necessary to manage and govern the implementations.
13. Manage, evaluate, control, and update: strategy and initiatives— understand and define the performance measures, milestones, bud-

geting implications, and risk mitigation aspects of strategic initiative implementation.

National Institutes of Health (NIH)

As an example of strategic direction and guiding principles, see the guiding principles below, developed by the NIH Center for Information Technology (CIT) *Strategic Plan, 2007*. Technology is changing at a rapid pace, and CIT is careful to ensure technology is used as a tool to support NIH's business goals. In addition to recognizing internal and external drivers, CIT operates using five guiding principles.

Principle 1: Deliver robust IT services that foster creative discoveries and innovative research strategies to promote the protection of health.

- Rationale: The NIH interfaces with many collaborators around the world and supports a premiere clinical center. Therefore, it is imperative that CIT's services are robust and are available to meet demands.

Principle 2: Collaborate with customers to develop solutions that transform biomedical research.

- Rationale: CIT's primary mission is to support NIH's institutes and centers and their varying missions. Consequently, CIT must develop solutions that seamlessly meet customer expectations.

Principle 3: Deliver flexible and cost-effective products/services that add value to our customers.

- Rationale: With limited resources, it is imperative that CIT develops and supports cost-effective, flexible, and reusable services.

Principle 4: Provide a secure information infrastructure that encourages collaboration and information sharing.

- Rationale: Security and privacy are ongoing concerns for organizations. Therefore, CIT will implement appropriate security controls to protect data assets and privacy.

Principle 5: Develop solutions that adhere to NIH and HHS (Health and Human Services) enterprise architecture (EA).

- Rationale: Effectively leveraging enterprise IT resources is key to containing IT costs and promoting data sharing. Therefore, CIT will implement and use EA.

Strategic Planning Critical Success Factors

Critical success factor (CSF) is the term for an element that is essential for an organization or project to achieve its mission. It is a critical factor or activity required for ensuring success. The term was initially used in the world of data analysis and business analysis but is now used in all successful strategy development planning.

The concept of "success factors" was developed by Dr. Ronald Daniel of McKinsey & Company in 1961 and has been refined and finely tuned since then. Within any organization, there are essential but limited factors that will be critical to the success of that organization and its undertakings. If objectives related to those factors are not achieved, the undertaking and perhaps even the organization will fail. That is why it is important to identify the critical success factors both to direct your course of action and measure the success of the outcome.

Establishing a sound strategic planning program is not an easy or short task. As a matter of fact, getting a program firmly established can take years, not days or months. Afterward comes the task of maintaining the program. Areas identified as critical success factors, needing to be constantly maintained, to which ongoing attention should be given are:

- Leadership: Never underestimate the role of leadership. Leadership is responsible for championing the cause, for "getting the ball rolling" and keeping it rolling. Without strong leadership, the program won't succeed. Leadership must be dedicated 24 hours a day, 7 days a week. Good leaders recognize that their success, and the success of their organization, is tied to the quality with which they serve their customers. Senior leadership must be personally involved in all aspects of strategic planning. Effective leadership demands clear, consistent, and visible commitment by leaders throughout the organization. Chief executives should personally explain or cascade the strategic vision throughout the organization, through town hall meetings with employees and customers, executive workshops, video telecasts to all hands with real-time, call-in capabilities, and other direct methods.
- Commitment: Everyone involved—especially those in leadership positions—needs to be committed to the program. The degree of commitment to the program will determine its degree of success. Commitment to the program should be nonstop, not for just certain periods of time. Faltering commitment will erode the program. Organizations need to commit with a sense of urgency. It has been said that there are two types of companies—the quick and the dead. The impetus to move, or to move

more aggressively, to a greater customer focus is the result of one of two things: a cataclysmic event or a newfound leadership commitment. Both bring a very real sense of urgency to the organization.

- Involvement: Performance-based management is inclusive, not exclusive. Thus, it should involve all "interested" parties. Specifically, stakeholders, customers, and employees should be involved where applicable. Involvement is an area that can "fall by the wayside." Management may assume that they know what stakeholders, customers, and/or employees think, want, or need and, thus, "leave them out of the equation." Don't make this mistake. Keep all involved who should be involved.
- Communication: Communication is a partner to involvement. Communication is not something that can be done once in a while but something that needs to be done on a continual basis. Communicating what's being planned, what's expected to happen, what's happened, and what corrections are being made as a result of what happened keeps everyone informed. It also keeps the program at the forefront. Effective communication in the development and deployment of the strategic plan is one of the hallmarks of successful companies and agencies. Top leaders must clearly convey the organization's mission, strategic direction, and vision to employees and external customers. A clear, concise statement that communicates what the organization is and is not increases the likelihood for buy-in from both employees and external customers. External communication (with the customer) is a must. Best-in-class organizations establish formal relationships with customers to better understand their needs and expectations to be able to include these needs in their visioning. The employee having direct interface with the customer also feeds customer requirements up the chain for inclusion in the strategic plan.
- Feedback: An ongoing feedback process will help to make adjustments to the program to keep it operating efficiently. Also, seeking and using feedback from stakeholders, customers, and employees lets them know that their opinion is valued and that they are involved in the process.
- Resources: A sound performance-driven management program must be adequately resourced. Otherwise, it can't function properly. Resources include people, money, and equipment. All must be appropriately stocked.
- Customer identification: Customer identification is important to performance-driven management. Failing to identify and meet the needs of a customer could be disastrous. Always keep the customer in mind.
- Learning and growth: Performance-driven management is not a stagnant process. It requires learning and growth. Thus, the organization must

keep pace with emerging technologies and trends in business management.

- Environmental scanning: As pointed out above, performance-driven management is not a stagnant process. Furthermore, performance-driven management does not operate in a stagnant environment. Both the external and internal environments must be monitored constantly for threats to and opportunities for the organization.
- Sense of purpose: An established performance-driven management program may become "routine," operating out of habit rather than with a sense of purpose. It's important for the organization to maintain a clear sense of purpose for its program.
- Organizational capacity: A focus on organizational capacity—the commitment of people to an organizational ideal as a necessary ingredient of success—supports a new or continued emphasis on process management as a way of ensuring that inefficient and ineffective processes do not get in the way of the drive to success. It would be wise to maintain this focus. Successful leadership requires not only the time, efforts, and personal abilities of chief executives but also the creation of a framework for success. Successful organizations recognize the importance not only of senior executive leadership but also of creating and sustaining an organizational leadership system that facilitates, develops, and rewards leaders at all levels of the organization. Best-in-class organizations are structured and operated to encourage participation and innovation by all employees, regardless of level.

Summary

Now that you have developed your business strategy, you have to be sure that it is going to work and achieve the required benefits. You are going to have to put measurement systems and protocols in place that can quantify the benefits achieved as the strategy is executed. This is what step 2 is all about, and it is critically important. Measurement will validate the investment in projects if performance benefits can be demonstrated, and just as important, measurement will tell you if the project is still on track. If benefits are not being achieved, the project is running behind schedule, or is exceeding budget, you will have the tools you need to make the necessary changes so that it gets back on track.

2

It's All about Business Performance

- Define business performance goals
- Develop performance framework
- Determine appropriate measures for business improvement and investment
- Develop baseline and target values

Overview

PERFORMANCE, THE CURRENT DAY-TO-DAY operational performance of an organization, provides the baseline for measuring improvements. Projects are successful when you can see measurable performance improvements because of the investment made.

Alignment of business operational (versus HR/personnel) performance measures assures the optimization of workflow across all process and organizational boundaries. These performance measures are customer focused and assess the enterprise-level capability of a process to provide value from the customer's perspective. Customers do not "see" the process boundaries through which their products flow, but they care about the attributes of the product delivered to them. The last step in establishing an integrated performance measurement system is to ensure organizational commitment to the system.

Performance measures, implemented properly, will drive greater accountability, visibility, and transparency. Not only do measures provide managers and executives with a tool to gauge organizational progress, but also, when well crafted and implemented, they can inspire and motivate all employees, set direction for the organization, and encourage alignment from top to bottom. There is a key relationship between strategy and results—execution. As illustrated in figure 2.1, strategy, goals, and objectives set the direction of the organization, and the relationship is evaluated, tracked, and refined using performance measures.

Again, figure 2.1 illustrates the four phases for developing a performance measurement system. The first phase is strategy, which identifies your goals and objectives—these should have been developed in step 1. Once these have been identified (phase 2), you can use them to identify and define performance measures, the focus of step 2/phase 3—and you can apply these measures to your outcomes. The results provide the feedback (phase 4), which can be used to ensure that the right measures are being implemented and that your goals and objectives are being met. All of this information is then fed back into phase 1 to validate the strategy. As with performance-driven management (PDM) and the five-step process, each phase is dependent on the others—producing a continuous loop, which allows best practices to be implemented and enables an ongoing process of continual improvement and enhancement to be developed.

Performance measures give life to the mission, vision, and strategy by providing a focus that lets each employee know how he or she contributes to the success of the company and its stakeholders' measurable expectations. It leads to improved profitability and growth in the private sector (outcomes) and improved mission performance and efficiency in the public sector.

There are huge demands on the investment pool, so any investment must be used effectively to achieve maximum results. There can be several types of performance improvement, and the right investment can result in multiple gains. These gains could be increased efficiency and output, increased quality and functionality, and increased function. Another gain could be maintenance of the baseline against performance degradation due to aging equipment or unanticipated volume growth. All of these are benefits if they result in a performance that is better, faster, and/or cheaper.

Performance measurement, in simplest terms, is the comparison of actual levels of performance to preestablished target levels of performance. To be effective, performance measurement must be linked to the organizational strategic plan. Performance-based management essentially uses performance measurement information to manage and improve performance and to demonstrate what has been accomplished. In other words,

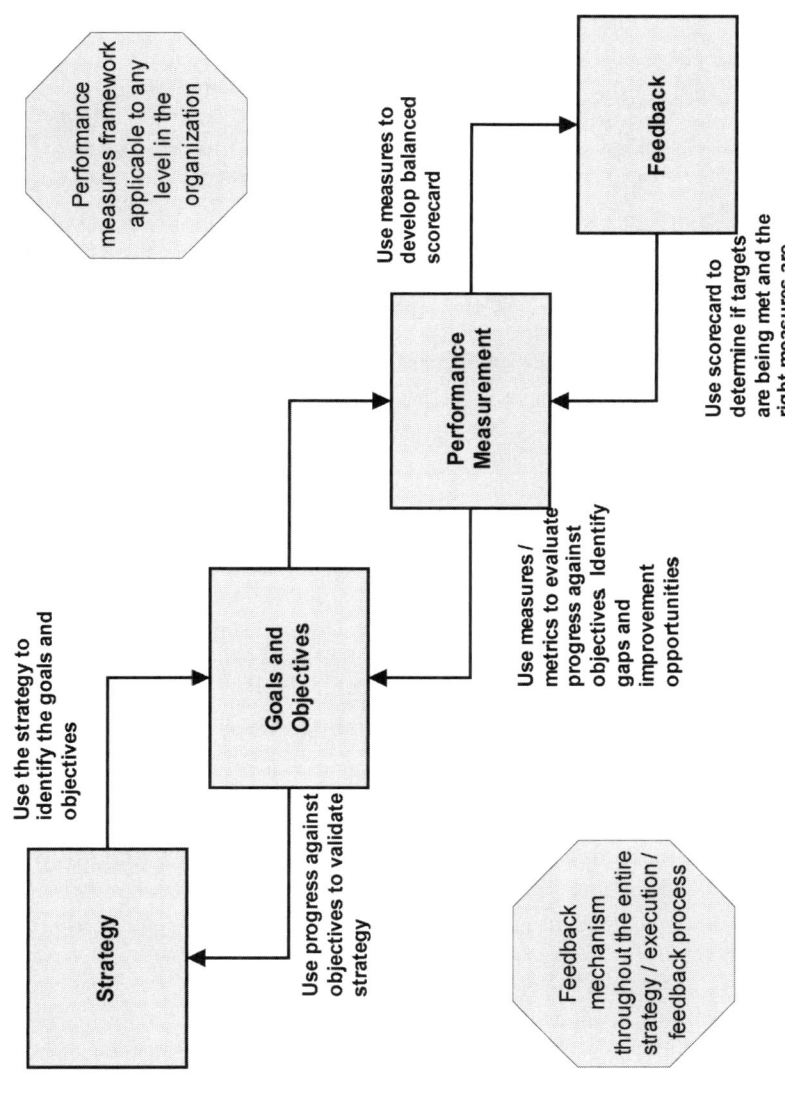

Performance measures framework applicable to any level in the organization

Use measures to develop balanced scorecard

Feedback

Use scorecard to determine if targets are being met and the right measures are being taken

Performance Measurement

Use measures / metrics to evaluate progress against objectives Identify gaps and improvement opportunities

Use the strategy to identify the goals and objectives

Goals and Objectives

Use progress against objectives to validate strategy

Strategy

Feedback mechanism throughout the entire strategy / execution / feedback process

FIGURE 2.1
Annotated Strategy/Feedback Loop

performance measurement is a critical component of performance-based management.

"A prerequisite for having a sensible performance measurement system is that some kind of agreement exists on agency or program goals and how to achieve the goals. That is step one; the performance measurement system is step two. So first have agreement on what to accomplish at the agency level, which is often called a strategic plan, or at the program level, which can be called a strategic plan if the program is large enough or may be called an operational plan, if the program is smaller. The measurement system is relevant only in the context of some degree of agreement on what goals we are shooting for and how we are trying to get there. That tells us what kind of measures will be useful in managing for performance and communicating what performance is desired and what performance we are achieving." (Wholey 1998)

Performance measurement has many beneficial uses. For example, it can be used to:

• Set goals and standards
• Detect and correct problems
• Manage, describe, and improve processes
• Document accomplishments
• Gain insight into, and make judgments about, the effectiveness and efficiency of programs, processes, and people
• Determine whether organizations are fulfilling their vision and meeting their customer-focused strategic goals
• Provide measurable results to demonstrate progress toward goals and objectives
• Determine the effectiveness of your part of your group/department/division/organization

Develop Business Performance Objectives

Business performance goals are driven by the strategic plan. There are a wide range of definitions for performance objective, performance goal, performance measure, performance measurement, and performance management. To frame the dialog and to move forward with a common baseline, certain key concepts need to be clearly defined and understood, such as:

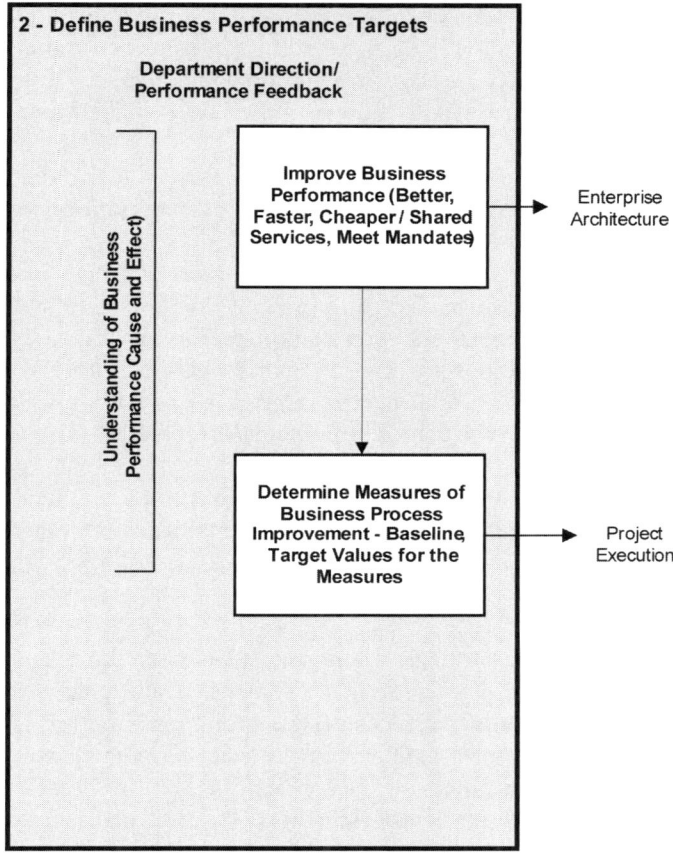

FIGURE 2.2
Overview of Step 2

- Performance objective: This is a critical success factor in achieving the organization's mission, vision, and strategy, which if not achieved would likely result in a significant decrease in customer satisfaction, system performance, employee satisfaction or retention, or effective financial management.
- Performance target or goal: A target level of activity expressed as a tangible, quantified measure, against which actual achievement can be compared.
- Performance measure: A quantitative or qualitative characterization of performance.

- Performance measurement: A process of assessing progress toward achieving predetermined goals, including information on the efficiency with which resources are transformed into goods and services (outputs), the quality of those outputs (how well they are delivered to clients and the extent to which clients are satisfied) and outcomes (the results of a program activity compared to its intended purpose), and the effectiveness of operations in terms of their specific contributions to program objectives.
- Performance management: The use of performance measurement information to effect positive change in organizational culture, systems, and processes by helping to set agreed-upon performance goals, allocating and prioritizing resources, informing managers to either confirm or change current policy or program directions to meet those goals, and sharing results of performance in pursuing those goals.

There are a number of sources that should be examined as a first step in establishing performance objectives. These sources typically provide a strategic perspective in developing a set of objectives and "critical few" performance measures. These components are:

- The strategic plan: Strategic plans (see step 1) set the foundation for effective performance measurement systems. Traditional performance measurement systems that focus on the wrong set of performance measures can actually undermine an organization's strategic mission by perpetuating shortsighted business practices. For this reason, it is appropriate to discuss the critical elements of strategic plans and review the compatibility of strategic plans to an integrated performance measurement system.
- Key business processes: Processes and their activities are the means to achieve the outcomes—the end results—of the strategic plan. But, usually, there are many processes and activities within an organization, each potentially needing performance measures. With this reality in mind, the secret to a successful integrated performance measurement system is to clearly identify the organization's "key" business processes, that is, those having the most impact on the success or failure of the organization's goals. The primary objective should be to keep the number of key processes to a manageable yet useful level. Too many can lead to an overwhelming number of measures and resulting data. Too few can lead to inadequate information on which to base business decisions.
- Stakeholder needs: If they have a stake in the output of the process, they should have input to the process.

- Senior management: In many organizations, leadership commitment to the development and use of performance measures is a critical element in the success of the performance measurement system.
- Employee involvement: When developing an integrated performance measurement system, don't forget to involve your employees in the process. After all, they are the ones who directly contribute to the input, output, outcome, performance, process, and every other aspect of the organizational operation. Employee involvement is one of the best ways to create a positive culture that thrives on performance measurement. When employees have input into all phases of creating a performance measurement system, buy-in is established as part of the process. The level and timing of employee involvement should be individually tailored depending on the size and structure of the organization.
- Accountability for measures: Successful deployment of an integrated performance measurement system is related strongly to developing a successful system of accountability, that is, managers and employees alike "buy in" to performance measurement by assuming responsibility for some part of the performance measurement process.
- A conceptual framework: A conceptual framework can help in deciding what to measure. For example, measuring organizational performance can be linked to the strategic planning process. Or you can use a balanced set of measures to ensure that senior leaders can get a quick comprehensive assessment of the organization in a single report. A family of measures can be used to align measurement across levels of the organizations.
- Communication: Communication is crucial for establishing and maintaining a performance measurement system. It should be multidirectional, running top-down, bottom-up, and horizontally within and across the organization.
- A sense of urgency: The impetus to move—or move more aggressively—to a new or enhanced performance measurement and performance management system is generally the result of a cataclysmic event—most frequently, a circumstance threatening the organization's marketplace survival. One of several scenarios may precede initiating a performance measurement system within an organization.

Each performance objective should be supported by at least one measure that will indicate an organization's performance against that objective. Measures should be precisely defined, including the population to be measured, the method of measurement, the data source, and the time period for the measurement. Measures should be written as mathematical formulae, wherever possible.

Once you have determined your objectives and goals, you have to develop a framework that provides an ongoing mechanism to track and quantify progress. This framework must be designed so that it can define the scope of measures needed and support development of specific measures. The framework then becomes an essential tool to evaluate performance.

Develop Performance Framework

The balanced scorecard (BSC) offers the best basis for developing a performance management system coupled with the line-of-sight process, which provides linkage from strategy to specific measurable results.

Balanced Scorecard

A balanced scorecard is a performance measurement program that acts as a change catalyst within an organization. It promotes innovation, encourages alignment throughout the enterprise, and changes the way the organization behaves toward accomplishing strategic goals and objectives. There are numerous approaches used by the federal government and commercial sector to measure performance. One technique widely leveraged and considered a best practice in both the commercial sector and the federal government is the BSC.

BSC is an approach that helps organizations translate strategy into operational objectives that drive both behavior and performance. It can help organizations create future value by understanding results and identifying improvement opportunities through implementing a double-loop feedback process. The BSC was developed by Robert Kaplan, a Harvard professor, and David Norton, a management consultant. In 1990, Kaplan and Norton led a research study of a dozen commercial companies, exploring new performance measurement methods. Representatives of these companies, along with Kaplan and Norton were convinced that relying solely on financial measures was limiting the organization's ability to create value. According to Kaplan and Norton, more than 75 percent of the average firm's market value is derived from intangible assets that traditional financial metrics don't capture.

The outcome of the study was the development of the BSC, which captures an organization's activity from four perspectives:

- *Financial*—Is the organization creating value for its shareholder?
- *Customer*—How is the organization performing from the perspective of those who purchase the organization's products and services?

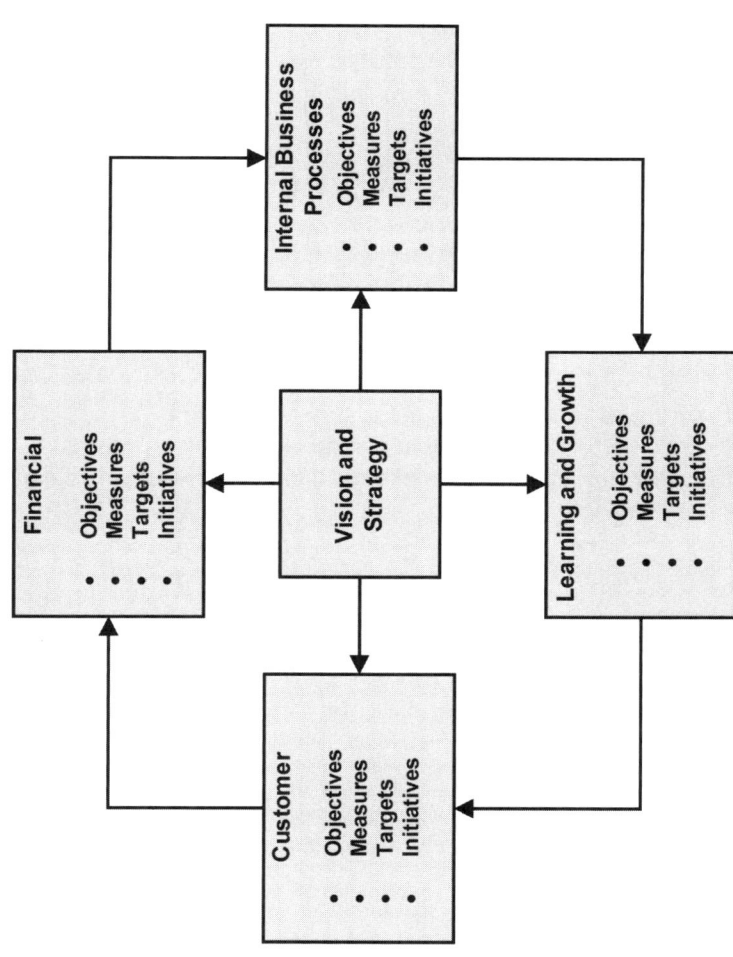

FIGURE 2.3
Balanced Scorecard Overview

- *Learning and growth*—Is the company improving its ability to innovate and learn?
- *Internal business processes*—How is the organization managing its internal business processes to meet its client expectations? Is throughput improving? This perspective also evaluates other processes, such as fulfillment, customer retention, financial planning, and so forth.

This strategic management approach balances: short- and long-term objectives, financial and nonfinancial measures, lagging and leading indicators, and external and internal performance.

The Defense Finance and Accounting Service (DFAS), BMW, Motorola, DuPont, the Defense Logistics Agency (DLA), the Department of the Army, CIGNA, Fulton County Schools, and others have successfully implemented the BSC principles and methodology to drive results in their organization.

The BSC can be leveraged by government agencies, including defense, state and local government, service organizations, and manufacturers. These organizations have employed the BSC to:

- Clarify strategies and communicate to the organization
- Identify key internal processes that will drive strategic success
- Align investments in people, technology, and organizational capital for the greatest impact

U.S. Army Medical School

On December 20, 2007, the U.S. Army surgeon general and commander of the U.S. Army Medical Command, Lieutenant General Eric B. Schoomaker sent a memo to all his senior commanders. He wrote: "We will continue to use the Balanced Scorecard (BSC) as the principal tool by which we guide and track the Command as we improve operational and fiscal effectiveness and better meet the needs of our patients and stakeholders. The BSC Strategy Map communicates our organization's mission, vision, and the means and ways on which we will focus our performance to best attain the needs important to mission accomplishment."

He added, "Use the BSC as a guide in all command and management functions. With conscious, disciplined application, it truly works!"

As shown in figure 2.4, the BSC drives business metrics/measures, which in turn drive performance targets. These targets are then achieved through strategic initiatives.

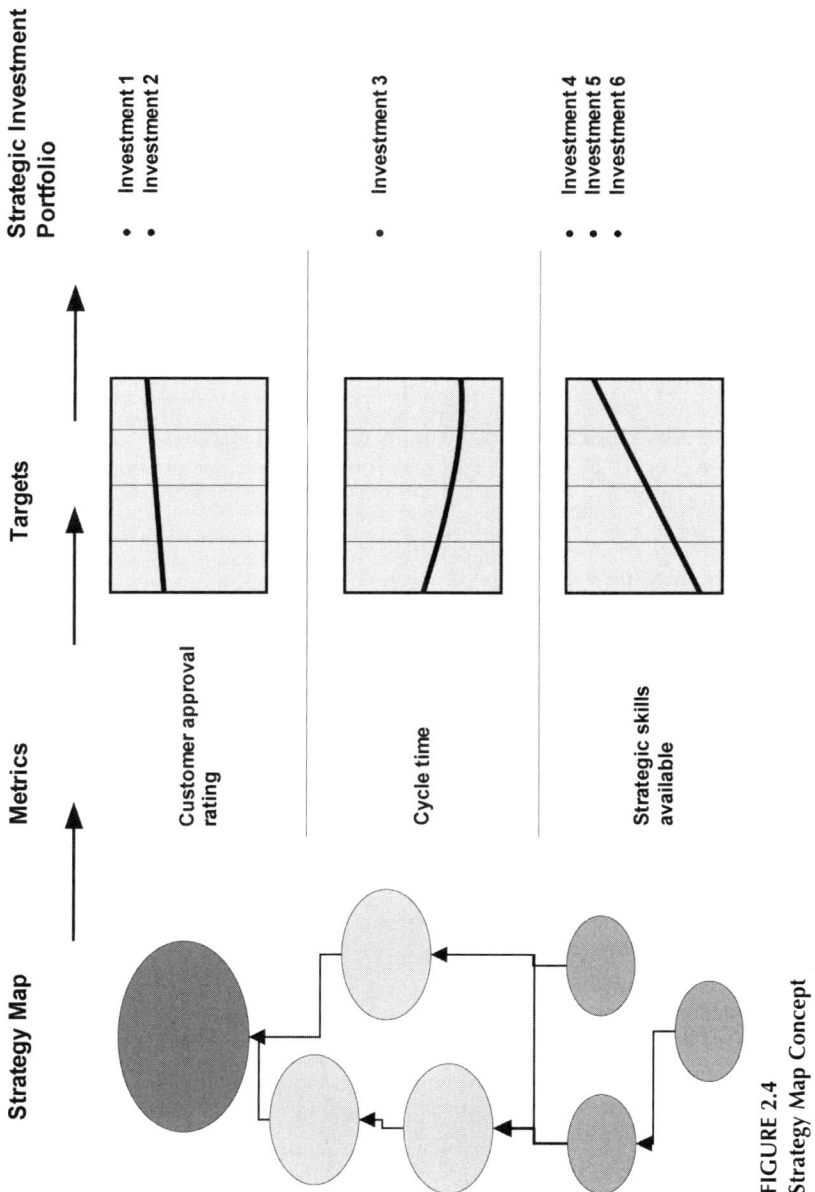

Strategic Investment Portfolio

- Investment 1
- Investment 2

- Investment 3

- Investment 4
- Investment 5
- Investment 6

Targets

Metrics

Customer approval rating

Cycle time

Strategic skills available

Strategy Map

FIGURE 2.4
Strategy Map Concept

Develop Appropriate Measures

It is important to focus on developing appropriate measures in order to define the benefits to be realized, create the metric, start the data-gathering process, and develop a clear line of sight—an unobstructed path that takes you from strategy to tangible measurement. The term comes from the old days of wireless when transmission towers had to be in sight of each other in order for a radio signal to be sent from one and received by the other. The analogy is a good one because in order for the project to succeed, you have to have a clear view (understanding) of how you are going to get there.

In the past, IT projects were left to the IT project manager who followed the well-tried dictum of "design, develop, test, and deliver." For major IT projects, this is no longer enough. The IT project manager is just one member of a representative integrated project team that works together to achieve the right outcomes.

Figure 2.5 describes the overall incorporation of metrics/measures in the strategic process. It illustrates the separate feedback loops for output and outcome measures.

Getting Organized

The BSC elements selected will guide your strategic focus as you begin to develop your performance measures. However, before you go about this task, you need to "get yourself organized." Specific steps to take are:

- Establish the performance measurement team. The team should be made up of the people who actually do the work to be measured and the people who are very familiar with the work to be measured. It is important that each person understands the task and his or her role in its accomplishment.
- Gain an understanding of the jargon. Performance measurement jargon can be very confusing but needs to be understood and agreed to by the performance measurement team.
- Consider the "considerations." The "considerations" are: keep the number of performance measures at each management level to a minimum, develop clear and understandable objectives and performance measures, determine if the cost of the measure is worth the gain, consider the cost of attaining the next level of improvement, assure that the measure is comprehensive, consider performing a risk evaluation, consider the weight of conflicting performance measures, and develop consistent performance measures that promote teamwork.

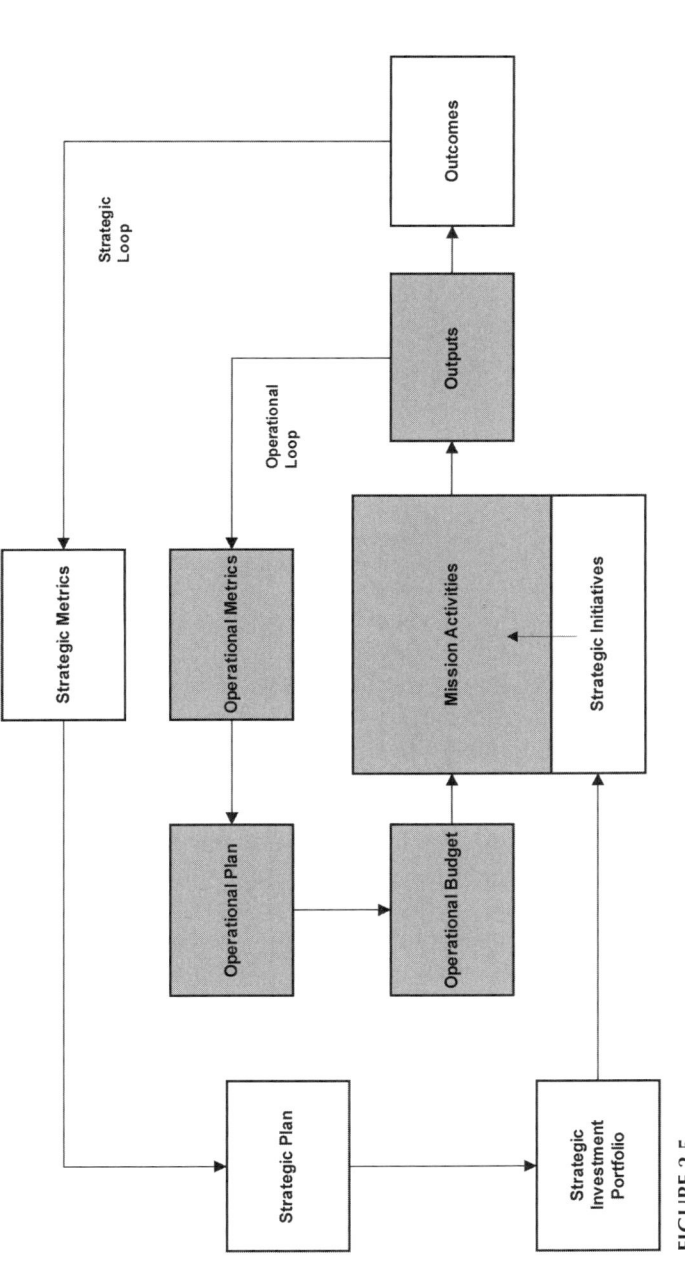

FIGURE 2.5
Performance Metric Driven Strategy

- Know how to check/test your measures. After you have developed your performance measures, you need to check/test them for soundness (i.e., completeness, repeatability, applicability, usefulness, etc.). Knowing how to perform these checks/tests and, thus, knowing what to look for in a performance measure, will help develop sound performance measures from the start.
- Take a look at how other organizations measure performance. Now that your team is organized and ready to develop its performance measures, take one last important step: look at what other organizations similar to yours have done and are doing with regard to their performance measurement system. The point here is to eliminate your team's "reinventing the wheel" and, thus, save you valuable time and resources (and spare you many headaches!). The odds run high that you will be able to find another organization to share useful information that your team (and organization) can adopt and adapt to its particular circumstances.

Common guidance for developing performance measures is embodied in the SMART acronym (Specific, Measurable, Accountable, Results Oriented, Time Bound). The SMART criteria are used to determine the usefulness, validity, and accuracy of the performance measures to be used by the program at all levels. For a performance measure to be effective, it must be:

- Specific: The performance measure has to indicate exactly what result is expected so that the performance can be judged accurately. The specificity of the measure is aided by clear definitions and standards for data collection, standardization, and reporting across program lines and among program employees involved in use of the measurement.
- Measurable: The intended result has to be something that can be measured and reported in quantitative and/or clear qualitative terms. This characteristic is achieved when programs set numeric targets or employ an evaluative approach that can ascertain in a definitive manner whether performance expectations have been met.
- Accountable: The performance measure has to be "owned" by a specific program line or employee base. Accountability is more than clarifying who is charged with achieving the result; it requires that management has devised targets based on what reasonably can be produced by the program during a given period of time. Accountability cannot be achieved if targets are unreasonable from the start.
- Results oriented: The performance measure must be aligned to the line of sight and track an important value or benefit needed to advance the

strategies and achieve the end results of the program. A performance measurement meets this test if it (1) measures an end or intermediate outcome, or (2) links to another measure already existing within a program that measures an intermediate or end outcome.
- Time bound: The performance measure must set a specific time frame for the results to be produced as well as allow for the reporting of performance in a timely manner. In this case, the program must have measures to provide fresh enough data to be used by management for adjustments in the program and corrective action if necessary. (Down 1981).

Additionally, measures should possess the following characteristics:

- Objective—not judgment calls
- Controllable—the results are substantially in the hands of the organization with the effects of potential outside influences minimized
- Simple—easily understood and measuring only one thing
- Timely—frequently available indicators of recent or current performance
- Accurate—reliable, precise, sensitive indicators of results
- Graded—trackable data available before system failure—not binary yes/no measures
- Cost-effective—providing data worth the cost of gathering it
- Useful—providing data necessary for the organization to manage the business
- Motivating—achieving the targets should drive good business decisions, not overexpenditure, overcompliance, or other suboptimization

Although the focus of strategic measures is most often on outcomes or outputs, some measures could be focused on inputs or other types of measures. The text below describes the different types of measures.

- Outcome measure: An assessment of the results of a program compared to its intended purpose. Outcome measurement cannot be done until the results expected from a program or activity has been first defined. As such, an outcome is a statement of basic expectations, often grounded in a statute, directive, or other document. Outcome measurement also cannot be done until a program (of fixed duration) is completed, or until a program (which is continuing indefinitely) has reached a point of maturity or steady-state operations. The measurement of incremental progress toward a specific outcome goal is sometimes referred to as an intermediate outcome.

- Output measure: Strictly defined, output is the goods and services produced by a program or organization and provided to the public or to other programs or organizations. Output may be measured either as the total quantity of a good or service produced or may be limited to those goods or services with certain attributes (e.g., number of timely and accurate benefit payments). Some output measures are developed and used independent of any outcome measure. The number of output measures will generally exceed the number of outcome measures, and both outcome and output measures can be set out as performance goals or performance indicators.
- Process measure: These measures quantify process attributes (e.g., paper flow, consultation), attribute measures (e.g., timeliness, accuracy, customer satisfaction), and measures of efficiency or effectiveness.
- Input measure: Measures of what an agency or manager has available to carry out the program or activity (i.e., achieve an outcome or output). These can include employees, funding, equipment or facilities, supplies on hand, goods or services received, work processes, or rules. When calculating efficiency, input is defined as the resources used.

Other dimensions of measures normally include the following:

- Core measures: These are measures an organization expects all elements to employ where applicable. The formulae and methods for core measures shall be maintained as standard as is practicable from site to site.
- Optional measures: These are measures suggested, but not required, and may be useful indicators for assessing progress toward the predetermined core objective.
- Local measures: These are measures that have site or contractor specificity, which each site may identify and include as part of their BSC.

Most performance measures can be grouped into one of the following six general categories. However, certain organizations may develop their own categories as appropriate depending on the organization's mission:

- Effectiveness: A process characteristic indicating the degree to which the process output (work product) conforms to requirements (are we doing the right things?).
- Efficiency: A process characteristic indicating the degree to which the process produces the required output at minimum resource cost (are we doing things right?).

- Quality: The degree to which a product or service meets customer requirements and expectations.
- Timeliness: Measures whether a unit of work was done correctly and on time. Criteria must be established to define what constitutes timeliness for a given unit of work. The criterion is usually based on customer requirements.
- Productivity: The value added by the process divided by the value of the labor and capital consumed.
- Safety: Measures the overall health of the organization and the working environment of its employees.

Initial Selection, Addition, and Deletion of Performance Measures

Many reasons exist for selecting a particular performance measure. In most instances, however, the reason for selecting a measure should fall within one or more of the following:

- BSC-driven: Measures driven by specific areas as defined in the BSC.
- Customer-focused: In most organizations, customer perception of product/ service cost, quality, timeliness, and service-provider responsiveness plays a significant role in organizational success. As a result, performance measures should be created that monitor product/service cost, quality, "speed," and service.
- Strategic considerations: Senior management is responsible for guiding organizational performance in a direction that will ensure accomplishment of strategic goals. Once strategic goals are defined, performance measures can be developed that will help stimulate performance toward achievement of predetermined objectives and in the desired strategic direction.
- Critical few: Performance measures should constitute those which are determined critical to achieving customer satisfaction and service, as well as organizational, informational, workforce, and business process improvements and other strategic objectives. Too many measures will diffuse the focus of the organization and the measurement process.

As an example, the Department of Energy (DOE) was one of the early federal government adopters of the BSC. See figure 2.6 for an example of DOE's development of performance measures along with performance targets.

The core measures used in the federal procurement and contractor purchasing models were established by cooperation between DOE headquarters

Objective	Measure	Target
Use of Electronic Commerce:	*Use of Electronic Commerce:*	
Data Source: Electronic Small Purchase Systems, PADS, CUTS,IIPS, local tracking systems	1. Percent of purchase and delivery orders issued through electronic commerce as a percentage of total simplified acquisition actions	33% for FY 2001 50% for FY 2002 60% for FY 2003
Data Generation: Data is tabulated from the listed tracking systems.	2. Percent of all synopses (for which widespread notice is required) and associated solicitations posted on FEDBIZOPPS. This measure will be tracked at HQ.	100% of actions over $25K
Data Verification: Procurement directors are responsible for accurately reporting results and retention of records in accordance with records management requirements. Records will be made available for compliance and/or HQ reviews.	3. Percent of all new competitive acquisition transactions of $100K conducted through electronic commerce.	30% for FY 2003 40% for FY 2004
Performance-Based Service Contracts	*Performance-Based Service Contracts:*	
Data Source: PADS Data Generation: Data is tabulated from PADS.	PBSCs awarded as a percentage of total eligible new service contract awards (applicable to actions over $100K).	66%
Data Verification: Procurement directors are responsible for accuracy of data entered into PADS. On a routine basis, HQ will randomly sample pre- and post-award actions and compare against the FAR PBSC standards.	Percent of total eligible service contract dollars obligated for PBSCs (applicable to all actions over $25K). This measure will be tracked at HQ.	60%

FIGURE 2.6
DOE Performance Measures and Targets

and DOE field elements (for the federal program) and DOE headquarters, DOE field elements, and contractor purchasing organizations (for the contractor purchasing program). Cooperation between participating parties is expected to continue in the creation and deletion of core performance measures. Although many factors exist that can influence any decision to add or delete a measure, the following criteria will be followed to the extent possible:

- *Each measure will be retained for multiple years, usually not less than three years.* Assessment of performance under the BSC methodology is dependent upon trend data established over time. A one-time-only assessment will provide a "snapshot" of current performance, but it does not provide a reliable assessment of where the organization is going. As a result, it does not make much sense to create a performance measure that will be utilized for one assessment period only. Therefore, in general, each core measure developed will be used for several years before any decision to delete is made.

- *In general, measures will be maintained for strategic purposes.* The BSC is a strategic tool whose objectives and measures are focused on strategic change. Therefore, when performance has reached stable levels of excellence, objectives and measures may be adjusted to focus on new directions and areas needing attention. However, because of the importance of excellent performance in certain areas (e.g., customer satisfaction, statutory and regulatory compliance), even when organizations achieve a high level of consistent performance, organizations still need to keep focused on these performance areas and have an assessment system that provides the organization with immediate notification if performance begins to slip.

- *DOE headquarters (federal program) or DOE headquarters or field element (contractor program) may mandate the inclusion of a performance measure.* In certain circumstances, DOE may require the inclusion of a measure without the participation or agreement of affected parties. These circumstances will be limited to instances where specific measurement is directed by law or regulation or is deemed critical to guide organizational performance in a direction necessary to accomplish strategic goals.

The guidelines above provide characteristics of performance measures that should be followed to develop the most effective and comprehensive performance measurement system for an organization. Selection of specific measures will be driven by the organization's strategy, performance objectives, and critical business elements.

Line of Sight

To be meaningful, performance measures need to link from strategy to quantified outcomes for an investment. A line of sight is the concept/tool for defining this linkage and achieving successful outcomes.

Project managers should consider broader agency goals and objectives in the development of IT investment performance indicators. In addition to guidance from the OMB, GAO audits and the annual performance plans, which track progress against the agency's strategic plan, should be used to help IT project managers develop measures that are in line with the priorities of the department. Alignment to the strategic plan and annual performance plans is necessary for reporting performance information as part of the OMB exhibit 300.

Figure 2.7 illustrates a full line of sight and the relationship of each line-of-sight element. The line of sight starts with a strategic goal, then links to a performance objective and a desired business result. The line of sight then continues by linking a specific measure to the desired business result and, finally, specific, quantified values associated with the measure. The example column provides a good illustration. Understanding of the line of sight for each measure is critical to ensuring that the measure is meaningful and will positively impact organizational business goals.

Process Improvement and Measures

Business performance results are generally achieved through one or more business processes. IT investments often relate to the effective enablement of business processes or business results. All business processes have fundamental elements—inputs, processes, and outputs. These elements are shown in figure 2.7 and described in the text that follows.

- Inputs: Inputs are the first step in a business process. The inputs are those things that enable the processes that produce the outputs of a process. Inputs are things like raw materials, resources, and so forth.
- Process/IT enablement: IT enablement may be technology and assets owned by a specific investment, or they may be external to the investment or its organization. To identify inputs, the following questions should be asked:
  - What are the relevant people, technology, and fixed assets?
  - How do these enablers contribute to outputs?
- Outputs: Outputs are the products or services provided by a business process. They should contribute directly or indirectly to an outcome. When identifying outputs, IT project managers should ask the following questions:

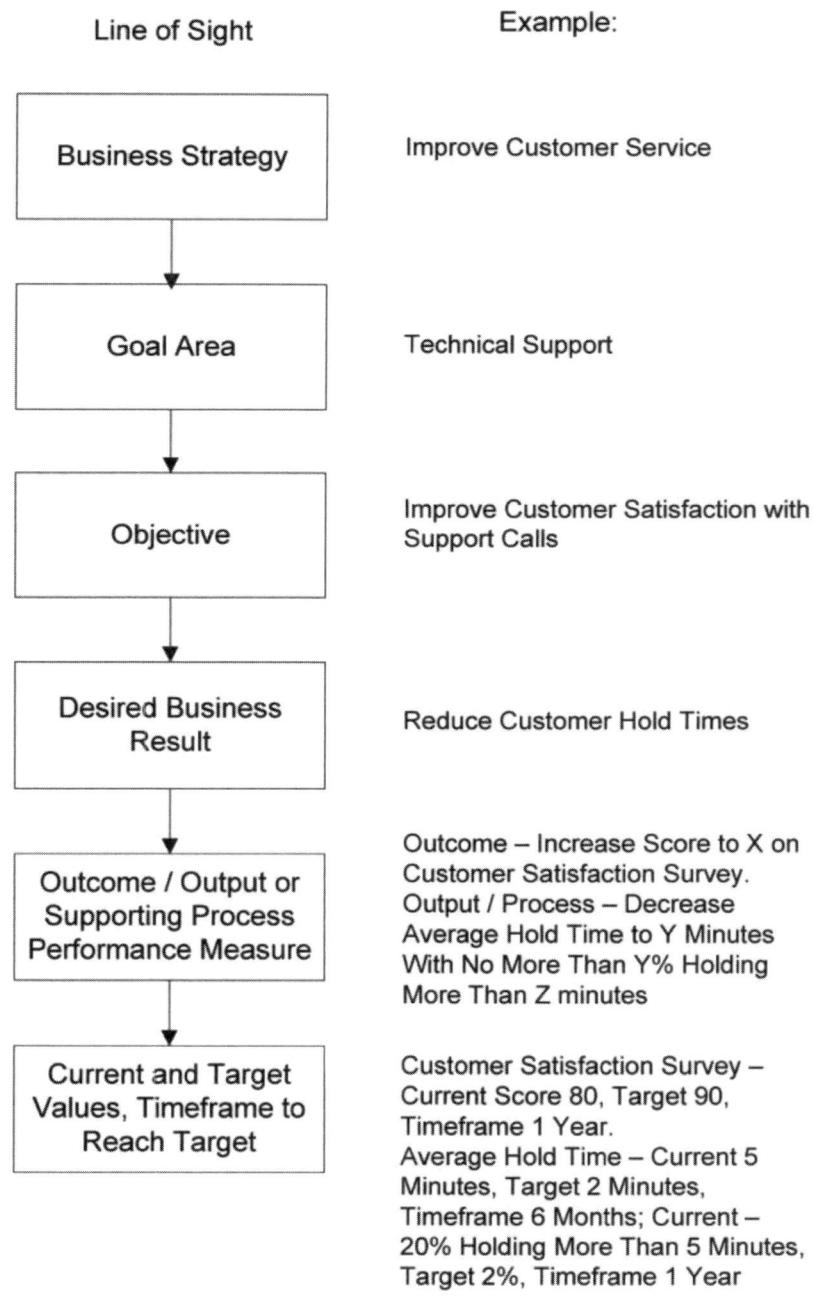

Line of Sight

Example:

| Business Strategy | Improve Customer Service |

| Goal Area | Technical Support |

| Objective | Improve Customer Satisfaction with Support Calls |

| Desired Business Result | Reduce Customer Hold Times |

| Outcome / Output or Supporting Process Performance Measure | Outcome – Increase Score to X on Customer Satisfaction Survey. Output / Process – Decrease Average Hold Time to Y Minutes With No More Than Y% Holding More Than Z minutes |

| Current and Target Values, Timeframe to Reach Target | Customer Satisfaction Survey – Current Score 80, Target 90, Timeframe 1 Year. Average Hold Time – Current 5 Minutes, Target 2 Minutes, Timeframe 6 Months; Current – 20% Holding More Than 5 Minutes, Target 2%, Timeframe 1 Year |

FIGURE 2.7
Performance Line of Sight

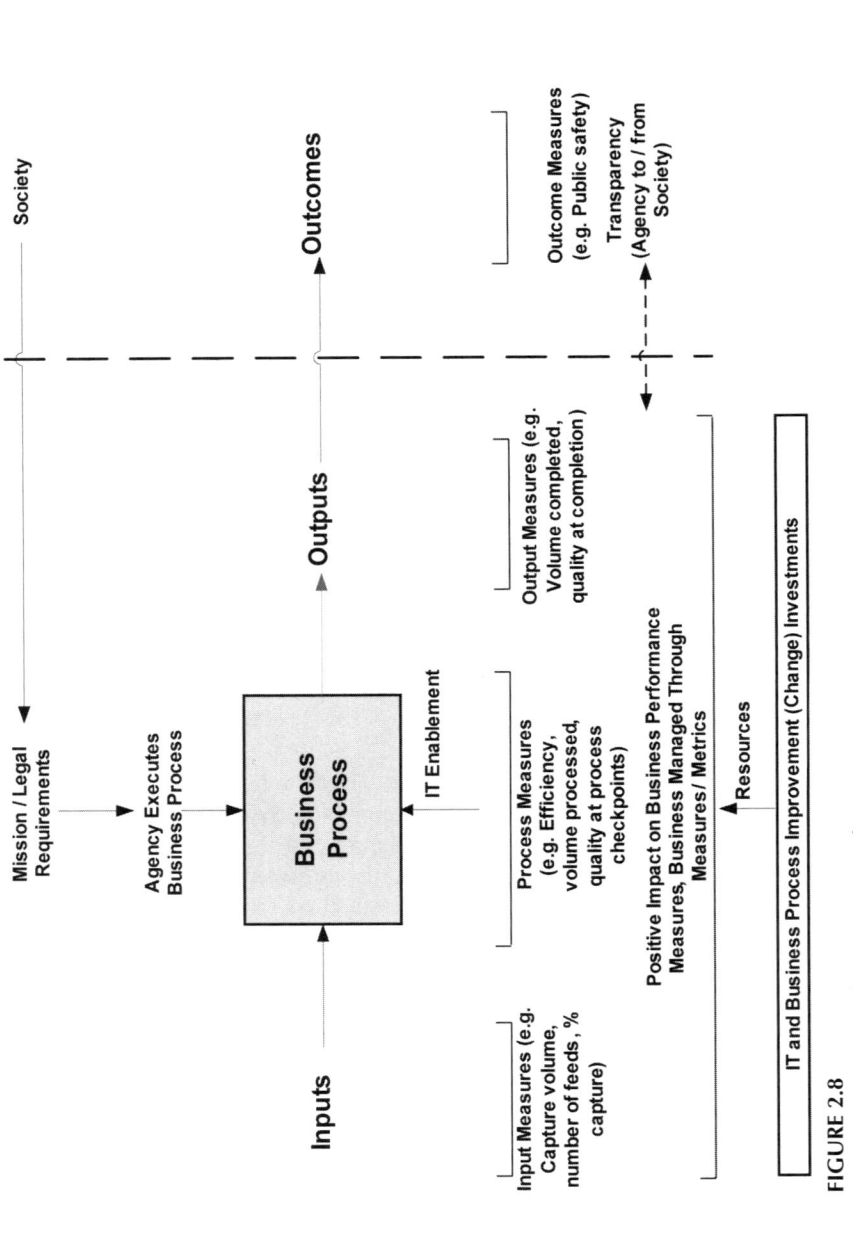

FIGURE 2.8
Business Process Performance Overview

o What are the measureable items produced as a direct result of the business process (i.e., number of loan applications completed for a bank)?

- Outcomes: Outcomes are the conditions created by an IT investment's success; they are results. Outcomes are the component that provides the best linkage to the higher level strategies and goals supported by the investment. For identifying outcomes, the following questions should be asked:

  o Who are the customers of the investment's processes?
  o How are these customers impacted by the products and services provided?
  o What is the purpose and mission of the investment and organization?

The process improvement continuum draws a clear connection from a process's inputs to outputs to outcomes. Once the process improvement continuum has been established, IT project managers and program managers should look for opportunities to measure the aspects of their IT investment's performance—IT projects enabling the overall process. Once this has been established, specific measures can be defined. Good process measures have the following characteristics:

- Informative: The measure helps to articulate success for the investment and the programs it supports. The measure demonstrates progress toward goals, closing performance gaps, and achieving critical results.
- Feasible: The data is currently being collected and available. The burden or cost of collecting new data for the measure is reasonable considering how informative it would be for managers and decision makers.
- Managed: Measures should be linked to the investment's business case, specifically any high-level milestones and the stated benefits outlined in the alternatives analysis.
- Complete: The entire list of measures collectively provides an accurate and broad enough "snapshot" of performance.

Develop Baseline and Target Values

Implied within every stage of the planning process is the ability to determine progress made toward the goals or targets. At this stage, it is important to begin quantifying the values for the measures. This includes both baseline (current) and target (goal) to be achieved through investments or other change activities.

To determine the baseline, current data is collected for each measure. The final form of the measures will depend upon the data available. Data will be analyzed to determine that acceptable quality data is available for all measures. Based on the data quality and other policy guidance, a starting point or baseline will be established.

Target values are then developed based on strategic goals and the ability to make reasonable progress from the baseline values. For example, if it takes 30 days to currently process an application, 15 days may be realistic for an initial goal, but subsequently, it may be easier to move from 15 days to 5 days than from 30 days to 5 days in one step. In general, target values should support the strategic and performance goals, no matter how aggressive, and the organization should then invest to meet these goals. Investments, including IT investments, are the way an organization can move business performance along toward its goals.

As an example, the DOE has established departmental expectations (desirable scores) for its core measures. Per their documents, these expectations or targets correlate to performance levels demonstrated by successful organizations. All sites shall strive to meet or exceed these expectations/targets. It is recognized that local situations are impacted by organizational alignment, structure, vision, strategic objectives, and current conditions.

Each site may establish short-term local targets for core, optional, and local measures. While these should provide aggressive "stretch" performance targets, they should be realistic. There is little benefit in creating unrealistic or unattainable targets for "optics." It is expected that when targets are set below departmental expectations, they will be set to stimulate substantial progress toward those expectations and will rise over time. Similarly, where organizations have already exceeded departmental expectations, targets in excess of national averages may be maintained as part of continuous improvement.

It is understood that performance should not be driven beyond what is necessary to be supportive of the organizational mission, taking into consideration funding and resource realities (e.g., though it is always desirable to drive cost-effectiveness, it is recognized there is a point in performance or cycle time beyond which improvement does no service to the customer and could drive unnecessary costs). Local targets may, therefore, not rise perpetually. When acceptable levels are achieved, these should be maintained and other performance areas emphasized whose improvement has greater strategic importance.

Pitfalls and Critical Success Factors

The development of performance measures is complex, and there are many challenges.

The Cause and Effect of Outcomes Are Not Easily Established

Outcomes can, and often do, reveal the impact of the program, but without collaborating data, it is difficult to demonstrate that your program was the cause of the outcome(s). The outcomes of public-sector services are inevitably affected by many events outside public control. In the weatherization assistance program, for example, it is not always easy to demonstrate energy savings because the changes introduced to homes may result in changes in the behavior of inhabitants that confounds the analysis. Assume, as a second example, that the goal of energy research is to encourage the development of new technologies that will be adopted by industry and result in energy savings. The outcome may not occur for decades, and while it may be possible to claim that the original research contributed to the final product, it will most likely not be the only contributing factor.

To determine the extent to which a program has affected the outcomes and to measure the impact, you need to do an in-depth analysis. Special program evaluations provide estimates of program impacts and help determine why some programs succeed and others do not. The cost of special program evaluations to demonstrate the causes and effects may outweigh the benefits of knowing more about causal relationships.

Though most benefits are expected to be related to your efforts and the original program plan, others may be viewed as serendipitous impacts. Such unplanned outcomes contribute to the value of programs and should be reflected in performance results appropriately.

Poor Results Do Not Necessarily Point to Poor Execution

If performance objectives are not being met, it is obvious that something is wrong, but performance information itself does not always provide the reason. Instead, it raises a flag requiring investigation.

Possibilities include performance expectations that were unrealistic or changed work priorities. Your organization should be able to explain performance results and to define and address the contributing factors.

Numerical Quotas Do Not Fix Defective Processes

There is also a danger when performance objectives become numerical quotas. The setting of numerical goals and quotas does nothing to accomplish improvements in the process. Identifying the challenges and changing the processes are what is needed to improve performance and achieve desired outcomes.

Measurements Only Approximate the Actual System

Performance measurement provides a valuable tool for management and continuous improvement. However, people might try to "game" the system in a way that will make their programs look good. Additionally, accurate data may not be available. These are among the reasons why you need to recognize the fact that the measured system is not the same as the actual system.

Performance Measures Do Not Ensure Compliance with Laws and Regulations

Performance measures help form the basis for sound performance-based management but do not provide information on adherence to laws and regulations or the effectiveness of internal controls. However, in federal circles, it is considered a valid performance measure if a law not previously complied with is now being followed. Because compliance and internal controls often have a direct effect on performance, care should be taken to supplement performance measurement with other oversight activities to ensure that controls are in place and working as intended and that activities are adhering to laws and regulations.

Other challenges include:

- Amassing too much data: It results in "information overload." So much so that managers and employees either will ignore the data or use it ineffectively.
- Focusing on the short-term: Most organizations only collect financial and operational data. They forget to focus on the longer-term measures—the very ones on which the Malcolm Baldrige National Quality Award focuses—of customer satisfaction, employee satisfaction, product/service quality, and public responsibility.
- Failing to base business decisions on the data: A lot of managers make decisions based on intuition and past experience rather than the data being reported to them. If the data is valid, it should be used appropriately.
- "Dumbing" the data: Sometimes data can be summarized so much that it becomes meaningless. If business decisions are going to be based on the data, then the data needs to be reported clearly and understandably.
- Measuring too little: Making business decisions with too little data is just as problematic as basing them on too much data. Some organizations (particularly smaller ones) tend to measure too few key variables to get the "whole picture" of the health of their organization. Mostly, their focus is on financial indicators. However, as with number 2 above,

there needs to be focus on longer-term measures, such as customer and employee satisfaction and market share.

- Collecting inconsistent, conflicting, and unnecessary data: All data should lead to some ultimate measure of success for the company. An example of conflicting measures would be measuring reduction of office space per staff while, at the same time, measuring staff satisfaction with facilities.
- Driving the wrong performance: Exceptional performance in one area could be disastrous in another. Mark Graham Brown tells a poignant anecdote about "chicken efficiency" in which the manager of a fast-food chicken restaurant scores a perfect 100 percent on his chicken efficiency measure (the ratio of how many pieces of chicken sold to the amount thrown away) by waiting until the chicken is ordered before cooking it. However, the end result of his actions was dissatisfied customers (from waiting too long) and lack of repeat business. Thus, the "chicken efficiency" was driving the wrong performance . . . and driving the customers away!
- Encouraging competition and discouraging teamwork: Comparing performance results of organizational unit to organizational unit, or one employee to another, sometimes creates fierce competition to be "number 1" at the expense of destroying a sense of teamwork. Remember to compare to stated performance goals.
- Establishing unrealistic and/or unreasonable measures: Measures must fit into the organization's budgetary and personnel constraints and must be cost-effective. They also must be achievable. Nothing can demoralize an employee quicker than a goal that never can be reached.
- Failing to link measures: Measures should be linked to the organization's strategic plan and should cascade down into the organization (horizontal and vertical linkage). Measures without linkage are like a boat without water. They're useless, and they're not going anywhere.
- Measuring progress too often or not often enough: There has to be a balance here. Measuring progress too often could result in unnecessary effort and excessive costs, resulting in little or no added value. On the other hand, not measuring progress often enough puts you in the situation where you don't know about potential problems until it's too late to take appropriate action.
- Ignoring the customer: Management often wants to measure only an organization's internal components and processes. That way they can "command and control" it. However, in reality, it is the customer who drives any organization's performance. As noted by the National Performance Review (1997), "most of the best-in-class organizations place customer satisfaction above all else."

- Asking the wrong questions/looking in the wrong places: Sometimes business executives ask who's to blame instead of asking what went wrong. They look for the answers in the people instead of the process. A faulty process makes employees look faulty.
- Confusing the purpose of the performance measurement system: The purpose of a performance measurement system is not merely to collect data but rather to collect data upon which to make critical business decisions that will in turn drive business improvement. Knowing that you're 10 pounds overweight is just knowledge of a fact. Taking improvement actions based on that knowledge is where "the truth" lies.

Best Practices

It can be quite a challenge for any organization, whether federal, public, or private, to establish a successful performance measurement process. However, the performance measurement benchmarking study report by the National Performance Review (NPR) identified several performance best practices that can assist an organization be successful in developing and maintaining its performance measurement process.

- Executive involvement: Leadership commitment to the development and use of performance measures is critical in the success of an organization's performance measurement process.
- Sense of urgency: The reason an organization usually implements a performance measurement process is generally the result of a potential threat to an organization's very survival.
- Alignment with strategic direction: Performance measurements are successful when measures are aligned with the organization's strategic mission, vision, and strategy.
- Conceptual framework: An organization's performance measurement process should be tied directly to its management process.
- Balanced set of measures: An organization's performance framework, such as the BSC, generally provides this.

Critical Success Factors for Performance Measurement and Management

1. Performance measurement systems must provide intelligence for decision makers, not just compile data. Performance measures should be limited to those that relate to strategic organizational goals and objectives and that provide timely, relevant, and concise information for use by decision makers—at all levels—to assess progress toward achieving predetermined

goals. Although each organization is unique in how performance results can best benefit the organization, several concepts appear to apply across the board. They include the following:

a. Assessment results must provide meaningful information. Management needs intelligent information for decision making. If properly constructed, the performance measures selected will result in data that is meaningful to decision makers in terms of improving organizational performance. The data generated should be timely, relevant, and concise. Assessment results should provide information on the efficiency of the production of goods and services, on how well current performance compares to intended programmatic purposes, and on the effectiveness of organizational activities and operations in terms of their specific contribution to program objectives. Numerous factors need to be considered when determining the effectiveness of assessment results. They include the following:

   - Does the data indicate any performance trends over time and over projects/functional areas?
   - Can the data be used to improve performance in areas other than the one(s) assessed?
   - Have the correct performance measures been selected for assessing desired performance?
   - Do the measures reflect priorities?
   - Do the results reflect an understandable causal relationship between performance effort and performance result?
   - If performance targets are not met, what inhibited successful performance?
   - If performance targets are significantly exceeded, are there additional benefits to the organization that can be gained in terms of reducing operating costs or improving performance?

b. Assessment results must be properly analyzed. Understanding what a particular result really means is important in determining whether or not it is useful to the organization. Data by itself is not useful information, but it can be when viewed from the context of organizational objectives, environmental conditions, and other factors.

   Proper analysis is imperative in determining whether or not performance indicators are effective and results are contributing to organizational objectives.

2. Results must be used or no one will take them seriously. This seems so obvious that it should not need to be stated. Nevertheless, assessments are often followed with little effective analysis of results or honest attempts at improved performance.

The following represent some of the ways that leading organizations, both public and private, use performance information to improve performance, manage risk, and support decision making:

a. Gap management: Performance results can be used to determine gaps between specific strategic objectives and/or annual goals and actual achievement. The root causes of these gaps are analyzed, and countermeasures are developed and implemented. Whenever there is a gap between current results and an organization's objectives, it is an opportunity for process improvement. Reengineering and redesign are a frequent response to the identification of gaps between objectives and achievement and are usually very effective, particularly when they include "process flow analysis," which requires a detailed examination of the existing process(es) and allows for exploration of alternate procedures within a process. Process flow analysis is especially useful when BSC results indicate performance gaps in the areas of timeliness, purchasing costs, or efficiency. Understanding which key processes need the most attention and then aggressively addressing the differences between current performance and the desired end state is a hallmark of successful organizations.

b. Self-diagnosis: A contracting or purchasing activity can use the information for "self-diagnosis." BSC data together with other reports and statistics can help the activity anticipate and resolve issues before they become problems or at least minimize the effect of problems by early action. Information from other reports and statistics may also indicate the need to adjust BSC strategies and measures.

c. Enhancing strategic feedback and learning: Kaplan and Norton recommend that, in addition to tracking progress on past results, managers can use the BSC to learn about the future. Managers should discuss not only how they achieved past results but also whether their expectations for the future remain on track. Changes in the environment (e.g., new technology, legislative initiatives, etc.) may create new opportunities or threats not anticipated when the managers developed their initial strategies. If an organization followed established strategies but did not achieve target results, managers should examine internal capabilities and assess whether the underlying strategies remain valid. Based on such analyses, managers may adjust or redirect their strategies or identify new strategies. This focus serves as a foundation for effective process improvement and risk management. It also completes a feedback loop that supports decision making at all levels of the organization.

d. Benchmarking: An organization can use the BSC to benchmark its performance against other organizations. Benchmarking helps to get a picture of how the organization's procurement function performs compared to others. It also serves as one input for developing target goals. However, the strength of benchmarking is not in identifying best performance but in learning best practices. That is, the organization should identify, study, analyze, and adapt the "best practices" that led to the "best performance." Understanding the best practices helps managers to make better informed decisions about where and how to change their organization. To make valid comparisons, the organization should consider how the other organization is both similar and different. Common factors to consider, whether selecting another agency or an industry for benchmarking, include:

- Is the total size and budget similar?
- Is the amount spent on acquisition comparable?
- Is the percent of total budget spent on acquisition similar?
- Does the other organization have a similar mission or perform work of comparable complexity?
- Are the products and services acquired similar?
- Several sources have information available for benchmark comparisons:
- An organization can compare its performance on the core measures identified in this BSC to other federal agencies that use the same measures.
- Other agencies may also have similar supplemental organization-specific measures.
- The Center for Advanced Purchasing Studies (CAPS) reports on numerous industries plus municipal governments and state/county governments on many standard benchmarks.

Maintaining an Integrated Performance Measurement System

For those who already have established an integrated performance measurement system, the real issue is managing a mature system. They might ask, "How do I maintain it?" The answer is that you maintain it like you would an automobile or an airplane—through a series of regularly scheduled maintenance checks (which are outlined below).

- Maintenance Check #1: Measurement System Components—At the beginning of this section, a list of nine key components of an integrated performance measurement system was provided. These components should be checked (reevaluated) annually to look for any changes within the component that would impact the system.
- Maintenance Check #2: The Performance Measurement Team—The performance measurement team is made up of the people who actually do the

work being measured and those who are very familiar with the work being measured. It is important to periodically check the following things about your team: (1) changes to the makeup of the team due to turnover, reassignment, and so forth; (2) "burnout" of team members due to stagnant, repetitive roles/responsibilities (perhaps a rotation of assignments is in order); and (3) understanding of roles/responsibilities and tasks by team members (all should understand them and agree to them).

• Maintenance Check #3: New Legal Requirements/Issues—The issuance of new laws, regulations, and orders can have significant impact on an organization and its mission. For the most part, adherence to these laws, regulations, and orders is a requirement, not an option. Therefore, it is imperative that an organization "stay on top" of legal developments and incorporate their requirements into the performance measurement system. It also is "a must" that these requirements be communicated thoroughly to employees and stakeholders.

• Maintenance Check #4: New Developments/Technology—It will be necessary to keep abreast of and review any new developments (theories, practices, etc.) and/or technology that has emerged in the performance measurement field since the time that your system was instituted. When assessing these new developments/technology, consider: (1) the impact (both positive and negative) the incorporation of these new developments and/or technology into your system would have on the organization and the system, (2) the value-added of these new developments and/or technology, and (3) the cost of these new developments and/or technology.

• Maintenance Check #5: Feedback! Feedback! Feedback!—Feedback may be the greatest asset for a maintenance check. Seek it and use it. Get it from your employees and your customers/stakeholders. In particular, get it from a benchmarking partner—a similar organization with a successful, mature measurement system. They can give you new ideas to "breathe life" into your system.

Federal Laws and Initiatives

The current business environment is very different from what it was five or even ten years ago. Technology and customer requirements have evolved, changing the competitive landscape and continuing the focus on operational efficiencies. What has not changed is the importance of performance measurement. The government's interest stems from the idea of using performance measurement results in the budgeting process. The 1949 Hoover Commission, during Harry S. Truman's administration, was an effort to improve the efficiency and effectiveness of government. Subsequent interest in performance measurement surfaced in both the military and commercial sector. Interestingly enough, the same gentleman influenced both arenas, Robert McNamara. McNamara was one of ten "whiz kids" recruited en masse from the U.S. Air Force by Ford Motor Company. Henry Ford II quickly dubbed these 10 intelligence officers as the whiz kids because they brought quantitative analysis, the science of modern management to Ford Motor Company. McNamara advanced to become the president of Ford Motor Company and later the secretary of defense during the Kennedy and Johnson administrations. President Obama's 2009 *Memorandum on Transparency and Open Government* (see "Obama Administration Initiatives" in the introduction), requires executive departments and agencies to take the following steps toward the goal of creating a more open government:

1. Publish government information online. To increase accountability, promote informed participation by the public, and create economic opportunity, each agency shall take prompt steps to expand access to information by making it available online in open formats. With respect to information, the presumption shall be in favor of openness (to the extent permitted by law and subject to valid privacy, confidentiality, security, or other restrictions).
   a. Agencies shall respect the presumption of openness by publishing information online (in addition to any other planned or mandated publication methods) and by preserving and maintaining electronic information, consistent with the Federal Records Act and other applicable law and policy. Timely publication of information is an essential component of transparency. Delays should not be viewed as an inevitable and insurmountable consequence of high demand.
   b. To the extent practicable and subject to valid restrictions, agencies should publish information online in an open format that can be retrieved, downloaded, indexed, and searched by commonly used web search applications. An open format is one that is platform independent, machine readable, and made available to the public without restrictions that would impede the reuse of that information.
   c. To the extent practical and subject to valid restrictions, agencies should proactively use modern technology to disseminate useful information, rather than waiting for specific requests under the Freedom of Information Act (FOIA).
   d. Within 45 days, each agency shall identify and publish online in an open format at least three high-value data sets and register those data sets via Data.gov. These must be data sets not previously available online or in a downloadable format.

e. Within 60 days, each agency shall create an Open Government webpage located at www.[agency].gov/open to serve as the gateway for agency activities related to the Open Government Directive and shall maintain and update that webpage in a timely fashion.

f. Each Open Government webpage shall incorporate a mechanism for the public to:
  i. Give feedback on and assessment of the quality of published information;
  ii. Provide input about which information to prioritize for publication; and
  iii. Provide input on the agency's Open Government plan.

g. Each agency shall respond to public input received on its Open Government webpage on a regular basis.

h. Each agency shall publish its annual FOIA report in an open format on its Open Government webpage in addition to any other planned dissemination methods.

i. Each agency with a significant pending backlog of outstanding Freedom of Information requests shall take steps to reduce any such backlog by 10 percent each year.

j. Each agency shall comply with guidance on implementing specific presidential Open Government initiatives, such as Data.gov, eRulemaking, IT Dashboard, Recovery.gov, and USAspending.gov.

2. Improve the quality of government information. To improve the quality of government information available to the public, senior leaders should make certain that the information conforms to OMB guidance on information quality and that adequate systems and processes are in place within the agencies to promote such conformity.

a. Within 45 days, each agency, in consultation with the OMB, shall designate a high-level senior official to be accountable for the quality and objectivity of, and internal controls over, the federal spending information publicly disseminated through such public venues as USAspending .gov or other similar websites. The official shall participate in the agency's Senior Management Council, or similar governance structure, for the agency-wide internal control assessment pursuant to the Federal Managers' Financial Integrity Act.

b. Within 60 days, the deputy director for management at the OMB will issue, through separate guidance or as part of any planned comprehensive management guidance, a framework for the quality of federal spending information publicly disseminated through such public venues as USAspending.gov or other similar websites. The framework shall require agencies to submit plans with details of the internal controls implemented over information quality, including system and process changes, and the integration of these controls within the agency's existing infrastructure. An assessment will later be made as to whether additional guidance on implementing OMB guidance on information quality is necessary to cover other types of government information disseminated to the public.

c. Within 120 days, the deputy director for management at the OMB will issue, through separate guidance or as part of any planned comprehensive management guidance, a longer-term comprehensive strategy for federal spending transparency, including the Federal Funding Accountability Transparency Act and the American Reinvestment and Recovery Act. This guidance will identify the method for agencies to report quarterly on their progress toward improving their information quality.

3. Create and institutionalize a culture of open government. To create an unprecedented and sustained level of openness and accountability in every agency, senior leaders should strive to incorporate the values of transparency, participation, and collaboration into the ongoing work of their agency. Achieving a more open government will require the various professional disciplines within the government—such as policy, legal, procurement, finance, and technology operations—to work together to define and to develop open government solutions. Integration of various disciplines facilitates organization-wide and lasting change in the way that government works.

a. Within 120 days, each agency shall develop and publish on its Open Government webpage an Open Government plan that will describe how it will improve transparency and integrate public participation and collaboration into its activities.

b. Within 60 days, the federal chief information officer and the federal chief technology officer shall create an Open Government dashboard on www.whitehouse.gov/open. The Open Government dashboard will make available each agency's Open Government plan, together with aggregate statistics and visualizations designed to provide an assessment of the state of open government in the executive branch and progress over time toward meeting the deadlines for action outlined in this directive.

c. Within 45 days, the deputy director for management at the OMB, the federal chief information officer, and the federal chief technology officer will establish a working group that focuses on transparency, accountability, participation, and collaboration within the federal government. This group, with senior level representation from program and management offices throughout the government, will serve several critical functions, including:

    i. Providing a forum to share best practices on innovative ideas to promote transparency, including system and process solutions for information collection, aggregation, validation, and dissemination;

    ii. Coordinating efforts to implement existing mandates for federal spending transparency, including the Federal Funding Accountability Transparency Act and the American Reinvestment and Recovery Act; and

    iii. Providing a forum to share best practices on innovative ideas to promote participation and collaboration, including how to experiment with new technologies, take advantage of the expertise and insight of people both inside and outside the federal government, and form high-impact collaborations with researchers, the private sector, and civil society.

    d. Within 90 days, the deputy director for management at the OMB will issue, through separate guidance or as part of any planned comprehensive management guidance, a framework for how agencies can use challenges, prizes, and other incentive-backed strategies to find innovative or cost-effective solutions to improving open government.

4. Create an enabling policy framework for open government. Emerging technologies open new forms of communication between a government and the people. It is important that policies evolve to realize the potential of technology for open government.

Within 120 days, the administrator of the Office of Information and Regulatory Affairs (OIRA), in consultation with the federal chief information officer and the federal chief technology officer, will review existing OMB policies, such as Paperwork Reduction Act guidance and privacy guidance, to identify impediments to open government and to the use of new technologies and, where necessary, issue clarifying guidance and/or propose revisions to such policies, to promote greater openness in government.

Nothing in this directive shall be construed to supersede existing requirements for review and clearance of pre-decisional information by the director of the OMB relating to legislative, budgetary, administrative, and regulatory materials. Moreover, nothing in this directive shall be construed to suggest that the presumption of openness precludes the legitimate protection of information whose release would threaten national security, invade personal privacy, breach confidentiality, or damage other genuinely compelling interests.

Summary

When this step has been completed, your performance measures have been determined. Now you have to identify the investments that will drive the desired performance improvements and justify funding for those investments. That is what step 3 is about. You have to prove to your investment source that the project is going to achieve results according to measures that have been defined. Demand for funding is always high, and your project is unlikely to be the only one on the table. That is why it is critical that the organization completes steps 1 and 2 so that you can align your project with the appropriate performance measures, knowing that your project is going to work and that you have the systems in place to keep it on track and deliver the desired benefits.

3

Invest for Results

- Portfolio candidates
- Enterprise architecture
- Investment portfolio
- Business case
- Portfolio selection—what projects do you want to do

Overview

ONCE THE ORGANIZATIONS' STRATEGY is determined and performance objectives and measures are in place, the stage is set for identifying candidate investments that will move the organization forward to meet the performance objectives. This is shown at a high level in the step 3 diagram (see figure 3.1). These candidate investments must drive performance improvements and could also be new phases of already approved investments and operations and maintenance investments to maintain existing performance levels.

The detailed performance-driven management (PDM) approach for investing for results is shown in figure 3.1. Performance objectives identified in step 2 provide a basis for identifying candidate investments to drive those performance improvements. Ideas for investments can come from stakeholders who are familiar with the business issues at hand. Investment concepts can also be generated from a structured enterprise architecture (EA) approach (business and IT) that looks across the enterprise or business segment and identifies investments that can leverage commonality and standardization.

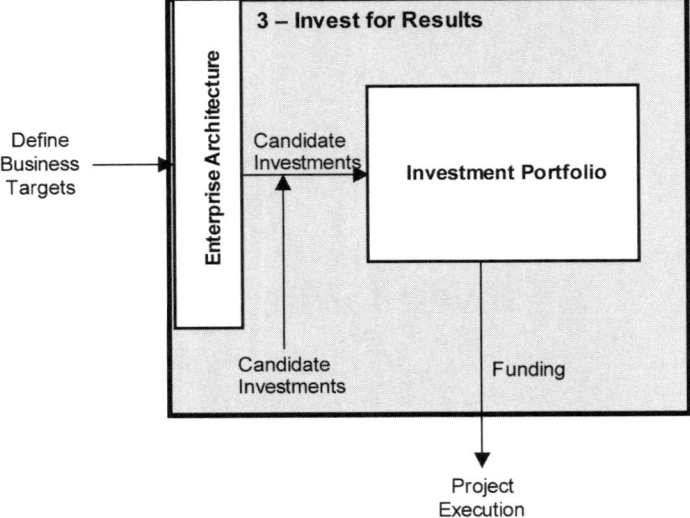

FIGURE 3.1
Overview of Step 3

Investments identified from any source come together conceptually to form a portfolio of candidate investments, which could range from transformational investments to nondiscretionary operations support (to maintain operations at current levels to maintain current performance levels).

Business cases are then developed for the investments. These business cases are the lynchpin of the PDM approach because they define the investment cost and benefits to be realized—the value proposition of the investment. The unique PDM aspect is that the business case defines the cause and effect between the investment and movement of measurable performance indicators and that this can often be validated through analysis and simulation. This provides the basis for the periodic reassessment of the business case throughout the project life cycle.

Once complete, the business cases position the investments to compete for scarce funds. Ideally, the investments with the highest return on investment (ROI) (financial and nonfinancial) are then selected for funding and execution. The development of the business case and selection of investments is considered a key part of the Capital Planning and Investment Control (CPIC) process in the federal government. The office of management and budget (OMB) has mandated this process, but it is critical that the business cases be done thoroughly with strong analysis for this process to be successful.

As part of the selection process, the investment is confirmed to be in compliance with the organization's business and IT EA. After selection, the investment/project is funded and the execution phase begins.

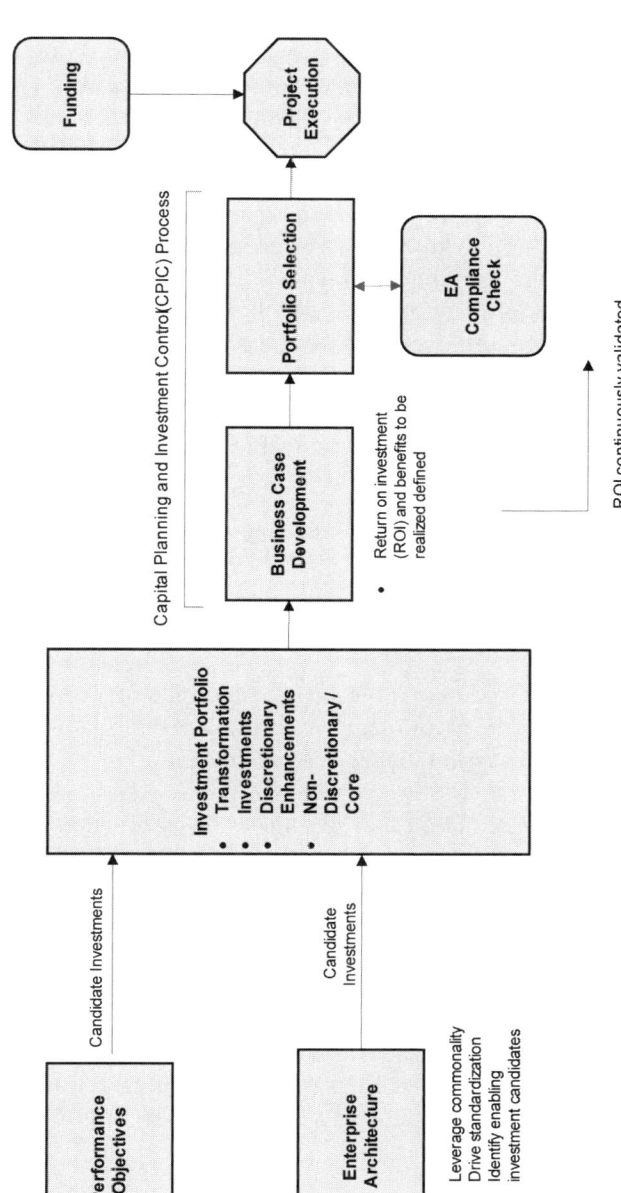

Funding

Project Execution

Capital Planning and Investment Control(CPIC) Process

Portfolio Selection

EA Compliance Check

Business Case Development

- Return on investment (ROI) and benefits to be realized defined

ROI continuously validated during project execution

Investment Portfolio
- Transformation Investments
- Discretionary Enhancements
- Non-Discretionary / Core

Candidate Investments

Performance Objectives

Candidate Investments

Enterprise Architecture

- Leverage commonality
- Drive standardization
- Identify enabling investment candidates

FIGURE 3.2
Step 3 Detailed Process

The business case that you develop in this step is the centerpiece of the PDM approach because it drives everything else. It assesses investment alternatives and develops a recommendation. It should not be confused with a business plan. Above all, it sets out the goals you need to achieve and provides a reference point throughout the project implementation phase.

EA guides and constrains how you do this from an IT and business perspective. EA helps you identify projects—both new and existing ones—that will help you achieve the required performance benefits. Having identified the potential projects, you need to know how you are going to implement—this is transitioning, which requires a sequencing plan that is a result of the portfolio selection process. Some of these projects may be started immediately; others may not be implemented until further down the road, in which case they will need revalidating before work starts.

The PDM approach is consistent with the OMB's architect, invest, implement concept. The key points of that process are described below:

- Architect
  - Develop and maintain the EA as the shared view of the current and future state of the agency
  - Define and prioritize EA segments as part of an EA transition strategy that defines the sequencing of individual segments according to business priority
  - Develop segment architecture to provide a bridge between the enterprise strategy and the investment in and implementation of individual business and information management solutions
- Invest
  - Define the implementation and funding strategy for individual solutions identified in the EA transition strategy and described in the segment architecture
  - Create the program management plan to implement the individual solutions identified in the implementation and funding strategy
- Implement
  - Execute projects according to the program management plans
  - Measure performance to determine how well the implemented solutions achieve the desired results and mission outcomes and provide feedback into the enterprise and segment architecture development processes

As part of this process, chief architects, and the EA practice as a whole, must provide valuable, results-driven information at varying levels of detail to support business performance improvement.

Portfolio Candidate Investments

After performance targets have been developed in step 2, the organization is positioned to develop candidate investment ideas to move performance toward the targets. This movement can be in any of the business areas identified—from finance and cost cutting, to driving strategic growth. These investments, if approved, are then implemented through one or more projects. There are several levels of investments, driving differing levels of performance improvement impact. All potential organizational investments can be categorized as follows:

- Nondiscretionary and operational spending normally dominate IT budgets so that modest savings in these areas can often fund more transformative or focused investments with greater performance improvement impact.
- Funding may then be diverted to discretionary projects, which bring added value or increase competitiveness.
- The choice of investments made by an organization is a trade-off between the investment types noted above to steadily improve performance in an optimal way.

TABLE 3.1
Investment Portfolio Levels

Investment Level	Description	Performance Impact
Transformative	The result of a strategic decision and deemed necessary when an organization's modestly enhanced infrastructure would still limit its ability to meet objectives	Wide-ranging, a game changer
Focused	The result of a decision to improve the performance of a given business process	Significant performance improvement but focused on a single or limited number of business processes
Discretionary	The result of a decision to enhance already existing capabilities to improve a performance aspect	Modest performance improvement to an aspect of a business process
Nondiscretionary	Required to maintain existing performance levels or comply with laws and regulations	Prevents degradation of existing acceptable performance levels
Operational	Required to operate on a daily basis	None—simply provides the resources to operate at existing performance levels

Organizational candidate investment ideas come from analysis of the strategic plan defined in step 1 and the performance targets defined in step 2. Creative thinking combined with knowledge of mission/business operations can identify candidate investments that can move the organizational performance measures toward their target values. Candidate investments can come from a variety of sources:

- Stakeholders
- Employees
- Executives
- Consultants and analysts
- General public
- Government and regulators (compliance can necessitate nondiscretionary investments)

The candidate investment ideas need to be compiled by investment analysts and screened through a governance process to create a set of candidate investments considered appropriate for the next step, development of a business case.

Additional investment candidates can come through an architectural analysis that looks across the organization of a particular business area (segment) to identify and leverage commonality for additional performance improvements. This architectural analysis is generally called EA and is focused on the enablement of the business through IT.

Enterprise Architecture

Enterprise, segment, and solution architecture provide different business perspectives by varying the level of detail and addressing related but distinct concerns. Just as enterprises are themselves hierarchically organized, so are the different views provided by each type of architecture.

By definition, EA is fundamentally concerned with identifying and leveraging common or shared assets, whether they are business processes, investments, data, systems, or technologies. EA is driven by strategy, it helps an organization identify whether its business and IT resources are properly aligned to the agency mission and strategic goals and objectives. From an investment perspective, EA is used to identify candidate investments for the IT investment portfolio as a whole. Consequently, the primary stakeholders of the EA are the senior managers and executives tasked with ensuring the agency fulfills its mission as effectively and efficiently as possible.

Since the scope of an enterprise can be so vast, the segment architecture concept has been developed to facilitate architectural focus on a particular core mission area, business service, or enterprise service. From an investment perspective, segment architecture drives investments for a business area supporting a core mission area or common or shared service.

Segment architecture is related to EA through three principles: structure, reuse, and alignment. First, segment architecture inherits the framework used by the EA; although, it may be extended and specialized to meet the specific needs of a core mission area or common or shared service. Second, segment architecture reuses important assets defined at the enterprise level including: data, common business processes and investments, and applications and technologies. Third, segment architecture aligns with elements defined at the enterprise level, such as business strategies, mandates, standards, and performance goals.

Solution architecture defines agency IT assets, such as applications or components used to automate and improve a specific solution. The scope of a solution architecture is typically limited to a single project and is used to implement all or part of a system or business solution. The primary stakeholders for solution architecture are system users and developers.

Solution architecture is commonly related to segment architecture and EA through definitions and constraints. For example, segment architecture provides definitions of data or service interfaces used within a core mission area or service, which are accessed by individual solutions. Equally, a solution may be constrained to specific technologies and standards that are defined at the enterprise level.

The remainder of this section describes approaches related to enterprise and segment architecture, which are closely related. Both enterprise and segment architecture result in identifying investment candidates for business case development and investment selection.

Benefits of the Enterprise and Segment Architecture

- Provides a framework to measure performance and validate target benefits (e.g., cost savings, cost avoidance, improved mission performance, technology standardization)
- Accelerates the initiation of individual implementation projects and program activities
- Increases alignment of the IT portfolio with cross-agency initiatives supporting opportunities for enterprise and government-wide collaboration and reuse
- Consolidates IT investments around core mission areas, business services, and enterprise services, simplifying the allocation of agency resources and increasing the efficiency and effectiveness of IT investments

- Improves government-wide collaboration, identifying opportunities to reuse common or shared business processes, data, and services
- Increases the frequency and quality of interactions between EA program staff and business and technical stakeholders improving business and IT planning and decision making
- Improves alignment of business and IT transformation initiatives with agency EA-identifying opportunities to share assets and apply enterprise and government-wide standards
- Promotes the development and approval of results-oriented architecture in advance of IT investment and budget formulation, improving decision making and portfolio management
- Increases alignment of IT business cases and agency budgets with the agency mission/vision
- Improves the quality of supporting documentation for IT investment business cases and budget formulation
- Enhances life-cycle management and governance processes by providing a shared vision for business and IT transformation
- Increases the alignment of business processes, information assets, and IT solutions with the agency EA and relevant cross-agency initiatives, increasing operational efficiency and effectiveness

Architectural Terms

- Target architecture: The target architecture represents the future vision for the agency and is also known as a "blueprint" or "to-be" architecture. The target architecture should already be designed before a sequencing plan is created, since the target is the endpoint for the transition strategy. As the target architecture is periodically updated, the sequencing plan should also be updated. An "interim target" represents a coordinated, discretionary upgrade or change to existing operations, functionality, or technology support and can be useful in coordinating numerous multi-year initiatives in the transition strategy.
- Baseline architecture: The baseline architecture represents the current state of the organization and is also known as an "as-is" architecture. The baseline architecture should be completed to the extent it supports the business needs of the organization and can sufficiently serve as the starting point for the transition strategy.
- Project: A discrete, planned effort to achieve a specific goal or result within a brief time frame. A project manager is accountable for each project as it moves through the investment process and implementation.

- Sequencing plan: Describes the technically required sequence of EA-identified projects. Shows interactions between projects and dependencies between programs and segments; the sequencing plan is not intended to replace ongoing project management or to track agency budgets down to the project level.
- Transition plan: Describes the specific funded projects planned with milestones and benefits realization time frames. Also identifies dependencies between projects.
- Performance improvement summary: Provides a consolidated view of agency performance improvement and cost reduction milestones. This is not a separate plan—it summarizes the performance goals and planned results from each project or program identified in the transition plan, including EA-identified investments. Specific program milestones can be events or outcomes leading to performance improvements. The performance improvements listed in the summary plan should match performance metrics in the OMB 300s.

As a quick recap, step 1 delivers the strategy, step 2 develops the performance measures, and now in step 3, you have to come up with your performance-driven business case. In order to do this, you have to develop a list of potential programs and project ideas before you can go after investments to pay for them. Developing this list should be an across-the-board effort because you need input from all relevant groups, users, and individuals and need to be informed by the enterprise and segment architectures. This input can come from an individual who has a great idea, a business steering committee, or a particular department. Many organizations have set up special committees to look at their ongoing investment needs and how these fit in with their overall business plan and strategy.

Note: As discussed in the previous chapter, success in achieving your goals is measured by reaching a target performance measure. It is important, however, to limit the number of goals and target measures. The aim should be one primary goal and no more than three secondary goals, with appropriate performance targets or focus areas. If there are too many goals and measures to meet, they will likely conflict with one another—progress in one area could decrease performance in another. As you act to achieve one goal or target, you may well be blurring or offsetting progress on another. The aim throughout is to maintain a forward momentum with your measurements—that is, progress—not lapsing backward.

Once the strategic analysis has been conducted, it can be integrated with your EA.

- EA both guides and constrains the business case, and IT development and investments are validated against the EA before being approved
- The focus is to identify projects—both new and current—that provide benefits and leverage commonality
- The EA provides the information needed to develop a sequencing plan

EA is one of several practice areas that must be executed effectively to achieve improvements in agency mission performance and other measurement areas. EA helps to organize, constrain, and clarify the relationships between agency strategic goals, investments, business solutions, and measurable performance improvements—*but it is just one link in a chain of integrated practice areas.* To achieve target performance improvements, the EA practice must be strong and fully integrated with other practice areas, including strategic planning, performance management, CPIC, and program and project management.

A single agency contains both core mission area segments and business service segments. Enterprise services are those crosscutting services spanning multiple segments. Segments can be leveraged within an agency, across several agencies, or the entire federal government.

> Note: EA-driven investments are more likely to identify, leverage, and drive commonality across an enterprise—and to a lesser degree across a segment. Also, if the EA is done in accordance with the enterprise's strategic performance goals, the proposed investments are more likely to help drive overall performance improvements. Leveraging commonality can significantly reduce costs, that is, not doing two systems that duplicate each other or increasing the ability to share information across the enterprise.

Architecture Development Activities

The steps in the development of enterprise and solution architecture are well documented in many texts and in the Federal Segment Architecture Methodology. This section addresses the highlights and provides thoughts on the advantages of various approaches used. Major steps are as follows:

TABLE 3.2
Architectural Analysis Summary

Activity	Stakeholder(s)	Deliverables
Develop concept diagram describing segment scope and current operational environment	- Program manager - Business owners (SME) - Enterprise architect	- One-page "as is" or baseline illustration and summary text description
Identify new or revised requirements and change drivers	- Program manager - Business owners (SME) - Enterprise architect	- Summary list of change drivers and associated information sources
Compile baseline segment architecture and segment assets	- Program manager - Business owners (SME) - Enterprise architect	- Baseline segment architecture (across all architectural layers) - Legacy system portfolio - Segment investment portfolio - Current staff resources
Identify and document opportunities for improvement	- Program manager - Business owners (SME) - Enterprise architect	- Annotated baseline concept diagram - Ordered list of opportunities for improvement
Illustrate segment vision	- Program manager - Business owners (SME) - Enterprise architect	- Vision diagram - Vision statement

TABLE 3.3
Architecture Definition Summary

Activity	Stakeholder(s)	Deliverables
Establish the performance goals for the enterprise or segment	- Program manager - Business owners (SME) - Enterprise architect	- Performance layer of the target architecture
Conduct analysis to evaluate design alternatives for achieving the performance goals	- Program manager - Business owners (SME) - Enterprise architect	- Market research - Alternatives analysis - Architectural concepts
Develop the target architecture	- Program manager - Business owners (SME) - Enterprise architect	- Business, data, services, and technology layers of the target segment architecture

(continued)

TABLE 3.3 (*continued*)

Develop sequencing plan/ transition strategy	- Program manager - Business owners (SME) - Enterprise architect	- List of projects to be executed - Transition strategy including a project sequencing plan
Reconcile the target segment architecture to the agency EA	- Program manager - Business owners (SME) - Enterprise architect - Chief architect	- Reconciled enterprise architecture and segment architecture

TABLE 3.4
Architecture Maintenance Summary

Activity	*Stakeholder(s)*	*Deliverables*
Update list of architectural change drivers	- Program manager - Business owners (SME) - Enterprise architect	- Summary list of change drivers and associated information sources
Analyze and prioritize change drivers	- Program manager - Business owners (SME) - Enterprise architect	- Priority list of architectural change drivers
Determine impact of priority change drivers on segment work products and the program management plan	- Program manager - Enterprise architect	- Updated target architecture, sequencing and transition plans

Segment Architecture

Segment architecture creates visibility to other enterprise segments and cross-agency initiatives, describing opportunities to reuse or provide common solutions. The segment architecture transition plan describes dependencies between related initiatives. It also contributes to a common understanding of what the segment is responsible for and how the segment supports the goals and objectives of the agency as a whole.

Segment architecture is reviewed and approved in the context of the agency EA and is consistent with common or shared elements, including standard business processes, data, applications, and technologies. Business requirements identified at the segment architecture level and solution architecture level are used to update the agency EA and EA transition strategy.

Segment architecture drives investment planning and resource allocation for a core mission area or common or shared service. Sufficient resources are identified and justified to execute the segment transition strategy and achieve measurable performance improvements.

> Segment architectures should be used to organize investments and business priorities within the EA. Segment architectures should not be used to create an additional layer of capital planning approval, unless such a layer already exists for a segment architecture that is operated by a single organizational unit (i.e., component agency, operating division, etc.). The intent of using segment architectures is not to complicate the capital planning process and other agency governance processes but rather to assist with grouping and prioritizing various agency initiatives that move through these processes.

Segment architecture work products support life-cycle processes, including IT investment management, program and project management, and systems development. New and revised business and information requirements are continuously identified as the segment moves though each life-cycle phase and as business and information management solutions are funded and developed to meet stakeholder requirements. Consequently, segment architecture work products must be maintained to reflect these inputs.

Architectural Analysis

The purpose of this step is to define a simple and concise vision for the enterprise segment and relate the vision to the agency strategic plan. During this step, the integrated program team (IPT) considers current change drivers, including key strategic, legislative, and management requirements, to identify opportunities to achieve performance improvements. The primary questions to be answered during this step are:

- *What is the scope of the segment?*

This question is answered by developing a simple conceptual diagram and summary description defining the current scope of the enterprise segment and the existing operational environment (including stakeholders, processes, applications, and information exchanges). Defining segment scope helps build consensus within the IPT on the range of opportunities for improvement and helps focus IPT working sessions. Whenever possible, the IPT should use the EA knowledge base to compile information on segment scope and the current operating environment.

• *What are the primary change drivers impacting the segment?*

This question is answered by identifying and describing new or revised business requirements and other change drivers impacting the segment. Change drivers help justify segment architecture development and implementation and include both strategic requirements and tactical requirements, such as legislative changes, the identification of performance gaps, and changes in stakeholder requirements. The IPT should consider a broad range of inputs when identifying change drivers, including the agency strategic plan, EA, executive directions, audit findings, performance assessments, stakeholder surveys, and other inputs.

• *What are the current segment systems and resources?*

This question is answered by compiling information describing the baseline or "as-is" architecture for the segment. Baseline information is compiled for each architectural layer—performance, business, data, services, and technology—plus current systems, investments, and personnel. Information should be collected to a sufficient level of detail to support the identification of performance improvement opportunities (e.g., improved service to citizens, improved mission performance, cost savings/avoidance, technology standardization, and improved management and use of information).

• *What are the deficiencies or inhibitors to success within the segment?*

This question is answered by reviewing current segment assets and change drivers to identify and document opportunities to improve agency performance and achieve measurable results. Candidate opportunities should be linked to relevant change drivers and prioritized based upon their relationship to specific deficiencies, such as audit findings, inspector general (IG) or Government Accountability Office (GAO) recommendations, and PART (Program Assessment Rating Tool) ratings, and their association with legislative mandates, mission priorities, performance goals, and other criteria. The IPT can update the simple diagram and text description describing segment scope to illustrate and describe priority opportunities for improvement within the context of the current operating environment.

• *What is our vision for the segment?*

This question is answered by creating a simple one-page graphic illustrating the vision for the segment. The conceptual diagram should describe the proposed operating environment, including planned changes to stakeholder interactions, business processes, information sharing, applications, and technology to resolve documented deficiencies and achieve measurable performance improvements. The concept graphic should be complemented by a summary vision statement describing the proposed operating environment and relevant links to strategic goals and objectives.

Segment Architecture Definition

Segment architecture definition provides a simple and powerful technique for the chief architect and EA program staff members to collaborate with business stakeholders to implement the agency EA and deliver value to core mission areas. The segment architecture process and associated work products outline a methodology to ask and answer questions about business and information management requirements and make informed decisions about the nature and priority of opportunities to implement target segment architecture and achieve performance goals. The resulting segment architecture is a shared vision for business and IT transformation within a core mission area or common service.

Segment architecture development is conducted by an IPT with activities and meetings led by a program manager. The program manager, business subject matter experts, and enterprise architects participate in each phase of segment architecture development, but the composition of the IPT evolves as the segment moves through each phase of the segment architecture process. For example, IT investment management staff members participate during the "define" phase to support the development of an IT-investment business case. Similarly, technical project managers and system engineers participate to support the "operate" phase and development of solution architecture.

Segment architecture development is controlled by EA governance and management processes across each phase of the performance improvement life cycle. Governance and management processes are implemented to:

- Review segment architecture work product content and format standards to promote reconciliation with the agency EA and relevant cross-agency initiatives
- Validate opportunities for agency-level and cross-agency collaboration and reuse, including the implementation of relevant cross-agency initiatives
- Review and approve segment architecture in advance of IT investment and project execution
- Capture segment-level business and information management requirements to update and maintain the agency EA
- Capture lessons learned to improve the segment architecture process and standard work products

The development and maintenance of the agency EA and EA transition strategy identify and define enterprise segments and prioritize opportunities to develop and implement segment architecture.

Segment Development in the Absence of an EA

If the agency EA and EA transition strategy have not been developed to a sufficient level of detail to support segment identification and prioritization, EA program staff can execute the following steps to identify candidate segments and initiate segment architecture development with business stakeholders. Stakeholder commitment must be attained to support each step in this process and ensure business and technical subject matter experts are assigned to initiate, develop, and maintain segment architecture.

> *Define and prioritize business and information management needs and architectural change drivers.*

This step identifies key business and information management requirements and significant strategic, policy, legislative, management, and performance drivers impacting on the agency. Elements of the approach to define requirements and drivers include:

- Review major IT investments and business transformation and modernization initiatives currently underway within the organization to identify relevant requirements and drivers.
- Compile information on current "pain points" to identify opportunities for performance improvement for core mission areas or common services. Pain points can come from audit findings, documented performance gaps, PART scores, stakeholder satisfaction surveys, or other sources.

> *Define, review, and prioritize candidate opportunities to improve agency performance.*

This step highlights business needs and change drivers offering the most significant opportunities to increase the efficiency and effectiveness of agency operations.

Elements of the approach to define and prioritize candidate opportunities include:

- Identify criteria to evaluate, prioritize, and select opportunities. Evaluation criteria include (but are not limited to) the impact of opportunities on agency performance, the relative complexity and/or dif-

ficulty to fulfill business needs and address change drivers, legislative or executive mandates, and relevant program and project dependencies.
• Apply evaluation criteria to prioritize opportunities.

Identify candidate segment(s).

This step maps priority opportunities (business needs and change drivers) to the agency business model and service model to identify candidate segments. Core mission areas and business services are identified in the business model, and enterprise services are identified in the services model.

Business needs and change drivers are also mapped to cross-agency initiatives to identify common or reusable services or solutions that can be applied to meet agency requirements. Common or reusable services support development of segment architecture and implementation of business and information management solutions to achieve performance improvements.

Select a segment and identify resources needed to develop segment architecture.

This step identifies management support and business and technical expertise required to execute segment architecture development and integration. Based upon the scope of the selected segment, resources can be identified from multiple program areas and support offices. At minimum, candidate resources should be identified for the following roles:

• Management sponsor(s) or champion(s)
• Qualified program manager
• Candidate IPT members (business and technical subject matter experts)

Establish segment architecture IPT.

This step formally initiates the segment architecture development process by establishing the IPT. Meetings are conducted with the business champion(s) and other principal stakeholders to review resource requirements and the schedule to complete segment architecture development and to assign business and technical subject matter experts to the IPT.

Perform redundancy and gap analyses.

The purpose of performing redundancy and gap analyses is to identify opportunities for improvement in the baseline architecture and to identify "gaps" between the baseline and target architectures. These analyses should focus on assessing value to the agency mission, identifying performance gaps, and cost-cutting or cost-avoidance opportunities. The agency-wide target architecture should already have been designed using the business needs of the organization as the primary drivers and to implement the goals and objectives in the agency's strategic plan. Opportunities identified by these analyses can be addressed by candidate investments.

Some examples of baseline redundancies and gaps between the baseline and target include but are not limited to:

- Gaps
  - Target performance measure, driven by a business need, cannot be achieved using existing business processes and information systems.
  - Target information sharing requirements cannot be achieved with current data sharing methods and standards.
  - Target cost-efficiency for department-wide services cannot be achieved with the existing business processes, applications, and organizational structure.
  - Target architecture includes flexible operations that are not supported by the current information systems, services, and business processes.
- Redundancy
  - Baseline analysis identifies redundant information systems providing the same capabilities in different organizational units.
  - Baseline analysis identifies redundant technology products and standards in use by various organizational units within the department or agency.

After completion of the investment management and budget formulation processes, the transition strategy will need to be updated based on the actual funding decisions for the agency. Once agency appropriations are final, the transition strategy must be updated to reflect funding decisions and budget "trade-offs" for the agency. Program scope, implementation schedules, cross-program dependencies, achievement of performance milestones, and other impacts should be assessed and adjusted accordingly in the transition strategy. In the PDM approach, the agency strategy and architecture should drive identification of candidate investments, not the other way around.

Transition Strategy and Sequencing

A primary output from the agency EA sequencing plan is candidate investments for the IT investment portfolio that can be traced back to a business-approved architectural portfolio. Once segments are identified, segment architectures are defined, and programs with projects are architected to implement them, agency planners should consider these programs and projects as proposed investments for the investment management process (i.e., capital planning process).

The EA transition strategy should include clear linkage between initiatives identified in the transition strategy and specific investments in the agency's investment portfolio. In accordance with guidance provided in OMB Circular A-11, agency investments and unique project identifier (UPI) codes should be matched to the appropriate segment architectures described in the EA transition strategy.

> Performance Management—The programs identified in the transition strategy should be linked to specific program performance goals. Coupled with the dependency relationships in the sequencing plan, this provides the ability to assess the performance impact of changes across programs.

For example, one program has its budget modified—the dependency between this program and another program shows the impact this budget adjustment will have on the ability of the second program to meet a planned performance objective. For guidance on how to define an effective performance measure, see OMB Circular A-11.

Performance management should be a primary consideration when transition strategy initiatives are proposed for funding in the budget process. Effects on performance goals across the agency, as shown by the dependencies between programs in the sequencing plan, should be considered in agency budget decisions.

> ### Federal Specific EA Transition Requirements
>
> **Annual OMB EA Assessment**
> As the transition strategy is updated each year, the agency's success in achieving performance milestones will be assessed against the previous year's plan during the annual EA assessment performed by the OMB. For more information on how the OMB will assess agency transition strategy progress, refer to the OMB's *Enterprise Architecture Assessment Framework*.
>
> **Quarterly OMB EA Progress Reports**
> The EA program plan is the agency's annual plan for developing and implementing the agency EA. Development of segment architectures should be identified in this plan so EA resources will be assigned to create segment architectures. Progress against an agency's EA program plan will be assessed using the quarterly EA reporting process implemented by the OMB. For more information on the definition of EA progress milestones, refer to *Guidance for Quarterly Reporting Requirements* located at: www.cio.gov/documents/quarterly_ea_reporting_2007.pdf.

Solution Architecture

Solution architecture addresses specific problems and requirements, EA looks at the overall picture, segment architecture breaks it down even more, and solution architecture looks at specific problems and generally architects specific investments or projects. It comes into its own in the implementation phase and is generally completed during the design phase.

Investment Portfolio

Once the candidate investments have been identified through analysis of performance objectives and enterprise/segment architecture, these candidate investments need to be screened through a governance process to determine which investments have significant potential and should have business cases developed.

An investment screening process should prescribe the amount of documentation and level of analytical rigor, depending on the project's type (i.e., transformational, focused, discretionary) and phase (i.e., initial concept, new, ongoing, and operational). For instance, when senior managers analyze initial concept proposals, the questions and documentation would be different from that required for a project that is ready to be awarded and implemented.

For example, one best-practice company required more documentation and greater analytical rigor if a proposal would replace or change an operational system vital to keeping the company running or if the concept matched a company-wide strategic goal. Lower-impact proposals that would only affect an office or had a nonstrategic objective were not scrutinized in as much detail.

If a project proposal does not meet all the essential requirements necessary for its type and phase, it should be returned to the originating business-unit sponsor indicating problems, issues, or documentation that needs further work or clarification.

Following are some of the questions that can be used to screen projects for relevancy to the agency's mission and for technical and organizational feasibility. If the answer to any of these questions is "no," a project should not receive further consideration and should be returned to the originating unit. Projects that meet these criteria should continue to the business case phase.

Key Questions to Consider in Screening a Proposal

- Is the investment clearly relevant to mission priorities outlined in the agency's strategic or business plan?

- Will this investment move organization performance measures toward their target values?
- Is the investment feasible to design and execute given the agency's demonstrated capability to deliver?
- What is the cause and effect of this investment (high-level) cost for benefits realized?
- Can this investment be implemented within acceptable risk parameters?
- Has another agency done this type of investment before? If so, have lessons learned been incorporated into the investment plan and consideration given to using their system for the investment's requirements?
- Does the investment conform to the agency's EA?
- Will the investment be executed in well-defined stages, including decision points for validating, continuing, modifying, or canceling the investment?
- Other questions specific to the organization . . .

As part of the screening process, thought must be given to how major risks would be mitigated for the candidate investments. Investment risk mitigation covers a range of options but all seek to minimize the impact that a specific event or input will have on the return on a given investment. The process includes analyzing all factors—both internal and external—to determine which could have a negative impact and lead to a loss or less-than-expected ROI. It is all about minimizing the risk and maximizing the return.

Figure 3.3 illustrates the full scope and impact of an investment and how risk can be mitigated through a complete understanding of the investments' cause-and-effect relationships. At a high level, the cause-and-effect relationships of a candidate investment should be understood sufficiently for an investment to pass through screening to the business case phase.

Additionally, consider that when investing for results, the organization must have clear, unequivocal prioritized goals. It is helpful to prioritization if there is one goal that is the most important—the one that overrides all the others. The organization's goal is realizing the project outcomes and the benefits that this brings, and the aim is to achieve this in the most efficient and effective manner possible.

Business Case

The PDM approach is based on and driven by the business case. The business case sets out the business reasons for the IT investment and demonstrates

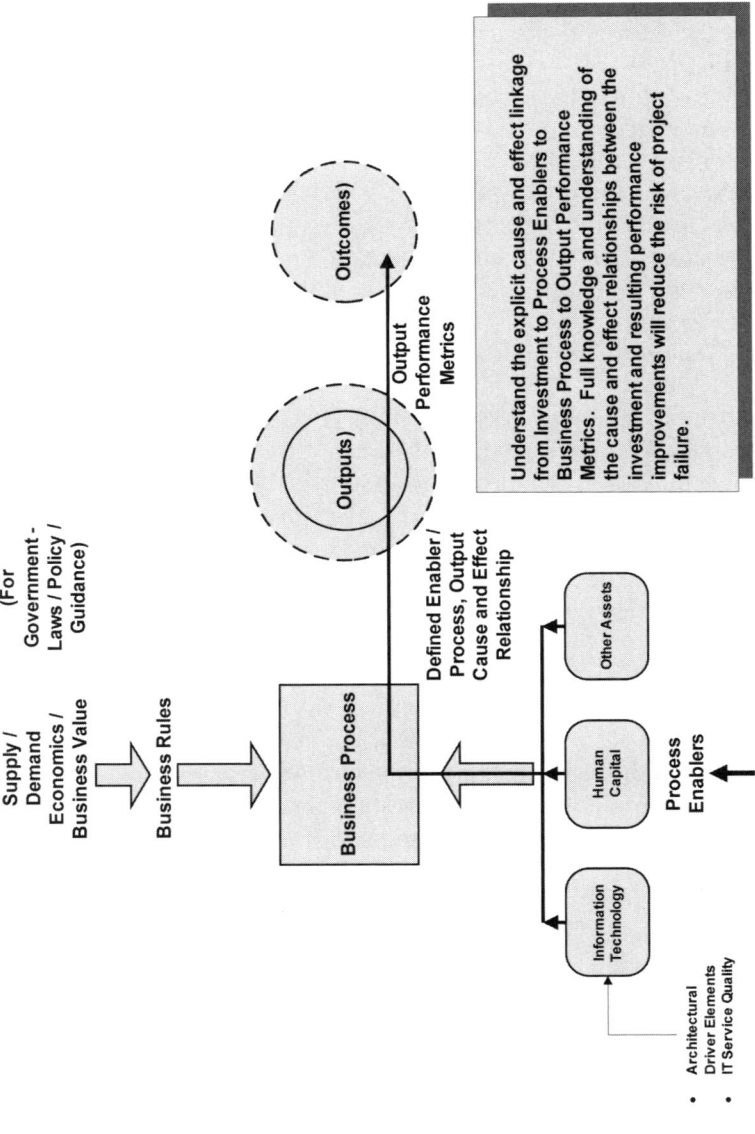

Supply / Demand Economics / Business Value

Business Rules

(For Government - Laws / Policy / Guidance)

Business Process

Defined Enabler / Process, Output Cause and Effect Relationship

(Outputs)

Output Performance Metrics

(Outcomes)

Understand the explicit cause and effect linkage from Investment to Process Enablers to Business Process to Output Performance Metrics. Full knowledge and understanding of the cause and effect relationships between the investment and resulting performance improvements will reduce the risk of project failure.

Information Technology

- Architectural
- Driver Elements
- IT Service Quality

Human Capital

Other Assets

Process Enablers

Investment to Improve Process Performance by Changing the Status Quo

FIGURE 3.3

Investment Cause-and-Effect Relationships

convincingly how best the objectives (benefits) can be achieved. The business case must satisfy four major requirements:

- Describe in detail the cause and effect of the investment and benefits realization
- Recommend the best business and technical approach selected from realistic alternative approach analysis
- Demonstrate ROI and the probability of various returns given the risk profile
- Provide an analytical basis for validating ROI and the likelihood of benefits realization throughout implementation

The basic questions to be answered as part of the business case are:

- What is the current situation?
- What happens if we do nothing?
- What options do we have to resolve the problem?
- What is the best-case scenario?
- What benefits accrue from resolving the problem?
- How long would it take to fix?
- What would it cost to fix?
- Can this cost be justified?

Elements of a Business Case Document

Every organization is likely to use a business case tailored to its own needs. However, there are elements that are common to almost all business cases.

- *Background*: A statement explaining what the investment is, why the business case has been prepared, what the source of the investment concept was.
- *Objectives*: A description of what has to be achieved along with performance measures that will be advanced through this investment.
- *Alternatives and analysis*: A business case should always analyze more than one alternative to choose the optimal approach. One alternative should be to continue as it is presently, with no change—the status quo.
- *Resources*: A list of the resources needed to deliver each alternative, including any costs of stopping existing work or diverting resources from current initiatives.
- *Costs*: A statement of how much each alternative will cost.
- *Risks*: An analysis of all the risks involved in each alternative and of the risks involved, if any, in doing nothing.

- *Benefits*: A description of the benefits that will accrue from undertaking each alternative and the timing of benefits realization. Benefits should be measurable (quantifiable) and should be stated in financial terms where possible.
- *Alternative*: A recommended alternative, including a justification and an outline of any risks.
- *Supporting data*: Appendixes and computer files containing the supporting data and analysis performed as part of the business case.

The business case is the cornerstone for PDM. It details the current situation and why the project is needed, why the investment will produce an ROI, what benefits will be achieved, and what is needed to achieve it. It is your road map to success—how to get from *a* to *b*—and your point of reference throughout implementation and after. During implementation, you use the business plan and the various measures put in place to ensure you stay on track, and once the project is completed, you use the plan to determine whether the expected benefits have been achieved. It also contributes to the development of a library of best practices—identifying what went well, what did not, and what improvements could be made.

The business case is a common presentation tool for describing the proposal. It identifies an existing business need and a proposed solution to meet the defined business need. Estimates are provided on how much the project will cost. The proposed solution defines the best solution to address the business need and includes an evaluation of all alternatives considered and a justification for the solution that is selected. The business case is also used to obtain management commitment and approval for investment in business change, including projects and programs, through rationale for the investment. The ongoing viability of a project or program will be monitored against the business case.

> A business case looks at a single investment, while a portfolio must be selected based on the optimal combination of investments for an organization.

There are three levels of business cases:

- *Strategic business case*: helps to connect initiatives/project proposals to corporate and service strategies and priorities
- *Full business case*: involves a full financial model and implementation plan for a preferred project option—the baseline for project approval and ongoing validation

- *Final business case*: confirms the detailed costs and benefits expected as a project goes forward

Business Case Approach

The following section provides a comprehensive approach to development of a business case and performance of business case analysis (BCA). It is derived from guidelines issued by the U.S. Air Force and, as such, includes elements relevant to government agencies as well as commercial organizations.

The content described in each section needs to be included in the documentation for a BCA. Note also that a BCA is scalable, depending on the decision being contemplated. When deciding upon the depth of a BCA, preparers of BCAs should keep in mind the decision-making audience, the time frame for the decision, and the implications of the proposed decision. In some cases, a top-level, preliminary, BCA of only three to five pages, prepared within a very short time (e.g., a week), is appropriate, while in other cases, a more extensive study is required. However, in all cases, the main body of the BCA should be succinct enough to allow decision makers to fully grasp the issues without becoming overwhelmed by details. The BCA should be limited to a maximum size of 20 to 40 pages (excluding attachments) and should be commensurate in breadth and depth with the magnitude of resources involved. The ultimate objective is to provide an analysis that effectively supports a timely decision-making process.

Sections

The following sections are included in each documented BCA:

- Executive summary
- Problem statement
- Assumptions
- Current state description—"status quo" or "as is"
- Future state description—"to be"
- Cost-benefit analysis
- Recommendation
- Funding
- Sensitivity and risk analyses
- Change management plan

Executive Summary

Provide a summary of the proposed investment decision. This section should focus on the key highlights that will then be expounded upon in the sections that follow the executive summary. The executive summary section should be no more than three pages in length.

Provide a short narrative identifying the unit that prepared the BCA, the recipient or customer, date, subject, project location, problem statement, project year, and period of analysis. In addition, provide any background information or history that will aid the reader in understanding the results of the analysis.

Present the name of each feasible alternative, its total investment cost, key financial metrics (e.g., net present value [NPV], return on investment [ROI], internal rate of return [IRR]), operational and combat metrics, benefits, constraints, and the risks. Constraints and risks that must be considered when determining costs include, for example: the need for legislation or military construction funding to make an alternative feasible, the need to possess or acquire technical data or licenses, the statutory requirements to analyze the impact on small businesses, the ability (and costs) to terminate existing contracts, the statutory requirement for a public-private competition if the work being performed by more than nine civilian employees will be converted to contract, and any legal prohibitions against elements of implementing a proposed alternative. In addition, provide the ranking of each alternative. Much of this information may be in a table format. Summarize how the recommended course of action will bring value (benefit) to the implementing organization, or describe the particular problem that the investment decision will solve. Value should be defined in general terms: how the particular investment enables the organization to achieve strategic goals. Value should also be defined in net quantitative benefits (e.g., monetary savings, ROI, payback period, improvement in operational and combat metrics) that the proposed investment is anticipated to generate.

Summarize the plan required for implementing the particular investment decision. Identify the key stakeholders and their responsibilities. Describe the implementation schedule. Summarize budget requirements.

Identify key assumptions upon which the analysis is based. Identify the analytical "trip points." In other words, to what extent would key assumptions have to fail such that the business case no longer makes sense? How likely is this to happen? What measures will be taken to mitigate the risk of failure? This discussion is a form of risk analysis and sensitivity analysis. If applicable, explain if there is a sensitivity "break point" or "crossover point" at which the proposed alternative would no longer be the recommended option but rather another alternative would arise as the preferred option. There are times when economic and noneconomic variables are so sensitive that they may affect the rank ordered list of alternatives.

Describe any measures that will be used to track the progress of the decision once implemented.

Problem Statement

A well-developed business case always begins with a problem statement that clearly and concisely defines the problem, requirement, or opportunity to be analyzed. What is the purpose of the analysis? What problem are you trying to solve? What is the scope of your analysis? Who is the decision maker? The problem statement helps define the framework of the analysis to be performed. Additionally, this statement should not assume a specific means of achieving the desired result but rather what the desired end-state is in as objective terms as possible (i.e., not biased toward any one alternative). Bias or unfounded assumptions in the problem statement undermine the analytical purpose of the BCA by jumping to conclusions. Having a clear and well-defined problem statement gives you a reference point to go back to when you proceed through your analysis. After reading this section, the decision maker should understand the purpose of the analysis and the framework of its conclusion. The problem statement should be limited to one page or less. If the problem statement does not accurately state the problem, then the whole BCA will be off on the wrong track and will address the wrong issue. If possible, drafts of a problem statement should be reviewed with the organization or senior leader requiring the BCA so that the intent of the analysis is clear up front. Such clarification can avoid unnecessary rework and make sure the analysis covers the assigned objective.

Assumptions

Assumptions are beliefs about what is true of a current or future state of affairs for a situation. Prior to formulating assumptions, what is known with certainty should be stated: facts, laws, defined criteria, ground rules, constraints, regulations, Office of the Secretary of Defense (OSD) or air force guidance, and any factor known to be true that may affect the current or future business conditions under consideration in the analysis. After stating what is known, list the assumptions about what is not known or about future states affecting business conditions. It is crucial to identify all key assumptions upon which the business case is based. Identifying assumptions is critical to conducting risk or sensitivity analysis on which alternative to recommend. Each major assumption should be evaluated for its impact on the business case should it be significantly changed. Assumptions are critical because not including a key assumption or changing key assumptions can directly influence which alternative is recommended.

Current State Description—"Status Quo" or "As Is"

Each investment decision will impact an existing process, whether the decision involves a material solution, such as procuring a new piece of equipment, or a nonmaterial solution, such as changing a mode of operation. Each decision should be evaluated in the context of the current status quo process that exists prior to the implementation of the proposed investment decision or new way of doing business. A description of the status quo state of operations is, thus, critical insofar as it establishes the foundation against which the proposed investment decision can be evaluated. For example, suppose a proposed investment will generate the production of six widgets per day. It is not possible to evaluate the value of this investment unless the "as is" production state (e.g., four widgets per day) is known. Requirements for the current state description are amplified in the following subsections. Status quo may also be thought of as the "as is" state.

Describe the current process or state of operations that the particular investment decision will impact. Provide a narrative description of the key elements of the process (the inputs, processes, and outputs), individuals or organizations performing the tasks, and the tools, systems, logistics or support functions, training, or other factors critical to the process. Include the customers and the requirement(s) that will be impacted by the decision. Where feasible, include process maps to the level of detail necessary to support this description.

Describe the users of the process output and why they value that output. Why is this output important to the implementing organization, its stakeholders, or its customers?

Identify the key performance indicators (KPIs) for the current process. Describe the cost, effectiveness, and efficiency of the current process. Cost might be addressed in terms of full-time equivalents (FTEs) of personnel, hours of work, or other specific cost elements (i.e., supplies, contracts, travel, etc.). Describe the effectiveness of the process in terms of accuracy, rework, or other measures. Discuss efficiency of the current process in terms of units per period of time, cost, excess by-products or waste, or other quantifiable measure. Use existing performance measures where possible, and describe the source and confidence level of any metrics developed over the course of the "as-is" process mapping/analysis.

Provide a brief root cause analysis: Describe the root cause(s) of the problem or desired improvement that the investment decision is focused on.

Describe the elements of the process (i.e., training, organization, equipment, personnel, etc.) that are the underlying root cause(s) of the process weakness or problem. At this point, it is important to point out that occasionally a status quo situation becomes unacceptable because it becomes contrary to new legislation or OSD or air force policy. In such cases, the status quo should still be stated and its costs estimated as a baseline for calculating costs and potential savings or additional funding needed for new alternatives. Also, an upgrade to the status quo may be one of the future alternatives to be considered.

Future State Description—"To Be"

For each alternative considered, describe the future state of operations that the proposed investment decision will help achieve. Future state may also be thought of as the "to be" state, as compared to the current state or status quo. There is a separate "to be" section for each alternative to the "to be" state considered.

Briefly describe the alternative considered. If an alternative was considered but dismissed as infeasible, discuss reasons for considering it infeasible.

> Note: EA-driven investments are more likely to identify, leverage, and drive commonality across an enterprise—and to a lesser degree across a segment. Also, if the EA is done in accordance with the enterprise's strategic performance goals, the proposed investments are more likely to help drive overall performance improvements. Leveraging commonality can significantly reduce costs, that is, not doing two systems that duplicate each other or increasing the ability to share information across the enterprise.

Follow the same outline as when describing the "as is" state. Explain how this "to be" alternative operates, how it provides value to the organization, and so forth. But also compare it to the current "as is" method. What makes it better? How does this alternative relate to the other "to be" scenarios examined? Explain the alternative solutions considered and why the final submitted alternative is recommended over all the competing alternatives. Basically, for each alternative, include: (a) a brief description of the alternative, (b) estimated costs, (c) estimated benefits, (d) alternative pros, (e) alternative cons, (f) relative merits when compared to the other alternatives, and (g) rationale for decision.

Cost-Benefit Analysis

Up to this point, a narrative of the different alternatives has been provided with some mention of costs and benefits. At this section, the narratives are translated into quantitative data. For each alternative, calculate the expected financial return on the initiative, including NPV, payback period, uniform annual cost, IRR, and ROI against which differing alternatives can be evaluated. Business case benefits and total costs to the government should be developed over the full-life cycle of the project (development, procurement, operation, support, and disposal) for each alternative. They should consider both tangible and intangible benefits and costs, as well as the strategic benefits to the air force from the investment decision. They should also address the consequences of doing nothing (status quo).

Methods for quantifying benefits: Costs are by their very nature quantifiable. Benefits may present a problem. Some benefits, such as an operational or combat metric (not mission capable rate, circular error probability, etc.), are easy to quantify. Others, such as "troop morale" or "customer satisfaction," may be more difficult. This can be overcome by using polling or a focus group to generate scores.

When trying to quantify areas that are not easily quantified, the important point to remember is to always be able to define the scores used. For example, morale could be rated as a 0 for "does not improve morale," 1 for "maintains current morale," or 2 for "improves current morale." The larger the span of ratings, the greater the difficulty in explaining what improvements an alternative would need to move up a point in the ratings scale. Any number of potential scoring methodologies can be devised. However, an example of a situation to avoid is where one alternative is rated 18 out of 20 and another is rated 19 out of 20 without any accompanying definition showing what made one alternative one point above the other.

Methods for weighting benefits: Another concern is that not all benefits may be equally important to the decision maker. In addition to a rating scale, the analysis may need a weighting scale. For example, is the benefit of morale improvement equal to safety improvement? Is safety improvement equal to targeting accuracy? Just as in determining a rating scale, the weighting scale needs to be defined and not just be a random listing of numbers or percentages. An example could be a 100 percent weight means the benefit is critical to success, a 75 percent weight indicates a benefit being above average in importance, while 50 percent shows moderate or importance, and 25 percent would mean the benefit is below average importance.

Methods for combining costs and benefits: Now that costs and benefits are quantified, they need to be combined in a meaningful way. The easiest is to first examine the alternatives ranked by cost and then by benefit. If the costs are equal but the benefits are not, then the alternative with the highest benefit would be picked. If the benefits between the alternatives are equal, the lowest cost solution would be chosen. However, most to all decisions will not be so easy. The typical decision will involve a balancing of costs and benefits. At this point, the analyst has a total cost for each alternative and a weighted total for the sum of various quantifiable (processing error reduction, etc.) and semi-quantifiable (morale scores based on surveys, etc.) benefits. The simplest way to link costs and benefits at this point is to establish a ratio of costs to benefits. This allows the analyst to compare the amount of incremental benefit gained by each additional dollar spent on an alternative. If one alternative does not stand out at this point, the solution will be to examine the cost-to-benefit ratio by individual benefits. If the benefits examined across several alternatives are square-foot work space area and reduction in processing errors, it may become apparent that errors are equally reduced across alternatives, but one alternative provides a disproportionate amount of workspace for the dollars required (square feet per dollar) than the others. At the same time, the alternative with the greater square feet per dollar is the most expensive. The question becomes "is the added work space benefit worth spending the extra dollars?" There is no simple formula for arriving at a decision. Ultimately, at the end of the analysis, an alternative must be rank ordered higher than the others based upon a combination of the total cost, benefits, and (in some cases, potential) risks associated with that alternative.

Risk is treated as a separate category for analysis While discussing costs, it is important to remember that the analysis must cover the life cycle of the project. In other words, the costs must cover what is needed to implement the alternative (construction, acquisition, training, etc.), as well as what is needed to sustain (utilities, annual maintenance, etc.) the alternative and what is needed to dispose of the alternative (remove hazardous waste, etc.), if there is a finite life to the alternative.

Life-cycle costs: Life-cycle costs (LCCs) are all the anticipated costs to the government associated with a project or program alternative throughout its life and include the cost of research and development, investment in mission and support equipment (hardware and software), initial inventories, training, data, facilities, and so forth and the operating, support, and, where applicable, demilitarization, detoxification, long-term waste storage, and disposal costs. All relevant resources required to achieve the stated objective throughout the alternative's useful life are to be shown in the analysis. Costs of each alternative that are required to meet the objective should be exhaustive.

Costs should be carefully analyzed to determine whether or not they are included under the scope of the objective. Closely associated costs that do not contribute to an objective may be excluded. The Department of Defense (DoD) position is that all costs of each alternative should be identified. In practice, it has been found that failing to identify all costs can easily lead to decisions being made on what, in reality, is incomplete and partial information.

If particular costs in a BCA are judged to be very small and difficult to measure due to lack of data, then a discussion of such costs should be included in
narrative format so that decision makers and reviewers will be aware of them.
The specific measure of LCC is the annual cost of the alternative discounted
to its present value and summed over the entire economic life of that alternative or, in other words, the present value of the total cost stream. Life-cycle
costing provides logical and comprehensive information on programs and
projects; its focus is on the total resource implications of program decisions,
implicitly considering the timing of expenditures. Compute LCCs for each
alternative:

Pilot costs: These are costs of developing a prototype solution and implementing it at one or more sites for testing. These costs may include:

- Development, installation, and modification of the system or process
- Training and lost productivity during learning
- Maintaining two separate systems during the pilot
- Program management to include oversight and measurement of desired
  changes
- Reversion to the old process if the pilot is unsuccessful

Implementation costs: Implementation costs include all investment costs
required to implement the alternative, which may include some or all of the
following:

- Hardware, software, installation, and integration with legacy systems
- Process development and modifications not discovered during the pilot
- Project management, including evaluating and staffing the new process
- Training, including lost productivity during learning
- Internal marketing to foster acceptance
- Acquisition of data (technical data) and licenses: This element needs to
  be considered as certain types of technical data (software code docu-
  mentation, schematics, etc.) are needed to ensure a competitive life-cycle
  support environment. If the air force does not possess technical data, life-
  cycle support is, by default, limited to what the vendor provides.
- Management of effects on human resources (e.g., hiring, relocation, re-
  training to other capabilities, reduction-in-force)
- Termination of existing contracts

Operational, maintenance, and sustainment costs: These costs represent the
ongoing costs to operate the system or process and may include some or all
of the following:

- Operations and maintenance
- Staffing and consultants
- Ongoing staff training
- Trouble-shooting and modifications as required
- Customer service and other transactions
- System upgrades and replacements over the life cycle

Note: Accurate estimation of costs is critical to success. An investment that is underestimated could go well and exceed budget while still providing a reasonable return, yet the investment could be terminated due to budget overruns. Although beyond the scope of this book, there are many good sources of detailed approaches to achieve accurate cost estimates. GAO's 2009 *GAO Cost Estimating and Assessment Guide* (GAO-09-3SP) is an excellent source.

Life-cycle benefits: Benefits may fall into one of several categories and may be monetary or nonmonetary. If costs exceed monetary benefits, other benefits must be clearly defined, and you must describe why the proposal is worth the additional cost to the air force. All benefits should be defined for the entire life of the solution. When benefits cannot be quantified, include a narrative description of benefits. The various types of benefits may include:

- Cost savings should have an identifiable dollar value. That value may or may not translate into budget terms and should be so identified in the business case. All calculations, assumptions, and methodology used to identify the savings should be included. Manpower and other cost data should be taken from AFI 65-503, *Cost and Planning Factors*, when possible. Savings fall into one of four categories:
  - Budget savings include those funds, manpower, or other resources that could be removed from the organization (or retained as an incentive) with no adverse impact on mission. These savings relate directly to a budget line or a historical expenditure rate that will cost less because of the new process or activity.
  - Cost avoidance savings are benefits from actions that reduce or eliminate the need for an increase in manpower or cost and would be necessary if present management practices continued. These include such things as price increases, replacement of aging or obsolete equipment, overtime pay due to increased workload resulting from poorly functioning processes or equipment, and so forth.
  - Opportunity cost is the cost of pursuing one alternative versus another. Opportunity cost can include, for example, the cost imposed by one

activity on another by diverting an existing asset from the latter to the former. If use of an existing asset would result in a cash outlay for some other project or activity, a cost that the government would not have otherwise incurred, that value should be included in the analysis as the cost of using that asset. Another example, if the air force decides to build a hospital on vacant land that it owns, the opportunity cost is another purpose, such as locating a different function's facility on that same parcel of land with construction funds instead. In building the hospital, the air force has forgone the ability to build an office building or hangar that was being planned on that land.

- ○ Productivity gains will allow fuller use of personnel or capital assets to achieve higher value with the same or reduced resources. This form of savings may, for example, result in fewer overtime hours that may or may not translate into actual budget savings. In some cases, funds or manpower may be redirected to other activities or reduced work hours.

- Strategic organizational benefits may be more difficult to quantify or may be unquantifiable/intangible in some situations but are often very critical when developing a business case. These benefits may be very important to the organization because of law, policy, or strategic objectives that direct the result or because of other organizational goals. Some examples of strategic benefits include:
  - ○ Attainment of the president's management agenda or most recent president's, secretary of defense's, secretary of the air force's, chief of staff of the air force's, or commander's initiatives
  - ○ Furtherance of the air force transformation goals
  - ○ Improving the effectiveness of operations resulting in higher customer satisfaction ratings
  - ○ A compression of average process cycle time by a factor of 4
  - ○ Work processes and workload that enable our people to accomplish routine organizational missions within a 40- to 50-hour workweek
  - ○ Empowerment of personnel and enrichment of job functions
  - ○ Increased morale
  - ○ A 20 percent shift in business operations dollars and people to war-fighting operations and new or modern war-fighting systems
  - ○ Progress on organizational strategic objectives
  - ○ Development of strategic partnerships
  - ○ Having a competitive support environment between several support contractors and organic capability
- Intangible benefits: Tangible but nonfinancial benefits may have the least cost visibility but may, nonetheless, be very important to the organization and need to be addressed. They may include:

- ○ Improved customer service
- ○ Improved internal and external communications
- ○ Improved management information
- ○ Improved operational information
- ○ Improved quality and accuracy of documents (reduced errors)
- ○ Reduced cycle time (improved effectiveness)

> Note: Measurement of benefits can be challenging and seem nearly impossible at times. There are many good sources on benefits measurement. The book *How to Measure Anything: Finding the Value of Intangibles in Business* by Douglas W. Hubbard is an excellent source of measurement ideas and approaches.

Recommendation

Explain the recommended alternative solution and why it is recommended over all the competing alternatives. Make reference to each rejected alternative and how it compares to the recommended alternative in costs and benefits, pros and cons, and relative merits. Give a rationale for the recommended alternative. Tasks within your explanation of the rationale for the recommendation include:

- Describe the proposed solution. Discuss the problem the initiative will solve and why this is considered a good solution related to the discussion of the current process Discuss whether this is a final solution or if follow-on projects are necessary to achieve full benefits.
- Describe the approach. Summarize how you went about solving or making progress on the problem. Did you use simulation, analytic models, prototype construction, or analysis of field data for an actual product? What was the extent of your analysis effort (did you look at one application program or 100 programs in 20 different programming languages)? What important variables did you control, ignore, or measure?
- Summarize best-practices research and conclusions. Usually recommended alternatives should reflect the best practices available in the business world or the government. Summarize your best-practice research, the best practices observed in other governmental or commercial organizations, and why they are better than the current process. Explain if there are any limitations on the air force implementing the best practice available due to laws, regulations, or DoD policy.

- Include performance measures, such as cost, effectiveness, and efficiency to support your case.
- Compare the current air force process to these best practices, and describe the amount of change required to match or exceed a logically selected benchmark practice, industry, or organization.
- Describe the users of the transformed process output and why they value that output.
- Highlight the key functionalities, requirements, and benefits to each user or customer. Why is this output better for the implementing organization, its stakeholders, its customers, or the air force in general? Does the transformed process offer better decision support to commanders? Do all users derive the same benefits, or are there variations? Compare and contrast the transformed process with the "as is" or status quo.
- Describe how the new process will work, including process maps at the level of detail necessary to support this explanation. Explain the differences in this process from the "as is" process.
- Describe the personnel resources required at each stage of implementation and sustainment, as well as any organizational changes that may be required. If support will be by contract, describe the type of support, and estimate the cost and type of contract. If any of the work will be performed by contract, discuss the risk of strikes that may disrupt performance and a contingency plan for continuity of operations during a short or extended strike.

Funding

Identify the amount of funding required for each phase of the recommended alternative (pilot, implement, and sustainment); identify the source for these funds and current funding status. Be sure you know, and account for, any restrictions associated with these funding sources. Your funding totals should reconcile to the cost estimate. The cost estimate provided the "price" of the alternative. This section merely breaks that resource need out by budget appropriation. Explain briefly the initiative's funding strategy. Include:

- What is the amount of funding from existing or previously submitted budgets for the existing operation that could be used for the new proposed operation?
- What is the amount of new funding, if any, needed to be requested by appropriation or major budget account?
- What is the rationale for requesting funds from these sources?
- What are any limitations on these funding sources?

- Will proposed funding require other existing or planned efforts or programs to go unfunded or have budgeted amounts reduced?
- What is the effect of funding impacts on organizations other than the office of primary responsibility (OPR) for the function or the organization proposing the new way of doing business?
- What is the risk of availability of funding source(s)?

Sensitivity and Risk Analyses

It is important to identify and analyze risks to determine which risks present the greatest threat to the initiative's successful outcome and inform senior leaders of risks to the proposed course of action as part of the decision-making process. Identify the risks, impacts, and potential mitigating strategies for the proposed plan of action. This should include an analysis on the impact to the business case if key assumptions do not hold. Risks may include technology that does not become available as predicted, lack of funding or other resources, lack of a workforce with requisite skills, and so forth. For each risk, assess the likelihood of that risk occurring, the potential impact on the project, and an approach to overcome or lessen the impact of the risk should it occur. Also, key variables should be analyzed to see how sensitive the recommended alternative is to changes in these key variables. Key variables to analyze include discount rate, inflation rate, prices, labor costs, and any variable the OPR judges to be a key player in the operation of the proposed alternative. For each identified risk, address the following:

- Were all phases and aspects of the initiative taken into account during the risk identification process?
- Has the likelihood of changes to key variables been assessed and variables changed in the analysis so that the sensitivity of the decision to changes in key variables is clear?
- Has the exposure of each identified risk been evaluated?
- Has a mitigation strategy been identified for each identified risk?
- Has a contingency strategy been defined for each identified risk?
- Has a trigger been established for each contingency strategy?
- Does the proposed initiative include tasks for actively monitoring for risks?
- Is there a process for tracking and reporting on risks?

Change Management Plan

For the recommended alternative only, provide a change management plan. A change management plan is developed to manage the organizational change that is associated with implementing a new initiative. A well-drafted change management plan should discuss any cultural changes required, shared visions between stakeholders, what necessitates the change, expected stakeholder resistances, leadership buy-in, communication strategies, and possible infrastructure changes. The plan is based on effective marketing of the project and the building of a partnership between the project management team and the user community. The plan should contain the following major elements:

1. Stakeholder action plan: Most proposed actions involve stakeholders, those who have an interest in a requirement or the means of achieving it. For the proposed alternative only, provide a stakeholder action plan. If the investment decision impacts stakeholders, address how the stakeholders will be informed, involved, convinced, or otherwise engaged in the new process to gain their support. It is important to remember that, depending on the process being changed, immediate stakeholders may be the Air Force Reserve Command (AFRC) and Air National Guard (ANG). If ANG and AFRC personnel rely on a process or automated system operated by active duty forces, they may very well be a stakeholder, and the impact to their organization must be considered.

   In addition, changing business processes affecting civilian personnel administration may require added analysis considering the union as a stakeholder. The critical point to keep in mind is to not overlook potential stakeholders in the process being changed. For each stakeholder, address the following:

   • What are their interests in the action plan?
   • Why should they be involved or to what extent?
   • What are any concerns they may have about the proposed alternative?
   • Were they represented in the development of the business case? If yes, how? If no, why not?
   • What might this stakeholder contribute to the implementation or planning process?

2. Communications plan: Communication is a major component of any successful project. Without effective communication, key stakeholders in a project may miss out on vital information and may not understand why change is needed. Customers might not be aware of the plans for a new way of doing business and may raise concerns about how the proposed alternative would meet their needs. The other military services, the Defense Finance and Accounting Service (DFAS), or the Joint Staff may need to be informed of the new way of doing business. Also, oversight groups such as the OSD, the OMB, or congressional staff may

need to be informed of the new way of doing business through the budget formulation process if not by any other means. In some cases, OSD or Joint Staff coordination or approval may be needed before adopting the new way of business, or congressional committees or subcommittees may need to approve it. The best way to approach communication is to develop a clearly planned approach or strategy. For the proposed alternative only, provide a communications plan. Address the means, methods, and messages, including who will issue messages, along with a schedule for delivery, to explain the initiative to stakeholders and other parties impacted by the proposed new way of doing business.

3. Training plan: Provide a training plan for the proposed alternative only. The training plan describes the strategies, activities, and tasks necessary to provide the individuals or organizations that will implement the new way of doing business the skills necessary to perform the new initiative successfully. The training plan helps to ensure that project outcomes are successfully achieved. The key to effective training and successful project implementation is to start the planning process early. If training needs are not considered until late in the implementation process, there may not be enough time to effectively prepare staff to implement the new process or to budget or contract for needed training. The training plan includes the following:

- A description of the scope of the training
- A description of the training objectives
- The training strategy
- Background information, such as a description of the desired skills outcome and a high-level overview of the curriculum
- The training requirements, such as the required skills, the audience(s), individuals, or positions needing specific training, and the required time frame
- The training roles and responsibilities
- A method for evaluating the training
- Existing sources for training
- Training resources: any additional or future resources that may be a source for training
- Costs of training (also should be included in rollup cost)
- Any constraints or limitations affecting the training
- A description of the training environment
- A description of the training materials
- A course outline
- A log for keeping track of who has received training
- A process for updating the training materials

- A recommendation on whether training should be accomplished in-house or by contractors
- Any budget implications of the proposed training

4. Implementation or action plan: Provide an implementation or action plan for the recommended alternative only. With a well-thought-out, high-level implementation or action plan, the project manager will be able to communicate and coordinate the tasks necessary for a successful transition throughout pilot, implementation, and sustainment phases. Implementation plans should have specific events tied to specific, achievable milestones that factor in technological, cost, and schedule risk. Identify the type of approach to implementing the preferred alternative, for example: one large project, a number of smaller projects, or a combination of both. The breakdown of the projects within this strategy can also be included where the "manageable chunks" or phases for each project have been identified. Deployment of complex projects or systems in modular units may reduce the risk of the failure of the new way of doing business. The OMB has directed this approach for large IT systems. Holding a walk-through of the implementation or action plan with all stakeholders is a good way to verify that all necessary tasks are accounted for, are in their proper sequence, and are assigned to appropriate organizations or individuals.

   BCA preparers must make sure the implementation plan is consistent with scheduled costs and budgets elsewhere in the BCA. When developing the implementation or action plan, consider the following:

   - Have dates been applied to all tasks?
   - Are the sequencing and timing of all the tasks correct?
   - Is there an assigned person or organization responsible for completing each task?
   - Have dependencies between tasks been identified and communicated to the resources affected by the dependency?
   - Has the plan been reviewed with all impacted stakeholders and resources assigned to the implementation or action tasks?
   - Has the initiative schedule been reviewed and updated based on the tasks and time frames identified in the implementation plan?
   - Is the implementation plan congruent with the funding profile?
   - Have other ongoing projects or processes been reviewed for possible changes based on the contents of this implementation plan?

5. Key performance measures and outcomes: A key aspect of any initiative is the ability to track results of the initiative over time. Determining perfor-

mance measures and outcomes (metrics) at the beginning of an initiative helps assure that the initiative stays true to the initial purpose and priorities. Defining the desired outcomes or acceptance criteria at the beginning of the initiative also clarifies the initiative's scope. For the recommended alternative only, provide key performance measures and outcomes. Using performance measures, establishes whether the initiative did indeed succeed and provides a starting point for developing future lessons learned. If the business process will change dramatically due to the initiative, then it's especially important to choose a basis of comparison that won't change. Some common measures to consider are program cost savings (requires baseline), business process time savings (requires baseline), amount of use that project outputs get (number of website hits, etc.), change in number of customer complaints (requires baseline), and nature of customer feedback (may require a survey, both before and after implementation). Each proposed metric should address the following:

- Do the performance measures directly target an initiative's objective?
- If the objective of a business operation has several parts, do the performance measures cover all parts of the objective?
- Does the measure use data that's readily available?
- If the measure uses data not readily available, what must be done to arrange to develop or receive the data, and is preparing to receive it feasible and manageable?
- How long will it take for changes to come about or to be able to capture meaningful data?
- Has baseline data been captured (necessary if changes are to be measured)?
- Is the basis for comparison consistent? (Is it comparing apples to apples?)
- Are possible seasonal variations in data accounted for in the time frame or reporting periods?

BCA Checklist

This checklist is designed to enhance consistency in BCA products.

1. Executive Summary
   a. Does the executive summary adequately state the problem, study objective, and significant criteria, assumptions, and constraints?
   b. Are the feasible alternatives clearly identified and differences explained?
   c. Is the recommended alternative adequately supported without reference to detailed study content?

2. Objective or Problem Statement
   a. Is the objective clear and specific?
   b. Is the objective realistic?
   c. Are any feasible alternative solutions excluded due to a bias in the objective statement?
3. Assumptions
   a. Are all assumptions recognized and identified?
   b. Are the assumptions realistic and properly supported?
   c. Are assumptions used only when actual facts are unavailable?
   d. Are assumptions unnecessarily restrictive thereby preventing consideration of feasible alternatives?
   e. Do assumptions include economic life and future changes in operations requirements?
   f. Are key facts, ground rules, laws, DoD or air force policies, and other constraints stated?
4. Alternatives
   a. Are all feasible alternatives considered?
   b. Were alternatives rejected before a full analysis was adequately documented?
   c. Are the alternatives significantly different as opposed to superficial restructuring of a single course of action?
   d. Was the status quo used as the baseline for alternative evaluation?
   e. Were other government agencies' capabilities to provide a product or service considered, where applicable?
   f. Were contracting alternatives considered (including public-private competition under OMB Circular A-76 or termination and consolidation of existing contracts)?
5. Cost Analysis
   a. Are all government direct and indirect costs included for each alternative?
   b. Do investment costs include transportation, installation, support, and training costs incurred before operational and building occupancy dates, and so forth?
   c. Are personnel costs all-inclusive; that is, specific skill levels, fringe benefits, overtime and shift differentials, and so forth? Are personnel costs broken out by rank/grade, number of employees in each category, and so forth?
   d. Are future equipment replacement costs included as investments as opposed to operations costs?
   e. Are available asset values considered, and are such values adequately documented?
   f. Are cost collection and aggregation methods correct?

g. Are estimating relationships and procedures identified and properly supported?

h. Are program or project costs expressed in constant dollars?

i. Where inflation or cost escalation is used, have the factors been identified and validated?

j. Are cash flows discounted at the proper discount rate?

k. Are cost and savings schedules realistic?

6. Benefit Analysis

a. Have all project results, outputs, benefits, or yields been included?

b. Are the benefits identified in measurable terms where possible?

c. Are benefit measuring techniques properly defined and supported?

d. Is benefit priority or ranking criteria clearly stated and used in the evaluation? Is any weighting scale consistently and reasonably applied?

e. Are negative results or outputs identified and adequately evaluated?

f. Are secondary benefits (not related to the objective) identified?

g. Do the benefits relate to the program and project objective?

h. Are all cost savings represented as a negative cost rather than as a benefit?

i. Are the benefits suitably tabulated, graphed, and so forth?

7. Comparison Selection Evaluation

a. Were alternative selection criteria applied consistently?

b. Are cost and benefit data suitably displayed to accurately depict relationships?

c. Were benefits quantified in support of the recommendation, and, if so, were they presented in the executive summary? (not always possible to quantify benefits)

d. Are the alternatives compared to a common baseline (minimum requirements level)?

e. Were alternative comparison techniques suitable for the program project being evaluated, that is, present value, payback period, uniform annual cost, and so forth?

f. Was a specific course of action recommended?

g. Does analysis data clearly support the recommendation?

h. Are significant differences between the recommended and other alternatives clearly identified?

8. Risk and Sensitivity Analyses

a. Were the effects of possible changes to the objective requirements evaluated?

b. Would the recommended alternative remain the same if key assumptions or criteria were varied within a feasible range?

c. Was the project schedule evaluated for both operational and cost impacts (slippages, advancements)?

9. Change Management Plan
   a. Does the change management plan detail all the steps that must be taken to move from the "as is" business situation to the proposed "to be" business situation?
   b. Do the plans for change management address all areas of change that could have a significant impact on adopting the new business plan?
   c. Do the planned changes take into account planned changes in other parts of air force operations that would affect the proposed business plan?
10. Stakeholders Action Plan
   a. Have the views of all stakeholders in the business operation been considered?
   b. Have all potential stakeholders been identified and considered to include the AFRC, ANG, union, other services (if selected alternative impacts joint operations), and local foreign nationals (if selected alternative impacts status-of-forces agreement)?
   c. Are there any actions needed by the various stakeholders in the business operation that have not been included?
11. Communication Plan
   a. Does the communication plan show a reasonable plan for spreading the word about the proposed business process to all affected parties?
12. Training Plan
   a. Have all the types of training needed to prepare the workforce or the customer population for the new way of doing business been identified?
   b. Have the objectives of each type of training been identified?
   c. Have sources of training been identified?
   d. Are any usual sources of training missing?
   e. Has the timeline for development and delivery of training been identified?
   f. Has funding for training been included, if needed, in the funding plan?
13. Implementation or Action Plan
   a. Is there an implementation plan that spells out in sufficient detail the actions different offices or organizations must take to implement the new way of doing business?
   b. Does the plan include reasonable steps that are sequenced in proper order to get from the "as is" to the "to be" state of business?
   c. Do steps in the action plan acknowledge any barriers to implementation and allow time and a reasonable plan of action to overcome implementation barriers?

14. Key Performance Measures and Outcomes
    a. Have performance measures and outcomes been identified that are appropriate for monitoring the business performance under the proposed new business plan?
15. Documentation
    a. Are the costs thoroughly documented in appendixes so an independent reviewer may replicate it? A key element of a good BCA is sufficient documentation of methods and sources used so that a reader not familiar with the analysis could arrive at essentially the same result. Without documentation, the BCA's appeal for acceptance is based on faith in the authority of the issuing agency.
    b. Is it possible to trace costs to their basic inputs, units of measure, sources derived from (website, the OPR, etc.), and as-of date for any special rates or factors?
    c. If costs, assumptions, or other input to the estimate is based upon expert opinion, does the supporting documentation include the individual's office symbol, email address, and phone number?
16. Coordination
    a. Has coordination of all participating offices and organizations been obtained?

Additional Thoughts on Business Cases and Their Importance

Business Cases Are Not Just about Money

Even if a hard-nosed financial calculation lies at the heart of an investment decision, the business case is always about more than just money. While it is true to say a good many business cases are built to maximize financial returns or efficiency savings, decisions to go ahead with a project—as well as where to rank it alongside other corporate initiatives—will reflect broader rationales, such as the strategic priorities of an authority.

The nature of public-sector organizations commonly means that a range of factors—particularly the generation of public value and social inclusion—will be considered in determining the most appropriate use of resources, particularly those related to investment capital.

Business Case Issues Are about Processes as Much as Products

Business cases are easily conceived of in terms of tangible documents—the reports that present the analyses and recommendations. The business is concerned with the overall process and the different stages and elements that go into decision making and project management. Business cases are managed dynamically through the whole life cycle of decision making and change.

Benefits to End-Users Should Be Central to Any Business Case

In putting forward the case for any government project, the benefits to customers/end-users will need to be considered. Of course, for many smaller projects (particularly technology upgrades) or back-office initiatives, there may be no obvious consequence so far as customer services are concerned. However, it is always advisable to explore and document potential contributions, even if they are only intermediate.

Service Managers Must Engage in the Business Case Process

Customer and service improvements will be more effectively addressed where service managers themselves take an active role in business case management. By being close to the customer and the potential service outcomes of projects, such managers are well placed to judge the benefits that a given investment will achieve.

Return on Investment (ROI)

The benefits derived from spending money on an investment are the ROI. The more benefits that are realized, the better the ROI. Actually working out the ROI can be complicated because it is not a simple computation, and there can be many intangibles. The obvious benefits can be listed and quantified. However, some benefits may not be apparent initially or may be long-term outcomes. If the project yields no benefits because it has strayed away from its stated goals, the investment is clearly a failure. On the other hand, if the project achieves all its goals and then some, the ROI was excellent. So, the ROI is not necessarily a single measure, it can be a range of calculations from failure at the bottom end of the scale to spectacular success at the top.

Validating the Business Case

To be successful in the PDM approach, business cases must include cause-and-effect analysis that evaluates cause and effect and incorporates the impact of risk. A business case done in this manner predicts a range of returns on investment and probabilities associated with each. This is the most realistic approach as there will be risk and variability among the elements that result in ROI. Reliance on a single point estimate of costs, benefits, and risks is naive (particularly for complex investments) and presents an uninformed and unrealistic perspective on the results an investment could provide. This could then lead to ill-informed decisions and early failure of an investment.

Two techniques for validating a business case and performing risk-based ongoing business case and ROI analysis are described—business process simulation and Monte Carlo analysis.

Business Process Simulation

It is important to understand the inevitable uncertainties inherent in any business case, and one way of doing this is to use a program to simulate possible results or outcomes. The core idea is to use random samples of inputs to explore and analyze the behavior of complex processes or systems. Computer models look at the lifetime of a project and simulate "what if" scenarios. It can identify both what and when things might happen, such as a critical overload or equipment failures, and it can sample a number of projects and predict interdependent issues that need addressing. Discreet event simulation is generally the most appropriate simulation technique for simulating business and IT processes.

In discrete-event simulation, the operation of a system is represented as a chronological sequence of events. Each event occurs at an instant in time and marks a change of state in the system. For example, if an elevator is simulated, an event could be "level 6 button pressed," with the resulting system state of "lift moving" and, eventually (unless one chooses to simulate the failure of the lift), "lift at level 6."

A common exercise in learning how to build discrete-event simulations is to model a queue, such as customers arriving at a bank to be served by a teller. In this example, the system entities are "customer queue" and "tellers." The system events are "customer arrival" and "customer departure." (The event of "teller begins service" can be part of the logic of the arrival and departure events.) The system states, which are changed by these events, are "number of customers in the queue" (an integer from 0 to n) and "teller status" (busy or idle). The random variables that need to be characterized to model this system stochastically are "customer inter-arrival time" and "teller service time."

A number of mechanisms have been proposed for carrying out discrete-event simulation; among them are the event-based, activity-based, process-based, and three-phase approaches (Pidd 1998).

The simulation must keep track of the current simulation time, in whatever measurement units are suitable for the system being modeled. In discrete-event simulations, as opposed to real-time simulations, time "hops" because events are instantaneous—the clock skips to the next event start time as the simulation proceeds.

The simulation maintains at least one list of simulation events. This is sometimes called the *pending event set* because it lists events that are pending as a result of previously simulated events but have yet to be simulated themselves. An event is described by the time at which it occurs and a type, indicating the code that will be used to simulate that event. It is common for the event code to be parameterized, in which case, the event description also contains parameters to the event code.

When events are instantaneous, activities that extend over time are modeled as sequences of events. Some simulation frameworks allow the time of an event to be specified as an interval, giving the start time and the end time of each event.

The graphical representation of business process information has also proven effective for presenting it to business stakeholders, including business analysts and system developers. Visual modeling languages used to represent business processes include Business Process Modeling Notation (BPMN) and the Unified Modeling Language (UML).

Techniques to model business process, such as the flow chart, functional flow block diagram, control flow diagram, Gantt chart, PERT diagram, and IDEF, have emerged since the beginning of the 20th century. The Gantt chart was among the first to arrive around 1900, the flow charts in the 1920s, functional flow block diagram and PERT in the 1950s, and data flow diagrams and IDEF in the 1970s. Among the modern methods are UML and BPMN. Still, these represent just a fraction of the methodologies used over the years to document business processes. The term "business process modeling" itself was coined in the 1960s in the field of systems engineering by S. Williams in his 1967 article "Business Process Modeling Improves Administrative Control." His idea was that techniques for obtaining a better understanding of physical control systems could be used in a similar way for business processes. It took until the 1990s before the term became popular.

In the 1990s, the term "process" became a new productivity paradigm. Companies were encouraged to think in *processes* instead of *functions* and *procedures*. Process thinking looks at the chain of events in the company from purchase to supply, from order retrieval to sales, and so forth. The traditional modeling tools were developed to picture time and costs, while modern methods focus on cross-function activities. These cross-functional activities have increased severely in number and importance due to the growth of complexity and dependencies. New methodologies, such as business process redesign, business process innovation, business process management, and integrated business planning, among others, are all "aiming at improving processes across the traditional functions that comprise a company."

A detailed description of discreet-event simulation can be found in many texts and is beyond the scope of this book.

Monte Carlo Analysis

Physicists at Los Alamos Scientific Laboratory in the 1940s were investigating radiation shielding and the distance that neutrons would likely travel through various materials. Despite having most of the necessary data, such as the average distance a neutron would travel in a substance before it collided with an atomic nucleus or how much energy the neutron was likely to give off following a collision, the problem could not be solved with analytical calculations. John von Neumann and Stanislaw Ulam suggested that the problem be solved by modeling the experiment on a computer using chance. Being secret, their work required a code name. Von Neumann chose the name "Monte Carlo." The name is a reference to the Monte Carlo Casino in Monaco where Ulam's uncle would borrow money to gamble.

The basic goal of a Monte Carlo analysis is to characterize quantitatively the uncertainty and variability in estimates of exposure or risk. A secondary goal is to identify key sources of variability and uncertainty and to quantify the relative contribution of these sources to the overall variance and range of model results.

There are several Monte Carlo methods that use computational algorithms that rely on repeated random sampling to compute their results. They all, however, follow the same pattern:

- Define a domain of possible inputs
- Generate inputs randomly from the domain using a certain specified probability distribution
- Perform a deterministic computation using the inputs
- Aggregate the results of the individual computations into the final result

An important bonus of a quantitative variability and uncertainty analysis is the process of interaction between the risk manager and other interested parties that makes risk assessment into a dynamic rather than a static process. Monte Carlo methods are useful for modeling phenomena with significant uncertainty in inputs, such as the calculation of risk in business.

One of the most important challenges facing the risk assessor is to communicate, effectively, the insights an analysis of variability and uncertainty provides. It is important for the risk assessor to remember that insights will generally be qualitative in nature even though the models they derive from are quantitative. Insights can include:

- An appreciation of the overall degree of variability and uncertainty and the confidence that can be placed in the analysis and its findings
- An understanding of the key sources of variability and key sources of uncertainty and their impacts on the analysis
- An understanding of the critical assumptions and their importance to the analysis and findings.
- An understanding of the unimportant assumptions and why they are unimportant.
- An understanding of the extent to which plausible alternative assumptions or models could affect any conclusions

The opposite of Monte Carlo simulation might be considered deterministic modeling using single-point estimates. Each uncertain variable within a model is assigned a "best guess" estimate. Various combinations of each input variable are manually chosen (such as, best case, worst case, and most likely case) and the results recorded for each "what if" scenario.

By contrast, Monte Carlo simulation considers random sampling of probability distribution functions as model inputs to produce hundreds or thousands of possible outcomes instead of a few discrete scenarios. The results provide probabilities of different outcomes occurring.

A publicly available approach that integrates business cases and revalidation is PRINCE2. PRINCE (which stands for Projects in Controlled Environments) was first developed by the U.K. government in 1989 as the standard approach to IT project management for central government. Since then, the method has been enhanced to become a generic, best-practice approach suitable for the management of all types of projects and has a proven record outside both IT and government sectors. PRINCE2 has been widely adopted and adapted by both the public and private sectors and is now the United Kingdom's de facto standard for project management. See appendix B for additional information.

Portfolio Selection

Approach for Successful Investment Selection

Selecting an investment introduces a defined process that an organization should use to select new IT project proposals and reselect ongoing projects. The purpose of this critical process is (1) to predefine a method for selecting new investment proposals, and (2) use this method to select new proposals. "New" proposals include both (1) previously submitted proposals that were not originally selected for funding, and (2) proposals that have never been submitted—new candidates.

Defining and implementing a selection process is a basic step toward implementing the mature IT critical processes for proposal and project selection. The key activities implemented within this critical process include (1) concurrent review of IT proposals by the organization's executives, (2) the use of predefined selection criteria to analyze the proposals, and (3) decision making by executives to fund some proposals and not others. The EA, where it exists, should be reflected in the selection criteria. Investments may come up outside of the EA, in which case their value must be considered under the same criteria as all other investments.

Investments that are not consistent with the current EA should either be assimilated into the EA or be provided a waiver. Reselection of ongoing projects is a very important part of this critical process. If a project is not meeting the goals and objectives that were established in the original selection, the investment board must make a decision on whether to continue to fund it.

Using a structured method to select new investments accomplishes several objectives. First, a structured method provides the organization's investment board, business units, and IT developers (whether they are internal IT staff or contractors) with a common understanding of the process and the cost, benefit, schedule, and risk criteria that will be used to select investments. Second, whether a business unit identifies a business need and develops an IT proposal itself or the organization's IT group develops the proposals, organizational roles and responsibilities will be defined for each participating unit involved in the project selection process. Lastly, the data required for decision making and the decision-making procedures should be predefined.

A documented selection process can help to ensure consistency when an organization is considering multiple investments for funding. Transparency in the process can help to create an environment that is objective, fair, and rational. Thus, potential investments will be judged solely on the merits of their contributions to the strategic goals of the organization without undue influence from outside the process.

A policy-driven, structured method for reselecting ongoing projects for further funding can also accomplish several objectives. A structured method provides the organization's investment board with a common understanding of how ongoing projects will be reselected for continued funding. Each ongoing project should be judged based on its success in meeting the investment outcomes that were stated in the policies and procedures for reselection. The information needed for decisions on project reselection should be predefined.

A documented reselection process ensures consistency when an organization is considering multiple investments for additional funding. Again, transparency in the process will create an environment that is objective, fair, and rational. Thus, ongoing investments will be judged solely on the merits of their current contributions to the strategic goals of the organization without undue influence from outside the process.

The process of selecting investments is not feasible unless the policies and procedures for selection and reselection take into account how much funding is available for IT investments. No decision to fund a project can be considered valid without considering what funds are available. It is, therefore, vitally important to include procedures for project funding in the documented policies and procedures for selecting investments.

There has to be criteria for analyzing, prioritizing, and selecting new investment opportunities established. Any decision-support process should be based on predetermined criteria. In order to maintain consistency, the criteria should include quantitative or qualitative measures for comparing projects.

Projects are compared with one another based on criteria such as investment size, project longevity, technical difficulty, project risk, business impact, customer needs, cost-benefit analysis, organizational impact, and expected improvement. The results of such a comparison will help the investment board analyze the potential risk and return of investing in a particular project and prioritize the portfolio of projects using a scoring mechanism that considers strengths and weaknesses. After a careful analysis of the various projects vying for funding, senior executives should be able to prioritize the list of investment proposals based on each investment's business case.

There should be consistent quantitative or qualitative measures for analyzing projects for reselection or, if necessary, termination. If corrective actions cannot be implemented to maintain the desired investment outcome, the project should be identified, based on developed criteria, for termination. The results of such an analysis will help the investment board determine the potential risk and return of continuing to fund an ongoing project and to prioritize the projects based on decision criteria. After a careful analysis of the various ongoing projects competing for continued funding, senior executives should be able to prioritize the list of existing investments for reselection based on supporting documentation.

The part of the process during which organizations tend to need the most help is in determining which projects to reselect and which to terminate. Competing priorities and differing objectives make it extremely difficult for IT decision-makers to determine where to allocate their scarce IT funds.

Faced with a changing laundry list of important and potential IT projects that exceeds budget parameters, managers need a predefined selection process that will help them choose among new and ongoing projects. To help ensure the selection and continuation of the most promising projects, ongoing projects should be reviewed continually along with new projects and "go" or "no go" decisions should be made using predefined selection criteria.

To make good investment decisions, an organization must be able to acquire pertinent information about each investment and store that information in a retrievable format, to be used in future investment decisions. During this critical process, the organization identifies its assets and creates a comprehensive repository of investment information. This repository of investment information is used to track the organization's resources to provide insights and trends about major IT cost and management drivers. The information in the repository serves to highlight lessons learned and to support current and future investment decisions. This critical process may be satisfied by the information contained in the current EA, augmented by additional information (e.g., financial information, risks, benefits, etc.) that the investment board may require to ensure that informed decisions are being made.

The repository can take many forms (e.g., a catalog, a list, IT system and software inventories, or a balance sheet), but regardless of form, the collection method should identify each IT investment and its associated components. An organization's "as is" architecture, along with its sequencing plan, can provide a resource for developing a list of existing investments.

The guiding principle for developing the information source is that it should be accessible where it is of the most value to those making decisions about IT investments. The information is particularly important when executing the critical processes for providing investment oversight, selecting an investment, creating the portfolio, and managing the succession of information systems. Additionally, beyond serving as a tool to aid in IT investment decision making, the IT information can also assist the organization with software licensing management, hardware life-cycle management, and system architecture plans.

Defining the portfolio criteria is the process of developing quantitative or qualitative factors, such as cost, benefit, schedule, and risk (CBSR), in order to compare and select projects for inclusion in the investment portfolio(s).

Portfolio selection criteria are a necessary part of an IT investment management process. Developing an IT investment portfolio involves defining appropriate IT investment CBSR criteria to ensure that the organization's strategic goals, objectives, and mission will be satisfied by the selected investments. If an EA, including a sequencing plan, exists, it should be used as the foundation for developing and updating the portfolio selection criteria. Portfolio selection criteria reflect the strategic and enterprise-wide focus of the organization and build on the criteria that are used to select individual IT projects. When IT projects are not considered in the context of a portfolio, criteria based on narrow, lower-level requirements may dominate enterprise-wide selection criteria. IT projects sometimes are selected on the basis of an isolated business need, the type and availability of funds, or the receptivity of management to a project proposal. Portfolio selection criteria build on the criteria that are used to select individual projects. The portfolio criteria focus on alignment with the organization's mission, organizational strategy, and line-of-business priorities. Portfolio selection criteria are used by the organization's investment board to select IT investments in the context of all other investments. These criteria should also be applied as uniformly as possible throughout the organization to ensure that decision making is consistent and that processes become institutionalized. When an organization's mission or business needs and strategies change, these criteria should be reexamined.

The selection criteria should be linked directly to the organization's broader mission, goals, performance measures, and priorities. This ensures that the selected IT investments will support these larger organizational tenets and purposes. It is important that the criteria also take into account the organization's EA in order to (1) avoid unwarranted overlap across investments, (2) ensure maximum systems interoperability, and (3) increase the assurance that investments align with strategy.

The selection criteria used for assessing and ranking individual investments and proposals should generally include the four essential investment elements: cost, benefit, schedule, and risk. The assessment may also include other criteria, which serves to enhance the evaluation of each investment's strategic alignment and synergy with other projects. Organizations typically focus on these four areas and develop multiple measures under each broad element:

- *Cost* may include LCCs broken apart into initial costs, ongoing development costs, and indirect costs.
- *Benefit* may include tangible benefits and intangible benefits estimated using a variety of techniques (e.g., cost/benefit analyses using net present value, ROI calculations).
- *Schedule* may include the life-cycle schedule and the schedule of benefits.
- *Risk* may include investment, organizational, funding, and technical risks.

The organization must determine how these criteria are to be used to select IT investments for the portfolio. Costs and benefits are both affected by risks. A risk-adjusted ROI could combine all of these categories. The selection criteria also may include a description of an investment's or proposal's minimum or maximum acceptable CBSR thresholds (e.g., a minimum acceptable ROI hurdle rate or a maximum acceptable schedule length).

Once an investment is selected, the investment could be implemented through one or more projects depending on the complexity of the investment and ownership of the various portions. An investment that is converted into multiple projects is often referred to as a program. In programs, all of the projects must contribute to the investment-level business case and contribute to moving the performance measures toward their target values. When an investment is converted into multiple projects, each project should have its own business case developed, defining its contribution to the overall program. Each project should then be managed through the PDM phases, accountable for its own business case (recognizing that there will be dependencies between projects). All projects emanating from an investment become part of the investment portfolio, grouped by the overall program.

Investment Portfolios

Taking a portfolio perspective enables the organization to consider its investments in a comprehensive manner so that the investments address not only the strategic goals, objectives, and mission of the organization but also the impact that projects have on one another. The organization develops its IT investment portfolio by combining all IT assets, resources, and investments that it owns, considering new proposals along with previously funded investments, and identifying the appropriate mix and synergies of IT investments that best meet its mission needs, organizational needs, technology needs, and priorities for improvement. The following elements are critical to portfolio analysis:

- Defining the portfolio criteria is the process of developing quantitative or qualitative factors, such as CBSR, in order to compare and select projects for inclusion in the investment portfolio(s).
- Creating the portfolio is the process of comparing worthwhile investments and then combining the investments selected into a funded portfolio.
- Portfolio review is the process that builds upon oversight by adding the element of portfolio performance to the organization's control process activities. (See also step 4.)
- Conducting post-implementation reviews (PIRs) is the process for reviewing IT projects in order to learn from past investments and initiatives by comparing actual results to estimates. PIRs also serve as vehicles for

evaluating the entire information technology investment management (ITIM) process. (See also step 5.)

Risk Mitigation

Risk mitigation involves prioritizing, evaluating, and implementing the appropriate risk-reducing controls recommended from the risk assessment process.

Because the elimination of all risk is usually impractical or close to impossible, it is the responsibility of senior management and functional and business managers to use the least-cost approach and implement the most appropriate controls to decrease mission risk to an acceptable level, with minimal adverse impact on the organization's resources and mission.

Risk Mitigation Options

Risk mitigation is a systematic methodology used by senior management to reduce mission risk. Risk mitigation can be achieved through any of the following risk mitigation options:

- Risk assumption: to accept the potential risk and continue operating the IT system or to implement controls to lower the risk to an acceptable level
- Risk avoidance: to avoid the risk by eliminating the risk cause and/or consequence (e.g., forgo certain functions of the system or shut down the system when risks are identified)
- Risk limitation: to limit the risk by implementing controls that minimize the adverse impact of a threat's exercising a vulnerability (e.g., use of supporting, preventive, detective controls)
- Risk planning: to manage risk by developing a risk mitigation plan that prioritizes, implements, and maintains controls
- Research and acknowledgment: to lower the risk of loss by acknowledging the vulnerability or flaw and researching controls to correct the vulnerability
- Risk transference: to transfer the risk by using other options to compensate for the loss, such as purchasing insurance

The goals and mission of an organization should be considered in selecting any of these risk mitigation options. It may not be practical to address all identified risks, so priority should be given to the threat and vulnerability pairs that have the potential to cause significant mission impact or harm.

Also, in safeguarding an organization's mission and its IT systems, because of each organization's unique environment and objectives, the option used to mitigate the risk and the methods used to implement controls may vary. The "best of breed" approach is to use appropriate technologies from among the various vendor security products, along with the appropriate risk mitigation option and no technical, administrative measures.

For more information on risk management see appendix C.

Recap

During steps 1 and 2, the organization identifies its business strategy and then puts in place measures to assess the benefits that should accrue. Step 3 looks at specific projects and analyzes each project's risks and returns before committing significant funds to any project. The purpose, of course, is to select the IT projects that will best support its mission needs. This process must be repeated each time funds are allocated to projects.

It is important that, as projects develop and investment expenditures continue, the project continues to meet mission needs at the expected levels of cost and risk. If the project is not meeting expectations or if problems have arisen, steps must be quickly taken to address the deficiencies. If mission needs have changed, the organization must adjust its objectives for the project and appropriately modify expected project outcomes.

Once a project has been designated for initial funding, it becomes the subject of evaluation throughout its lifetime. If a project is not meeting the goals and objectives that were originally established when it was selected or if the goals have been modified to reflect changes in mission objectives—and corrective actions are not succeeding—a decision must be made on whether to continue to fund the project. Ultimately, "deselection" can be one of the most difficult steps to implement, but it is necessary if funds can be better utilized elsewhere. Once projects are operating and being maintained, they must remain under constant review for reselection.

Governance Considerations—Building the Investment Foundation

The foundation for current and future investment success depends on establishing basic selection and control processes and includes:

- *Instituting the investment board* is the process for creating and defining the membership, guiding policies, operations, roles, responsibilities, and authorities for one or more investment boards within the organization.

- *Meeting business needs* is the process for developing a business case that identifies the key executive sponsor and business customers (or end users) and the business needs that the project will support.
- *Selecting an investment* introduces a defined process that an organization can use to select new project proposals and reselect ongoing projects.
- *Providing investment oversight* is a pivotal process whereby the organization monitors projects against cost and schedule expectations as well as anticipated benefits and risk exposure
- *Capturing investment information* is the process by which specific details about a particular investment are captured and maintained to provide asset-tracking data to executive decision makers.

The investment board is a key component in the investment management process. This critical process defines the membership, guiding policies, operations, roles, responsibilities, and authorities for each designated board and, if appropriate, each board's support staff. This definition provides the basis for each board's investment selection, control, and evaluation activities. The organization may choose to make this board the same board that provides executive guidance and support for the EA.

This overlap of responsibilities may enhance the ability of the board to ensure that investment decisions are consistent with the architecture and that it reflects the needs of the organization.

The enterprise-wide investment board is created to (1) define the investment board's structure and accompanying processes, and (2) implement the processes as they are defined. This board is comprised of senior executives, including the organization's head or a designee, the chief information officer (CIO) or other senior executive representing the CIO's interests, and heads of business units and supporting units, such as financial management. When the CIO is represented on the board by another senior executive, this executive must have knowledge of the CIO's management responsibilities and be able to fully represent the technical criteria that are being applied in the investment decision process. In cases where lower-level investment boards, comprised of individuals from across the organization, are chartered to carry out the responsibilities of the enterprise-wide investment board within their own business units, the enterprise-wide investment board still must maintain ultimate responsibility for the lower-level boards' activities. These subordinate boards should have the same broad representation as the enterprise-wide board, though at the subordinate unit's level. The enterprise-wide investment board is responsible not only for major systems that affect multiple departments and users, but also these enterprise-wide investments should be elevated to the enterprise-wide investment board to ensure buy-in from senior executives and users representing various departments. The enterprise-wide investment board should be actively involved in all investments and proposals that are high cost or high risk or have significant scope and duration.

Executive management is typically responsible for creating the investment board(s), defining their scope and resources, and specifying their membership. Establishing an investment management working group can benefit both the investment boards and project managers by coordinating requests for information and verifying and providing responses.

Depending on its size, structure, and culture, an organization may have more than one investment board. This critical process is based on the assumption that, for managerial reasons, the key practices in this critical process will be implemented consistently across each of these boards and that the organization will tailor each board's operations as part of this implementation.

Members of the investment board should have an understanding of the board's policies and procedures and the experience and skills to carry them out. Thus, the organization should consider introducing investment concepts to board members with little or no investment decision-making experience or relevant education in this area. Orientation sessions might be provided to board members in areas such as economic evaluation techniques, capital budgeting methods, performance measurement strategies, and risk management approaches. In addition, board members should be made aware of the specific processes for which they are responsible.

As the board responsible for defining and implementing the organization's investment management process, the enterprise-wide investment board should also have responsibility for developing the organization-specific investment guide. The board's work processes and decision-making processes (i.e., schedules, agendas, authorities, decision-making rules, etc.) are described and documented in the guidance. In addition, after the guide has been developed, the enterprise-wide investment board must actively maintain it, making sure that it always reflects the board's current structure and the processes that are being used to manage the selection, control, and evaluation of the organization's investments.

For the whole investment management process to function smoothly and effectively, each investment board must operate within its assigned authority and responsibility so that investments are properly aligned with the organization's objectives and are reviewed by the appropriate board.

Oversight

While the board should not micromanage each project in order to provide effective control, it should maintain adequate oversight and observe each project's performance and progress toward predefined cost and schedule expectations as well as each project's anticipated benefits and risk exposure. The board should expect that each project development team will be responsible for meeting project milestones within the expected cost parameters that have been established by the project's business case and cost/benefit analysis. The board should also employ early warning systems that enable it to take corrective actions at the first sign of cost, schedule, and performance slippages.

> Note: While a convincing business case has to be made for investment in every proposed project, a major element of the PDM method is whether that investment is able to move performance measures to their targets. The capability for an investment to do this, especially on strategic items, must be a key criterion for selection. That is what a performance-driven business case—and this book—is all about.

Investment Selection Maturity

The following section describes how an organization matures in investment selection over time.

Five Stages of IT Selection Maturity (source GAO/AIMD-10.1.23)

Stage 1 is characterized by ad hoc, unstructured, and unpredictable investment processes. For example, there is generally little relationship between the success or failure of one project and the success or failure of another project. If an IT project succeeds and is seen as a good investment, it is largely due to exceptional actions on the part of the project team, and thus, its success might be difficult to repeat. Investment processes that are important for success may be known but only to isolated teams; this process knowledge is not widely shared or institutionalized. The selection process is frequently rudimentary, poorly documented, and inconsistently applied.

The unstructured and unpredictable investment processes that characterize a stage 1 organization also mean that even if it recognizes that a given project is in trouble, it may not have adequate processes to consistently address and resolve the project's problems. Additionally, a focus on project results in terms of business benefits is often missing in these organizations.

One focus of stage 2 maturity is to establish basic selection capabilities. Basic selection capabilities are driven by the development of project selection criteria, including benefit and risk criteria, and an awareness of organizational priorities when identifying projects for funding. No longer are projects being funded solely on an ad hoc basis. The basic selection processes established in stage 2 lay the foundation for more mature selection capabilities in stage 3. Therefore, the organization also focuses on defining and developing its IT investment board(s), identifying the business needs or opportunities to be addressed by each IT project, and using this knowledge in the selection of new IT proposals.

An organization working to complete stage 2 should be starting to develop an ITIM decision-making process that utilizes its EA—to the extent that an EA exists. In addition, to gain further confidence that each investment is providing specific value to the organization, an organization's policies and procedures should provide for identifying the business needs and the associated users of each IT project.

An equally important focus is to attain repeatable, successful IT investment control techniques at the project level. For an organization to develop a sound IT investment process, it must first be able to control its investments so that they finish predictably within established schedule and budget ranges. In addition, it must be able to identify potential exposures to risk and put in place strategies to mitigate that risk. In the absence of predictable, repeatable, and reliable investment control processes, selected investments will be subject to a higher risk of failure despite rigorous analysis of the estimates used to justify them. Further, the absence of repeatable control processes will result in ineffective evaluation processes and contradictory efforts at process improvement.

Stage 3 critical processes depend specifically on the successful implementation of stage 2 critical processes. In order to operate successfully at stage 3, the organization must have in place the structure and repeatability of the project-centric management processes described above. In addition, the project-specific performance data being used for oversight and reselection in stage 2 are crucial for the successful management of the investment portfolio. The critical focus for stage 3 maturation is to establish a consistent, well-defined perspective on the IT investment portfolio and to maintain mature, integrated selection (and reselection), control, and evaluation processes. These processes will be evaluated during PIRs. Once IT projects have been selected and are meeting their scheduled performance expectations—as outlined in stage 2—the organization needs to develop an IT investment portfolio using an investment process that is consistent with its EA and employs sound selection criteria.

The development and use of portfolio selection criteria enable the organization to expand its focus from being primarily project-oriented to including the broader portfolio perspective. The portfolio perspective drives the organization to focus on the benefits gained from the synergies to be found among the investments in the entire collection, rather than just from the sum of the individual investments.

An organization at stage 4 maturity is focused on using evaluation techniques to improve its IT investment processes and portfolio(s) while maintaining mature control and selection processes. At this stage, the organization should also regularly analyze its investment portfolio(s) to ensure that its investments continue to be aligned with the most current version of its architecture, since small changes in either an investment itself or in the EA may have occurred over time without being recognized in periodic selection/ reselection decisions. As described in stage 3, PIRs typically identify lessons learned from an investment and determine whether the benefits anticipated in the business case for the investment have been achieved. Analyzing a number of PIRs serves as a basis for creating recommendations for changing and improving IT investment processes.

Stage 5: Once an organization has mastered the selection, control, and evaluation processes, it seeks to shape its strategic outcomes by (1) using its EA as a critical frame of reference to ensure alignment with the target architecture, (2) learning from other organizations, (3) continuously improving the manner in which it uses IT to support and improve its business outcomes, and (4) focusing on flexibility and becoming a more agile organization that relies on its architecture for its vision of the future and the ITIM as a critical means for implementing it. Thus, an organization with stage 5 maturity benchmarks its IT investment processes relative to other "best-in-class" organizations and conducts proactive monitoring for breakthrough information technologies that will allow it to significantly change and improve its business performance.

> Remember: Some projects may be selected for immediate start while others may be approved but not implemented for some time. In these cases, each of these projects will need to be revalidated before commencement to ensure that they still conform to the business case.

Summary

At the end of step 3, you must be able to answer the questions: What am I getting for the money I am spending, when am I going to get it, and what performance improvement will result?

- Investments that can achieve measurable benefits on the most important strategic items are the most desirable.

- The BCA provides the basis for approving investments and revalidating investments and projects as they move through implementation.
- The organization must understand the uncertainties inherent in any investment and conduct the necessary risk analysis and mitigation.
- If the business case is highly complex, use simulation and other analysis processes to understand the cause and effect of the investment before proceeding.

Now that you have selected your investments, they must be executed in order to produce the desired results, and this takes us to step 4.

4

Achieve Investment Results

- Project execution
- Project revalidation
- Management dashboards
- Implemented project

Overview

STEP 4 IS ALL ABOUT PROJECT VALIDATION against the original business case across the IT investment implementation life cycle.

Throughout the investment implementation, revalidation is the key to minimizing risk and achieving success. In steps 2 and 3, you put measures in place to monitor progress and performance and validate the specific investment business case. In step 4, you implement the investment in a manner to ensure that you stay on track and that the expected benefits and performance improvements are realized.

This is the most critical step in the process—because it is the one during which implementation takes place—and it does have its challenges. However, these challenges can be minimized if you have carefully followed the lessons learned in the previous steps. The aims of steps 1, 2, and 3 are to ensure that by the time that you reach step 4, you are absolutely sure what it is you aim to achieve with the investment/project and how you are going to do it. In steps 1 through 3, you completed your strategic review, developed and defined your performance measures, identified investment opportunities, and, both guided by and constrained by your enterprise architecture, selected the most appropriate projects for investment. Each investment was chosen based on the project's ability to improve organizational performance as defined and validated in the business case.

This means that you "thought through" the cause and effect of the project implementation and the business performance results, risks, and other factors as part of the project planning stage, incorporated whatever approaches are necessary to resolve or mitigate them and are now ready to implement in order to achieve your investment results.

> Note: The words "thought through" above are in quotation marks because this is the key message of this book. If you understand the cause and effect of the investment and its resulting positive impact on performance and specific performance measures, the project has the potential for a successful outcome. A project without this understanding has no basis for fully understanding what success is and how to validate for success and, therefore, has a much higher potential for failure.

As you work on implementing the project, you must make sure you have controls built in along the way to ensure you stay on track. It goes without saying that once you start executing the project, it can start to veer off course unless tight control and oversight is maintained. The goal of the performance-driven management (PDM) approach is to understand very early when a project is veering away from its specific objectives, in time to take corrective action and before large sums of money are spent on a project that already cannot deliver according to its business case.

The business case is the key document that describes the justification for setting up a project. It drives the project activities and demonstrates that the project continues to be viable. The business case developed in step 3 is continually updated throughout the project life cycle.

Figure 4.1 summarizes the major activities of step 4.

Project Execution

Overview

Once investments are selected, a project is typically initiated to focus the necessary resources to achieve the business results and associated performance improvements. Projects have three distinct phases. These are:

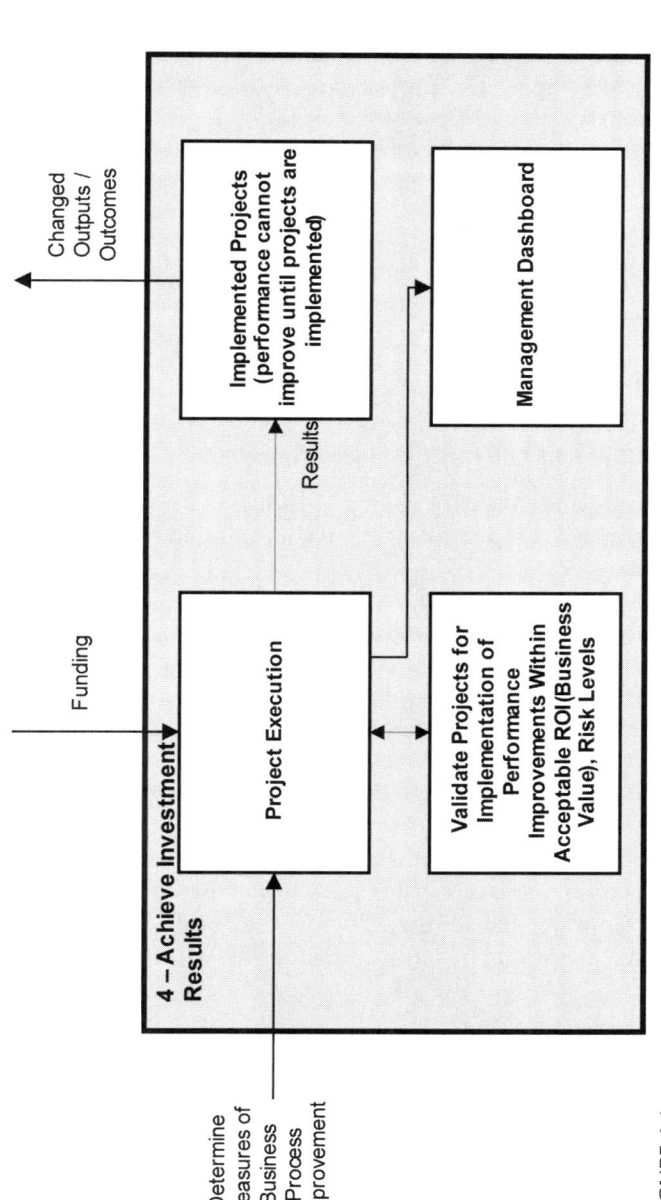

FIGURE 4.1
Overview of Step 4

- Preliminary: organizing, defining execution strategy, developing the work breakdown structure (WBS), defining project checkpoints and planned status at those checkpoints, and initiating the first project phase
- Operating: managing the project day-to-day execution, broken down into appropriate stages
- Closing: the end of the project, with assessments of how well the project was conducted and whether the expected benefits were achieved

An important task once the need for the project has been established is to determine how it is to be delivered; this helps to reduce risk. Depending on the project's scale and complexity, it may be appropriate to break it down into more manageable blocks of activity or stages or to implement the project in incremental steps.

Systems Development Life Cycle and Checkpoints

There are numerous types of change projects or investments that an organization can make. For the purposes of this book, they can be categorized into two types:

- Business projects: focused on business process improvement and building organizational capability
- IT projects: focused on providing new IT enablement capabilities and implementing these capabilities into the daily operations of the business

Each of these project types has in common the investment of organizational resources to improve business performance in a measurable way. They each have the three major phases discussed above. The major difference is that business projects do not have a major software and hardware component that requires programming and testing. The remainder of this section will focus on an approach specific to IT projects, since that is the focus of this book. However, the concepts are similar for business projects, with the exception of software and hardware implementation. The similarities will be pointed out, as appropriate.

The project phases or major steps provide an opportunity for project checkpoints at the end of each phase. These checkpoints provide a predetermined point for checking the project's progress before approving the next phase of activity. These checkpoints also provide an opportunity to reassess the business case—the focus of the PDM approach.

The systems development life cycle (SDLC) is specific to IT projects. It is a conceptual model used in project management that describes the stages involved in an information system development project, from an initial feasibility study through maintenance of the completed application.

Various SDLC methodologies have been developed to guide the processes involved, including the waterfall model (which was the original SDLC method), rapid application development (RAD), joint application development (JAD), the fountain model, the spiral model, build and fix, and synchronize-and-stabilize. Frequently, several models are combined into some sort of hybrid methodology. Documentation is crucial regardless of the type of model chosen or devised for any application and is usually done in parallel with the development process. Some methods work better for specific types of projects, but in the final analysis, the most important factor for the success of a project may be the ability for the project team to implement and deliver according to the business case and to manage the risks appropriately along the way.

In general, an SDLC methodology has the following steps:

- The system concept and solution architecture are developed.
- The new system requirements are defined.
- The proposed system is designed. Plans are laid out concerning the physical construction, hardware, operating systems, programming, communications, and security issues.
- The new system is developed. The new components and programs must be obtained and installed. Users of the system must be trained in its use, and all aspects of techical and business performance must be tested. If necessary, adjustments must be made at this stage.
- The system is put into use. This can be done in various ways. The new system can be phased in, according to application or location, and the old system gradually replaced. In some cases, it may be more cost-effective to shut down the old system and implement the new system all at once.
- Once the new system is up and running for a while, it should be exhaustively evaluated. Maintenance must be kept up rigorously at all times. Users of the system should be kept up-to-date concerning the latest modifications and procedures.

Note that a business project would have similar overall steps as above:

- The business capability concept and business solution architecture are developed.
- The new process/capability requirements are defined.
- The proposed process/capability is designed. Plans are laid out as needed concerning the physical construction, capability, business process, communications, human capital, and security issues.

- The new capability/process is developed. The new capability/process must be created and implemented. Users of the capability/process must be trained in its use, and all aspects of performance must be tested. If necessary, adjustments must be made at this stage.
- The capability/process is put into use. This can be done in various ways. The new capability/process can be phased in, according to workgroup or location, and the old capability/process gradually replaced. In some cases, it may be more cost-effective to implement the new capability/process all at once.
- Once the new capability/process is up and running for a while, it should be exhaustively evaluated. Enhancements should then be made as appropriate.

The SDLC is a logical process used to develop an information system, including requirements, validation, training, and user (stakeholder) ownership. Any SDLC should result in a high quality system that meets or exceeds customer expectations, reaches completion within time and cost estimates, works effectively and efficiently in the current and planned IT infrastructure, and is inexpensive to maintain and cost-effective to enhance.

SDLC includes important phases that are essential for developers, such as planning, analysis, design, and implementation, and are explained below. There are several SDLC models in existence. The oldest model, which was originally regarded as "the systems development life cycle" is the waterfall model: a sequence of stages in which the output of each stage becomes the input for the next. Other approaches, such as RAD and JAD, were developed to take advantage of rapid development technology available and deliver software functionality more quickly and at reduced cost. Figure 4.2 depicts the original waterfall model.

An exhaustive explanation of the SDLC can be found in many texts and is beyond the scope of this book. However, each phase does provide opportunities to revalidate the project and the business case to ensure that the project is staying on track. The following briefly describes each phase in that context:

Initiation: This phase occurs prior to investment selection (discussed in step 3). The purpose of this phase is to generate a high-level view of the intended investment and determine the goals of the investment/project. A feasibility study is sometimes used to present the project to upper management in an attempt to gain funding. Projects are typically evaluated in three areas of feasibility: economical, operational or organizational, and technical.

System concept development: This is the phase where an investment is fully analyzed and a business case developed (discussed in step 3). This becomes the baseline for the project going forward.

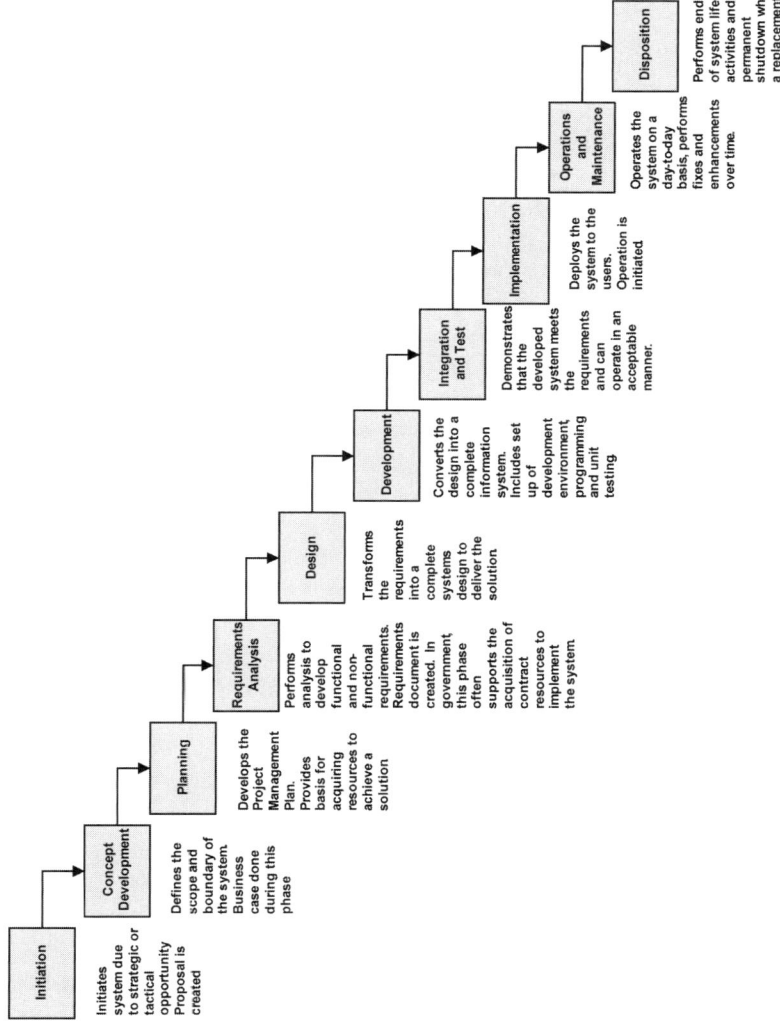

FIGURE 4.2
SDLC Waterfall Model

Planning: This is the early phase of the project where resources are gathered and focused on implementing the project and the detailed project approach and WBS are developed. During this phase, resource requirements and cost estimates are analyzed in more detail, the timing of benefits delivery is specifically determined, and project risks are documented. The end of this phase provides the first opportunity to revalidate the business case based on improved cost estimates, knowledge of benefits timing, and variability associated with risks. At this early stage, it is possible that the original business case can already be invalidated, with the costs potentially increasing; the projected ROI could already become more difficult to attain. The PDM approach can identify issues at this stage, potentially saving large sums of money that would be spent if the project proceeded, without the stakeholder's knowledge, in an already invalidated state.

Requirements analysis: In this phase, the detailed system requirements are determined and documented. This is the phase in which many IT projects become derailed. The requirements developed can often be poorly defined or begin to diverge from what the project needs to implement the planned benefits according to the business case. Functionality can grow beyond what was envisioned, lose focus on the key cause-and-effect enablement features, require more complex technology, or a host of other potential issues can arise. The result is the project's planned delivery of functionality can vary from what was envisioned in the business case, resulting in the potential for increased costs, reduced benefits, and higher risk. The PDM approach can also identify issues at this stage, potentially saving large sums of money that would be spent if the project proceeded, without the stakeholder's knowledge, in an already invalidated state. This is a critical phase—it is recommended that the business case be revalidated twice, once after the major functional requirements have been documented and once at the end of the phase.

In the government sector, after the requirements phase is completed, the subsequent phases (design, development, etc.) are typically put out for competitive bid. If the business case is already invalid, which in many cases it is, project failure in terms of the business case is guaranteed. Yet many contracts are awarded at this point, and projects proceed to their highest spending stages, already in trouble. The PDM approach is specifically intended to prevent these types of often spectacular failures (see book introduction).

Design: Systems design functions and operations are described in detail, including screen layouts, business rules, process diagrams, and other documentation. The output of this stage will describe the new system as a collection of modules or subsystems. The design stage takes as its initial input the requirements identified in the approved requirements document. For each requirement, a set of one or more design elements will be produced as a result of interviews, workshops, and/or prototype efforts. Design elements describe the desired software and hardware features in detail and generally include functional hierarchy diagrams, screen layout diagrams, tables of business rules, business process diagrams, and a complete entity-relationship diagram with a full data dictionary. These design elements are intended to describe the software in sufficient detail that skilled programmers may develop the software or modify commercial software with minimal additional input.

Functionality and risk can continue to change, potentially significantly as the design phase proceeds and more detailed specifications for the new system are developed, introducing additional potential for the project to veer away from the business case. This means design is another critical phase—it is recommended that the business case be revalidated twice during the design phase, once halfway through the design effort and once at the end of the phase. The design phase represents the last opportunity to revalidate the business case before system construction begins.

Development: Modular and subsystem programming software will be created during this stage. Unit testing and module testing are done in this stage by the developers. This stage is intermingled with the next in that individual modules will need testing before integration to the main project. At the end of this phase, the system is essentially complete. The business case should be revalidated at this stage to document the continuing tracking of the planned performance improvements. At the end of this phase, much of the development funds will have been expended, and this spending can be analyzed versus the estimates. If the business case has been continuously revalidated per the PDM approach, the cost estimates and actual costs should be very close.

Integration and test: The software is tested at various levels in software testing. System and user acceptance testing are often performed. This is a grey area as many different opinions exist as to what the stages of testing are and how much, if any, iteration and redefinition occurs. Iteration is not generally part of the waterfall model, but usually some occurs at this stage. The business case should only be revalidated if significant iterations occur.

Implementation: At this point, development is complete, and the system is implemented, rolled out across multiple functional or geographic areas and put into day-to-day use. The business case should only be revalidated if significant implementation changes occur. It is generally too late to cancel the project at this point, but adjustments can be made to improve the delivery with respect to the business case.

Operations, maintenance, and disposition: At this point, the system is implemented, and the project moves into a benefits realization phase. Performance improvement should be measured and compared to what was anticipated in the business case. A post-implementation review should be performed to identify lessons learned in business case estimation as well as project management.

PDM is relevant to all of the SDLC phases, but is particularly effective in the early phases, when discovery of a project veering from its approved business case can prevent large additional expenditures that are already ill advised but unknown without using the PDM approach. As such, PDM is most effective when deployed in the planning, requirements, and design phases. These are the stages when a project's foundation is formed, prior to the majority of the effort and expense. During these phases, it is early enough to adjust to a project beginning to depart from its business case before the majority of the funds are spent. In the later phases, PDM slowly becomes less impactful as the majority of the project is completed and funds are spent.

Agile Development

Agile software development is a set of software development methodologies based on iterative and incremental development, where requirements and solutions evolve through collaboration between self-organizing, cross-functional teams. Agile methods break tasks into small increments with minimal planning. Iterations are short time frames (time boxes) that typically last from one to four weeks. Each iteration involves a team working through a full software development cycle, including requirements analysis, design, coding, unit testing, and acceptance testing when a working product is demonstrated to stakeholders. This helps minimize overall risk and lets the project adapt to changes quickly. An iteration may not add enough functionality to warrant a implementable release, but the goal is to have an available release (with minimal bugs) at the end of each iteration. Multiple iterations may be required to release a product or new features.

Since agile development rapidly combines elements of the life cycle from requirements through testing, clear milestones for revalidating the business case are not as clear as the traditional life cycle described above. Since agile approaches typically involve many iterations for a given cycle time period, it is recommended that the business case be revalidated after a planned number of iterations as determined in the project planning phases. For example, if 4 sets of 15 iterations are planned, revalidate the business case after the first 2 sets or as needed if there is a significant change in cost, functional delivery, or risk.

One variation of agile is for organizations to time-box delivery (for example, a six-month time box) and to take whatever can be delivered within that time box. When this approach is used, it is recommended that the business case be revalidated after each time box, as significant variation can potentially occur within each time box, positioning each subsequent time box for additional cost, complexity, risk, and delayed benefits realization.

Agile development is often used as part of other approaches, such as RAD, which combines prototyping, JAD, and implementation of computer-aided software engineering (CASE) tools. The potential advantages of RAD are similar to agile—speed, reduced development cost, and active user involvement in the development process.

Work Breakdown Structure

To manage and control any SDLC initiative, each project will be required to establish some degree of a work breakdown structure (WBS) to capture and schedule the work necessary to complete the project. The WBS format is mostly left to the project manager to establish in a way that best describes the project work. There are some key areas that must be defined in the WBS as part of the SDLC policy. The WBS for a project using PDM should include PDM revalidations as planned activities within the project.

The high level of the WBS should identify the major phases and milestones of the project in a summary fashion, including revalidations. In addition, the upper level should provide an overview of the full scope and timeline of the project and will be part of the initial project description effort leading to project approval. The middle level of the WBS is based on the SDLC phases as a guide for WBS task development. The WBS elements should consist of milestones and "tasks," as opposed to "activities," and have a definitive period (usually two weeks or more). Each task must have a measurable output (e.g., document, decision, or analysis). A WBS task may rely on one or more activities (e.g., software engineering, systems engineering) and may require close coordination with other tasks, either internal or external to the project. Any part of the project needing support from contractors should have a statement of work (SOW) written to include the appropriate tasks from the SDLC phases. The development of a SOW does not occur during a specific phase of the SDLC but is developed up front to include the work from the SDLC process that may be conducted by external resources, such as contractors.

Baselines are an important part of the SDLC and should be denoted in the WBS. Revalidations should occur after the functional and allocated baselines are developed. Each baseline is considered as a milestone in the SDLC.

- Functional baseline: established after the requirements phase
- Allocated baseline: established after the design phase
- Product baseline: established after the detail design and development phase

TABLE 4.1
SDLC Advantages and Challenges

Advantages	Challenges
Control	Increased development time
Monitor large projects	Increased development cost
Detailed steps	Systems must be defined up front
Evaluate costs and completion targets	Rigidity
Documentation	Hard to estimate costs, setting up potential project overruns
Well-defined user input	User input is sometimes limited
Ease of maintenance	
Development and design standards	
Tolerates changes in MIS staffing	

- Updated product baseline: established after the production construction phase

At this point in time, a strict waterfall model for the SDLC may not be used, as many modern methodologies have superseded this thinking. Some will argue that the SDLC no longer applies to models like agile computing, but it is still a term widely in use in technology circles. The SDLC practice has advantages over traditional models of software development, in that it lends itself more to a structured environment and clear revalidation points. The disadvantage to using the SDLC methodology is when there is need for iterative development (i.e., web development or e-commerce) or when stakeholders need to review on a regular basis the software being designed. Either way, the PDM approach can be key to early discovery of divergence from the business case and provides a basis for making adjustments to meet business and investment requirements.

> Note: The PDM approach described in this book takes SDLC and its variations further by introducing multiple business case revalidations to reduce risk by leveraging the elements described in steps 1 through 3.

Project Execution Overview

The following section describes early project initiation activities to get the project off to a good start. It includes positioning to implement the PDM approach (assuming a high-quality business case has already been developed).

The activities described below will be broadly similar for most projects; although, the precise terminology and project documentation may vary.

Getting started is a short pre-project process, gathering basic information about why the project is needed, what the project should deliver, and so on. It plays an important role in reaching an agreed understanding of project scope and securing commitment from senior management.

The main objectives of this phase are:

- Ensure that the aims and business case for the project are known and agreed.
- Appoint the business owner of the project.
- Design an appropriate organization structure for the project and appoint individuals to the roles.
- Ensure that delegations and responsibilities are clearly understood and do not overlap, especially where roles are combined.
- Appoint role(s) for the day-to-day management of the project. For small or straightforward projects, there could be a single role combining the interfaces with the owner and with the project team (project sponsor/ project director combined with project manager).

The primary activities of project initiation include:

- Forming the project management team (including project board, if required). Project organization is an essential task in the start-up activities. The roles are assigned (owner/decision maker and other key roles), project management responsibilities assigned, and the project team assembled. If required, the project board members are nominated at this point. Delegated authority for each role is determined and reporting arrangements confirmed to ensure that everyone knows what is expected of him or her and that the routes for reporting are clear. Organization management should confirm their formal approval before the project continues and work begins.
- Deciding on the approach that will be taken within the project to provide a solution. Establish whether the project exists as a single/discrete entity, has relationships with other projects, or is part of a larger program of work. An important factor for success is to ensure that the project boundaries and interfaces with the wider business environment are clearly understood.
- Communication of a clear definition of the business case, scope, resources, responsibilities, and plans. This activity is dedicated to establishing a firm foundation and planning the work to be done. A key purpose

of this activity is to draw up an agreed way forward based on the initial scope to ensure there is a common understanding of the rationale and aims of the project. This includes planning how quality is achieved and the subsequent work will be conducted. The level of risk for the project needs to be determined at this point.

A project initiation document (PID—names may vary depending on organization) should be developed and used to provide a full and firm foundation for the initiation of the project and is created in the project initiation activity. The PID is a formal statement of the business case objectives and functional and operational requirements of the finished project. It should be in sufficient detail to enable the project team to execute the detailed design and specification of the work and is, therefore, an essential reference for the team.

The PID should be brief and should address the following questions:

- Does a firm basis exist on which to initiate a project?
- Does the business case accurately reflect the mandate for the project and the requirements of the business and the users?
- How will the customer assess the acceptability of the finished product(s)?
- Has a project approach been selected that maximizes the chance of achieving overall success for the project?
- Have business case revalidation points been defined?
- Are the project objectives, project approach, and strategies consistent with the organization's mission and values?

Suggested content for the PID includes:

- Project definition: explaining what the project needs to achieve, including:
  - Background
  - Project objectives and business case summary (covering time, cost, quality, scope, risk, and benefit performance goals)
  - Desired outcomes
  - Project scope and exclusions
  - Constraints and assumptions
  - Project tolerances for business case revalidation
  - The user(s) and any other known interested parties
- Interfaces
- Project product description: including the customer's quality expectations, user acceptance criteria, and operations and maintenance acceptance criteria

- Project approach: to define the approach that will be used within the project to deliver the business option selected from the business case, taking into consideration the operational environment into which the solution must fit
- Project management team structure: a chart showing who will be involved with the project
- Role descriptions for the project management team and any other key resources identified at this time
- Risk management strategy
- Project controls
- References to any associated documents or products

A PID can take a number of formats, including a document or presentation slides. This is an example of a PID fitness-for-purpose checklist:

- Does the PID correctly represent the project?
- Does it show a viable, achievable project that is in line with corporate strategy or overall program needs?
- Is the project management team structure complete, with names and titles?
- Have all the roles been considered, and are they backed up by agreed role descriptions?
- Are the relationships and lines of authority clear?
- Who will make the key decisions about the project based on the planned revalidations of the business case?
- If necessary, does the project management team structure say to whom the project board reports?
- Does it clearly show a control, reporting, and direction regime that can be implemented appropriately to the scale, risk, and importance of the project to corporate or program management?
- Do the controls cover the needs of the project board, project manager, and team managers and satisfy any delegated assurance requirements?
- Is it clear who will administer each control?

The PID should be a living document, adjusted as key elements of the project change. For small projects, a single document PID is appropriate. For large projects, it can be more appropriate for the PID to be a collection of stand-alone documents. The volatility of each element of the PID should be used to assess whether it should be stand-alone (e.g., elements that are likely to change frequently are best separated out). The PID is not necessarily one document but can be an index for a collection of documents, a document which cross-references to a number of other documents, or a collection of information in a project management tool. It is likely to be developed through several reiterations. It will have stable elements and dynamic ones, which will need to have new versions created as the project progresses.

The project plan provides a statement of how and when a project's objectives are to be achieved by showing the major products, milestones, activities, and resources required on the project. It is used as a baseline against which to monitor project progress and cost, stage by stage.

It provides updated planned project costs and provides a basis for the initial revalidation of the business case.

Suggested project plan contents include:

- Plan description: giving a brief description of what the plan covers
- Project prerequisites: containing any fundamental aspects that must be in place at the start of the project and any that must remain in place for the project to succeed
- External dependencies: identifying the products that must be provided to the project so that it can continue but which the project management team has no authority over and, therefore, cannot ensure delivery fits the project requirements
- Planning assumptions: concerning availability of resources, skills/competency requirements, and so forth
- Project-level Gantt chart or bar chart: identifying management stages (e.g., milestones and control points)
- Project-level WBS
- Product descriptions: defining what the project will deliver, including the required quality level
- Project-level activity network and product dependencies
- Project-level table of resource requirement
- Requested/assigned specific resources
- Project change budget (if appropriate)
- Project-level tolerance for business case revalidation
- Updated cost, benefit, performance, and risks for the project
- Contingency plans: explaining how it is intended to deal with the consequences of any risks that materialize

Project Management

Project management is much more than the tasks carried out by a project manager. Project management is a combination of the roles and responsibilities of individuals assigned to the project, the organizational structure that sets out clear reporting arrangements, and the set of processes to deliver the required outcome. It ensures that everyone involved knows what is expected of himself or herself and helps to keep cost, time, and risk under control.

Experience has shown that projects are inherently at risk—through overrunning on time and cost and/or failing to deliver a successful outcome. Such failures are almost invariably caused by:

- Poor project definition by the project's owner, perhaps because of insufficient consultation with stakeholders or their failure to be specific about requirements and desired outcomes
- Poorly developed and invalid business case or business case unknown—no basis from which to judge project success or failure
- Lack of ownership and personal accountability by senior management
- Inadequately skilled and experienced project management and project personnel
- Inadequate reporting arrangements and decision-making
- Inconsistent understanding of required project activities, roles, and responsibilities

Experienced project management helps to reduce and manage risk. It puts in place an organization where lines of accountability are short and the responsibilities of individuals are clearly defined. Its processes are clearly documented and repeatable so that those involved in the project can learn from the experiences of others.

The principles of project management are equally valuable for smaller and/or less complex projects. The nature of your project will determine the project management approach you need, which should be adapted as required.

Project Execution

After initiation, the project should be executed, phase by phase, as defined in the project plan. The complexity and context for the project will determine whether the implementation phase of the project is carried out in a single stage or broken down into two or more stages so that appropriate levels of management control can be applied. Each stage ends with a decision point on whether to continue with the project or not; this is a stage boundary, a control point in the project when the business case is revalidated and progress and deliverables are reviewed by senior management before approval to proceed to the next stage. Where applicable, these decision points are preceded by gateway reviews. Planning and controlling each stage as well as managing product delivery are key project management processes that are supported by project plans and reports against such plans. Monitoring and control activities need to be in place to ensure that a stage stays on course and responds to unexpected events.

Project Completion

At the end of the project, the customer organization will want to know how well it conducted the project and whether the expected benefits and performance improvements have been achieved. Project closure is a formally controlled process, whether the project was completed to plan or was stopped prematurely. A project is closed down on agreement by senior management to an end-of-project report and lessons-learned report.

A post-project review or post-implementation review should be undertaken subsequently to confirm whether the expected benefits have been delivered and realized. This information should be fed back to senior management as it will inform other projects underway or planned.

Project Revalidation

The PDM approach requires that the organization reassess each project at planned intervals to ensure that the ROI is within or better than an acceptable range. This is the critical value-add that PDM provides.

Frequent reassessment is critical to determine the current state of a project, uncover potential problems—perhaps scheduling issues or scope—and come up with appropriate solutions to address them. The aim is to keep the project on track and ensure its success.

The business case sets out a rationale for investment and, as such, must support robust analysis and realistic decision making. At its heart, the cost-benefit analysis traditionally seeks to establish that the (usually financial) returns justify the preferred option, that costs can be controlled, and that the risks can be effectively managed. A business case looks at movement of performance indicators—financial, process, or others.

In reality, not all benefits can be measured financially: qualitative or less-tangible benefits, which are often more difficult to measure, will also need to be identified, scoped, and tracked. Similarly, costs, risks, and benefits will change over time. For these reasons, a simple snapshot taken at the beginning of the project may not adequately reflect interdependencies or changes in external circumstances; consequently, a continuously updated business case must be the key input for reviewing progress toward outcomes and making the almost inevitable necessary adjustments.

Benefits management is the identification of potential benefits, their planning and tracking, the assignment of responsibilities and authorities, and their actual realization. There should be a benefits management strategy to ensure that benefits are achieved as expected. A post-implementation review should be conducted to assesses whether the benefits have been achieved, whether more could be done, and whether there are any opportunities for further improvements.

The four key questions for business case revalidation are as follows:

Are benefits on track to being realized?

- Categories of benefits
- Specific benefits
- Measurability of benefits realization
- Expected improvement of metric values toward target values

Is the cost and change for benefits realization—the cause and effect—proving valid?

- Update cost estimate, project risk profile
- Link specific project capability implementation stream to benefits
- Understand costs for measuring benefits, include in project implementation

Is the timing of benefits realization within an acceptable time frame?

- Link benefits realization to timing of operating capability implementation
- Allow for "start-up" and ramp up of benefits over time

Has the project risk profile changed?

Governance

For larger or more complex projects, there may be a project board chaired by the project owner. Membership of the project board, which is through formal appointment by the project owner, should be a single role representing key stakeholder interests (described in more detail below) and a single role addressing technical/supply issues (typically a representative from the supplier organization). The project board provides the owner with stakeholder/technical input to decisions affecting the project; ultimate authority and accountability resides with the project owner.

There will always need to be active project reporting to assure the owner that the project is employing good practice and making sure stakeholders are being consulted appropriately and their needs are being addressed, for example. The project is ultimately the responsibility of the project owner and will be included in the responsibilities of project board members or may be fulfilled by individuals external to the project acting on behalf of the owner.

In practice, some roles may be combined, subject to an overriding proviso that the person combining the roles possesses the requisite competencies, experience, expertise, and time. For example, the roles of project owner and project manager can be combined for smaller or straightforward projects, or project ownership and project sponsor/director can be combined where the responsibilities of both roles can be fulfilled by a single individual. Where roles are combined, the allocation of the functions must always be absolutely clear, with delegations and responsibilities that do not overlap. The role of project manager should be clearly defined and implemented and not simply another member of the project team. Where two roles are combined, the person appointed must have at least the authority and status of the "higher" role; however, it is important to note that the roles of investment decision maker and project sponsor/project director cannot be allocated to a single individual.

Any changes that are required during the life of the project must be formally planned and controlled to ensure that the impact of change stays within agreed parameters; there should be a documented change control procedure. The cost, time, and quality parameters associated with the project should be established before implementation and monitored throughout the life of the project. All proposed changes should be costed and their effect on the overall project established before they can be authorized to go ahead.

Ensure ROI Remains within an Acceptable Range

Completing a project is like a long car ride. You know where you want to go, and you have a map that shows you how best to get there. The problem is that there could be lots of roadwork and detours that you don't know about. That is why it is important to maintain a PID document. You use it like your road map, to ensure the business case put forward is still valid and to reconfirm performance benefits and timing—based on a more detailed cost and schedule analysis. It is also critical to monitor costs in relationship to the benefits to be realized.

If the project is on track and expected to yield the acceptable performance improvements spelled out in the business case, you can give yourself a pat on the back. If your review finds that the project is off track (i.e., it falls below the acceptable tolerance thresholds), you will have to reassess and modify the project to get it back on track or, in the worst-case scenario, to cancel it and go back to the drawing board.

The business case sets out a rationale for investment and, as such, must support the continuing robust analysis and realistic decision making. As previously discussed, if business case revalidations show you that the ROI is acceptable, then the project continues. However, if the ROI falls below—but still within an acceptable range—adjustments have to be made. If the ROI plummets, the project should be abandoned.

Many projects now include implementation of a number of mandatory elements in order to comply with the law, federal government requirements, and so on. Regular checks during the implementation process will ensure that you are in compliance or, if not, give you the opportunity to correct this. For projects involving mandatory elements that must be accomplished by law, these additional checks ensure that a project that is running off track will get the additional scrutiny needed in order to have the risks more actively addressed or, at a minimum, provide full disclosure regarding the costs and the risks of implementing a mandate.

> Note: The cost for validation of the business case or model is a fraction of the cost of the project going off track. The best way to ensure the project stays on track is to use proactive business-case-revalidation analysis techniques.

Revalidation Approach

To revalidate a business case, all elements of the business case must be reworked with the most current information and then the result compared to the original business case. This includes reestimating the cost, the benefits (movement of performance measures, benefits realization timing), risks, and cause-and-effect relationship between the investment and the benefits. If simulation was done as part of the original business case analysis, it should be updated with any new information added to the simulation. By reworking the costs and benefits independently, a valid updated business case can be developed for comparison against the original for validation.

- *Cost*: The business case cost estimate for the investment should be reworked, incorporating any changes and any enhanced analysis approaches. This is the most critical revalidation element, as cost estimates tend to increase as a project gets underway and more is known. Additionally, costs are often underestimated early on, often due to organization political and competitive reasons—the lower the cost of a project, the more likely the project is to be approved. The lower a competitive consulting bid is, the more likely it is to be accepted.

- *Schedule*: Update and reassess the realism of the project schedule, focusing particularly on when the implementation will take place and benefits will begin to accrue. Delays in schedule often occur and push out the date when benefits will be realized. This effectively lowers the ROI by elongating the financial "payback" time and creating an unplanned period during the project where the status quo continues, despite the project going on to improve it.

- *Cause and effect*: As more is learned about the project and the associated business processes, understanding of the cause and effect between the investment and its benefits should improve. In some cases, this will validate that the benefits will occur when the investment is completed. In other cases, this may bring understanding that the benefits will not occur as had been expected when the investment is completed. The cause-and-effect analysis/simulation performed in the business case should be updated to reconfirm the cause-and-effect relationship. If the cause and effect is proving not to be valid as expected, the project focus should be adjusted or replanned to meet the business case ROI framework.

- *Benefits*: The value and timing of the benefits should be reassessed. Often during the course of a project, new requirements can be added to the project's goals. Additionally, requirements that are not documented clearly can be implemented in unexpected ways or not implemented at all, resulting in functionality that does not match what the business case envisioned. Reworking the business case benefits (along with the associated costs) determines what the benefits are now likely to be and, along with any schedule changes, when the benefits will begin to accrue. This focus on benefits (movement of performance measures in a positive direction) will assure that the project keeps its "eye on the ball" and delivers effectively.

- *Risk*: Conditions change as a project progresses. Risks projected to be a factor on a project can be mitigated or disappear, while other risks can appear. It is essential that the project risk analysis, with respect to ROI and benefits realization, be reworked to incorporate the updated risk profile. This would typically be done by rerunning the Monte Carlo analysis or simulation done as part of the original business case, with updated variable values for the probabilities and standard deviations of events. This will provide a new benefit (and potentially cost) profile. This will enable the resulting updated variation in ROI to be examined—if the risks have greatly increased, it may be appropriate to adjust or replan the project.

- *ROI:* Once the costs, benefits, and risks have been reassessed, the new projected ROI for the project and the ROI's standard deviation (risk) can be determined and compared to the original or most recently approved ROI. If the ROI falls out of an acceptable range or the risk is too great, the project should be examined by the governing body and adjusted. This will allow the organization to apply resources more productively and avoid spending scarce funding on a project that is not destined to succeed.

Revalidation Example

An investment called PRISM is selected by the governing board of an organization. As a result, a project called PRISM is initiated. The project is to implement a new claims processing system. The benefits are to speed claim processing for customers by 50 percent (improved customer service, no financial value, per se) and reducing claim processing costs by 40 percent. The project is anticipated to cost $50 million and take two years to implement, after which the benefits will accrue immediately and continue into the future. See table 4.2, showing how the project unfolds and how the PDM approach can inform and reduce risk. The minimum acceptable financial return for the project is 2 percent—the need for a higher return is offset by the improved customer service.

Due to the revalidation of the business case, the impact of issues arising was determined early in the project, facilitating a fact-based cancellation and replanning, saving what would certainly have been money that would have been lost on a likely failed project.

Although, in this example, the project was cancelled, the organization still needs the benefits this project was to deliver. The organization will go "back to the drawing board" and create a new replanned project that will more effectively deliver the benefits.

Move Forward, Replan, or Cancel?

If you have revalidated the business case, you can move forward. If the revalidation determines that the cost of some phases of the project cannot be justified or that some risks outweigh the benefits, you will have to replan. That means going back to step 3 and developing a new business case that takes into account the issues flagged by the revalidation. In extreme cases, a thorough review of the business case may lead to the conclusion that the initiative

TABLE 4.2
Notional PDM Example

Stage Completed	$ Spent	Project Event(s)	Impact on Project	Projected ROI / Std Dev (SD)	Investment Decision
Concept development	$0.5M	Business case completed	Investment selected	10% ± 5%	Proceed
Planning	$1M	Costs up by 10%, additional workgroup will be impacted	Cost increase reduces ROI, risk up slightly due to new workgroup likely to resist changes	9% ± 5.5%	Proceed, ROI remains acceptable
50% of requirements analysis	$2M	Additional requirements discovered, this phase alone goes over budget—costs up by 10%	Updated cause and effect validates new requirements, cost increase reduces ROI, new requirements increase risk and extend schedule to 2.5 years	5% ± 6%	ROI acceptable, but it could become unacceptable—replan to reduce risk, schedule delay reduces ROI
Requirements analysis	$2M	Technology not fully proven during prototype, risk and cost increase due to mitigation needed	Cost increase reduces ROI yet again, risk increases	2% ± 8%	Minimum ROI now appears unlikely to be achieved, replan or cancel
50% of design	$8M	N/A	N/A	N/A	Project phase not conducted, funding saved
Design	$8M	N/A	N/A	N/A	Project phase not conducted, funding saved
Development, test, implementation	$100M	N/A	N/A	N/A	Project phase not conducted, funding saved

should be cancelled. This can be for several reasons, such as the business case is no longer valid, the project is no longer required, or it no longer meets the needs of the department and its customers. And, of course, perhaps the biggest reason of all, it will not deliver value for money.

Management Dashboards

As a project proceeds through to implementation, statistics on costs, schedule, and delivery will begin to accumulate. Earned value management (EVM) provides a structure for reporting costs and delivery against plan to evaluate the status of a project. Although this analysis is not proactive, like the PDM approach, the visibility of EVM data can provide a wide range of stakeholders with a view of the project and its status. Dashboards are a way to illustrate this EVM and related data in an understandable way during implementation. Dashboards are another tool to use to provide project visibility as an adjunct to the PDM approach.

EVM provides part of the solution but not the whole solution. EVM is a useful tool in ensuring that a project stays on track as far as cost, scheduling, and work in place are concerned, but it has to be stressed that it is not relevant to benefits realization, which is at the heart of the PDM process. A project could still be on track as far as EVM is concerned, but that could be irrelevant if it is not implementing the right thing (i.e., realizing the benefits). However, EVM does have a role to play in tracking the progress of the project when used in conjunction with the other elements that make up the PDM process.

The U.S. federal government has recently begun using an IT management dashboard to publically provide visibility into large federal IT projects. It allows the public to monitor IT investments across the federal government and has received many millions of hits.

> Note: It is important to reemphasize that the dashboard as a project tool is only as valuable as the information fed into it. If the data are old, the results have no relevance at all. Project information has to be fed in so that it is always as up-to-date as possible regarding cost, schedule, implementations of functionality, results, and so on.

The federal IT dashboard displays data received from agency reports to the Office of Management and Budget (OMB), including general information on over 7,000 federal IT investments and detailed data for nearly 800 of those investments that agencies classify as "major." The performance data used to track the 800 major IT investments are based on milestone information displayed in agency reports to the OMB. Agency CIOs are responsible for evaluating and updating select data on a monthly basis, which is accomplished through interfaces provided on the website.

However, it is not enough to simply shine a light on IT programs and hope that results will follow. In January 2010, TechStat accountability sessions, a good next step, were launched by the OMB. A TechStat accountability session is a face-to-face, evidence-based review of an IT program with OMB and agency leadership, powered by the IT dashboard and input from the public. TechStat sessions enable the government to turn around, halt, or terminate IT investments that do not produce dividends for the public. Investments are carefully analyzed with a focus on problem solving that leads to concrete action to improve performance, although this is not necessarily business case–based (to learn more, go to http://it.usaspending.gov).

IT dashboards have also become an important tool for monitoring performance of IT projects within organizations as well. They provide a visual overview of the project information, and obviously, to be totally effective, the data it displays have to be kept up-to-date. The big advantage of this tool is that it can deliver a range of quantifiable measurements, which indicate how well the project is doing, and it can provide actionable information to the right people at the right time either by alerting them onscreen or by printing out reports.

The President's Management Agenda (PMA 2002) established goals for each initiative, requiring each agency to establish a plan on how the goals would be achieved and provided an example of a dashboard. Progress was tracked and managed by the OMB. The results were published externally on a quarterly basis, using a simple traffic-light rating scheme defined by the OMB:

- Green = Implementation is proceeding according to plans agreed upon with the agencies
- Yellow = Some slippage or other issues requiring adjustment by the agency in order to achieve the initiative objective on a timely basis
- Red = Initiative is seriously in jeopardy and is unlikely to realize objectives absent significant management intervention

This is a good example of a scorecard. The Department of Transportation Scorecard illustrated on the next page (see figure 4.3) highlights the status (left side) and scores for progress (right side) for each agency scorecard initiative. For illustrative purposes, below is the March 31, 2008, scorecard.

President Obama's 2009 *Memorandum on Transparency and Open Government* (see "Obama Administration Initiatives" in the introduction), requires

President's Management Agenda Scorecard

INITIATIVE	STATUS (as of 3/31/2008)	PROGRESS (as of Second Quarter FY 2008)
Human Capital	Green	Green
Competitive Sourcing	Yellow	Green
Financial Performance	Yellow	Green
E-Government	Yellow	Green
Performance Improvement	Green	Green
Eliminating Improper Payments	Yellow	Green
Real Property	Green	Green

Green = Satisfactory
Yellow = Good Progress
Red = Unsatisfactory

FIGURE 4.3
Department of Transportation 2008 Scorecard

executive departments and agencies to take the following steps toward the goal of creating a more open government, including publishing dashboard information and other project and related data. The following describes the memorandum's directives:

1. *Publish government information online.* To increase accountability, promote informed participation by the public, and create economic opportunity, each agency shall take prompt steps to expand access to information by making it available online in open formats. With respect to information, the presumption shall be in favor of openness (to the extent permit-

ted by law and subject to valid privacy, confidentiality, security, or other restrictions).

a. Agencies shall respect the presumption of openness by publishing information online (in addition to any other planned or mandated publication methods) and by preserving and maintaining electronic information, consistent with the Federal Records Act and other applicable law and policy. Timely publication of information is an essential component of transparency. Delays should not be viewed as an inevitable and insurmountable consequence of high demand.

b. To the extent practicable and subject to valid restrictions, agencies should publish information online in an open format that can be retrieved, downloaded, indexed, and searched by commonly used web search applications. An open format is one that is platform independent, machine readable, and made available to the public without restrictions that would impede the reuse of that information.

c. To the extent practical and subject to valid restrictions, agencies should proactively use modern technology to disseminate useful information, rather than waiting for specific requests under the Freedom of Information Act (FOIA).

d. Within 45 days, each agency shall identify and publish online in an open format at least three high-value data sets and register those data sets via Data.gov. These must be data sets not previously available online or in a downloadable format.

e. Within 60 days, each agency shall create an Open Government webpage located at www.[agency].gov/open to serve as the gateway for agency activities related to the Open Government Directive and shall maintain and update that webpage in a timely fashion.

f. Each Open Government webpage shall incorporate a mechanism for the public to:
   i. Give feedback on and assessment of the quality of published information;
   ii. Provide input about which information to prioritize for publication; and
   iii. Provide input on the agency's Open Government plan.

g. Each agency shall respond to public input received on its Open Government webpage on a regular basis.

h. Each agency shall publish its annual FOIA report in an open format on its Open Government webpage in addition to any other planned dissemination methods.

i. Each agency with a significant pending backlog of outstanding Freedom of Information requests shall take steps to reduce any such backlog by 10 percent each year.

j. Each agency shall comply with guidance on implementing specific presidential Open Government initiatives, such as Data.gov, eRulemaking, IT Dashboard, Recovery.gov, and USAspending.gov.

2. *Improve the quality of government information.* To improve the quality of government information available to the public, senior leaders should make certain that the information conforms to OMB guidance on information quality and that adequate systems and processes are in place within the agencies to promote such conformity.

   a. Within 45 days, each agency, in consultation with the OMB, shall designate a high-level senior official to be accountable for the quality and objectivity of, and internal controls over, the federal spending information publicly disseminated through such public venues as USAspending .gov or other similar websites. The official shall participate in the agency's Senior Management Council, or similar governance structure, for the agency-wide internal control assessment pursuant to the Federal Managers' Financial Integrity Act.

   b. Within 60 days, the deputy director for management at the OMB will issue, through separate guidance or as part of any planned comprehensive management guidance, a framework for the quality of federal spending information publicly disseminated through such public venues as USAspending.gov or other similar websites. The framework shall require agencies to submit plans with details of the internal controls implemented over information quality, including system and process changes, and the integration of these controls within the agency's existing infrastructure. An assessment will later be made as to whether additional guidance on implementing OMB guidance on information quality is necessary to cover other types of government information disseminated to the public.

   c. Within 120 days, the deputy director for management at the OMB will issue, through separate guidance or as part of any planned comprehensive management guidance, a longer-term comprehensive strategy for federal spending transparency, including the Federal Funding Accountability Transparency Act and the American Reinvestment and Recovery Act. This guidance will identify the method for agencies to report quarterly on their progress toward improving their information quality.

3. *Create and institutionalize a culture of open government.* To create an unprecedented and sustained level of openness and accountability in every agency, senior leaders should strive to incorporate the values of transparency, participation, and collaboration into the ongoing work of their agency. Achieving a more open government will require the various professional disciplines within the government—such as policy, legal,

procurement, finance, and technology operations—to work together to define and to develop open government solutions. Integration of various disciplines facilitates organization-wide and lasting change in the way that government works.

a. Within 120 days, each agency shall develop and publish on its Open Government webpage, an Open Government plan that will describe how it will improve transparency and integrate public participation and collaboration into its activities.

b. Within 60 days, the federal chief information officer and the federal chief technology officer shall create an Open Government dashboard on www .whitehouse.gov/open. The Open Government dashboard will make available each agency's Open Government plan, together with aggregate statistics and visualizations designed to provide an assessment of the state of open government in the executive branch and progress over time toward meeting the deadlines for action outlined in this directive.

c. Within 45 days, the deputy director for management at the OMB, the federal chief information officer, and the federal chief technology officer will establish a working group that focuses on transparency, accountability, participation, and collaboration within the federal government. This group, with senior level representation from program and management offices throughout the government, will serve several critical functions, including:

   i. Providing a forum to share best practices on innovative ideas to promote transparency, including system and process solutions for information collection, aggregation, validation, and dissemination;

   ii. Coordinating efforts to implement existing mandates for federal spending transparency, including the Federal Funding Accountability Transparency Act and the American Reinvestment and Recovery Act; and

   iii. Providing a forum to share best practices on innovative ideas to promote participation and collaboration, including how to experiment with new technologies, take advantage of the expertise and insight of people both inside and outside the federal government, and form high-impact collaborations with researchers, the private sector, and civil society.

d. Within 90 days, the deputy director for management at the OMB will issue, through separate guidance or as part of any planned comprehensive management guidance, a framework for how agencies can use challenges, prizes, and other incentive-backed strategies to find innovative or cost-effective solutions to improving open government.

4. *Create an enabling policy framework for open government.* Emerging technologies open new forms of communication between a government and the people. It is important that policies evolve to realize the potential of technology for open government.

   a. Within 120 days, the administrator of the Office of Information and Regulatory Affairs (OIRA), in consultation with the federal chief information officer and the federal chief technology officer, will review existing OMB policies, such as Paperwork Reduction Act guidance and privacy guidance, to identify impediments to open government and to the use of new technologies and, where necessary, issue clarifying guidance and/or propose revisions to such policies, to promote greater openness in government.

Implemented Project

Once the project is implemented, the focus of project-related efforts needs to pivot, to focus on measuring the movement of the desired performance indicators—realizing the benefits. Additionally, documentation of a lessons learned report is critical for an organization to continuously improve.

There should be a post-implementation review (see step 5), which documents whether business benefits have been realized and provides recommendations for future improvements.

If the PDM approach is followed, and the project is managed correctly, the probability of a successful project that meets the business case goals will be increased, the probability of failure decreased.

Critical Success Factors for Investment Implementation

- Make sure that the business case thoroughly addresses all issues and, above all, meets your business needs
- Make sure that the business case is revalidated at planned checkpoints throughout the project
- If the project veers from the business case, replan or, in severe cases, cancel the project
- Make sure that all requirements are clear and unambiguous and aligned with the business case
- Make sure that all relevant options for delivery have been considered
- Make sure that all compliance and regulatory issues have been addressed

- Make sure you have the right skills, capabilities, and management expertise (including an experienced project manager) to ensure success
- Make sure that you are being realistic about your ability to achieve a successful outcome within the parameters of the allocated budget and agreed project implementation plan

At the end of step 4—the implementation phase—the project is much more likely to be successful if you have stayed true to the business case benefits and the projected ROI. The project has to be fully implemented and working in order for benefits to be realized, and of course, if it has veered off course, it will not deliver the necessary outcomes to achieve the benefits required. Making sure you have realized those benefits, fed that result back to the strategic planning process, and learned from the process so that best practices can be followed for future projects is what step 5 teaches us.

5

Realize the Benefits, and Close the Strategy Loop

- Post-implementation review
- Compare performance measure values to planned targets
- Assess overall outcome impact
- Close the loop on strategy—the feedback loop

Overview

STEP 5 IS ALL ABOUT BENEFITS realization, lessons learned, and closing the strategy loop. The project has been implemented, and this final step validates all the effort involved in steps 1 through 4 by clearly demonstrating that the changes implemented have led to measurably improved performance and achieved the goals set out in the original strategy and planning documents. This performance improvement and benefits realization need to be quantified using the performance measures identified in the business case.

The results of your measurement and evaluation enable you to go back to your original strategic planning to see how well you did. If all goals have been realized, you are right on track. If not, the strategy will need to be adjusted to meet those goals not yet realized. Measurements in step 5 link back to the strategic planning process in step 1 and the performance measures in step 2 so as to close the loop. The performance impact also contributes to the growing library of organizational knowledge and helps establish best practices.

The post-implementation review details what worked and what didn't, what could be done better, and how, by using the lessons learned, costs and time can be saved in future projects. The newly improved performance-measure values can be used to establish a new baseline for future projects.

Post-Implementation Review

A post-implementation review (PIR) is a formal review of a program or project after completion. It is used to answer the question: Did we achieve what we set out to do, in business terms, and if not, what should be done? The PIR is undertaken after there has been time to demonstrate the business benefits of the project. For a major change program, there could be several PIRs conducted over time.

The timing of the first PIR will depend on the predicted benefits stream brought about by the business change, as predicted in the business case. Although time must be allowed for benefits to accrue, it is important that the PIR is completed early enough to identify any problems. Remedial action can thus be taken promptly if predicted benefits are not realized. The initial PIR should usually be carried out 6 to 12 months after completion of the project.

The scope of the PIR will be dictated largely by the business case, which will have identified the areas of business change and where benefits were to be realized. As a minimum, the PIR will usually assess:

- Achievement (to date) of business case objectives
- Costs and benefits (to date) against forecast and other benefits realized and expected
- Continued alignment to the business strategy
- Effectiveness of revised business operations (functions, processes, staff numbers, etc.)
- Ways of maximizing benefits and minimizing cost and risk
- Sensitivity of the business service to expected business change
- Business and user satisfaction

A PIR is an essential component of the benefits management process. It checks, for the last time, whether benefits, including these set out in the business case, have been achieved and identifies opportunities for further improvement. Without a PIR, you cannot prove that your investment in the program of business change was worthwhile.

The investment owner, as the owner of the business case for change, is ultimately responsible for the PIR. Team members conducting the review will typically include:

- People with working knowledge of the business area under review and its processes

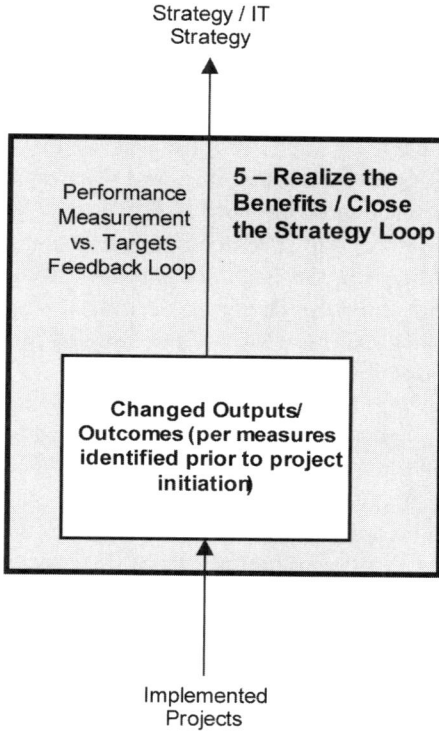

FIGURE 5.1
Overview of Step 5

- People with relevant technical knowledge
- Strategy planners with knowledge of the organization's business strategy and the business change contribution to it
- People involved in the everyday benefits management process

Business change projects vary in their scope, method of delivery, and the environment in which they are implemented. The reviews of such projects vary similarly. There is, however, a set of fundamental principles that apply to all projects; they have implications for the conduct of the review.

- The objective of the PIR is to ensure that the maximum benefit is obtained for the organization through the business change that the project made possible and to make recommendations if the benefits are not obtained.
- Reviews help organizations to assess the contribution of business change projects to business objectives—these objectives and the metrics that will

be applied to measure their achievement should be stated in your business and supporting strategies. In practice, these objectives are achieved through projects and programs of business change.

- PIRs are a key part of the benefits management process—benefits must be actively managed to be achieved; the PIR is a key element in the benefits management process because it is used to assess whether the changes that have taken place have improved effectiveness and to make recommendations for further improvements (program management).
- PIRs identify opportunities to improve the effectiveness of business change. Over time and with changing circumstances, the benefits profile will be altered. PIRs examine ways of maximizing benefits and minimizing costs on an ongoing basis.
- PIRs are not a one-off exercise—a program of business change may be in excess of 10 years, and the business system it supports may be in existence for an even longer period of time. The level of cost, risk, and benefit delivered by the change must be reviewed periodically, following the first PIR. It may be appropriate to conduct abridged PIRs after the full PIR, to address only those key areas that reflect business priorities.
- Reviews must be conducted in an open manner; organizations must be prepared to learn—to get the most value, reviews should be conducted openly, and participants must be prepared to make constructive criticism. It is only in this way that real lessons will be learned or improvements to business processes and supporting infrastructure made.

Recommendations need to be implemented by the organization if reviews are to add real value—recommendations for improvements should add value to the business. This will involve changing the way the business system or process operates in some way. Recommendations must be sufficiently robust for the organization to be able to act upon them. Importantly, good practice in project management and business operations should be included in recommendations for incorporating in the organization's guidelines for good practice.

There are a number of common issues that may be encountered in carrying out PIRs, and the review team needs to be aware of these (although, they may not be able to solve them). These include:

- More than one organization involved: This in an issue when there is no common standard for measuring and recording the benefits and costs.
- Lack of documentation: Much factual information will come from project documentation, especially the business case.

- Lack or inadequacy of baseline measures: For a PIR, measures of success can only be made accurately by comparing the level of performance before the project implementation against that at the time of the PIR. Hopefully, with the performance-driven management (PDM) approach and its focus on the business case, this is not an issue.
- Sensitivities: Examining the performance of project teams or current operations against a predicted level may lead to feelings of insecurity or grievance for those who were involved with the project or in the business area supported by the change.
- Management of expectations: Although the use of reviews will improve the effectiveness of the organization, the review team should ensure that they manage expectations of system enhancements or business change.
- The organization is too busy to do a PIR, and never gets it done: There should be policies to ensure that reviews are carried out as part of the organization's normal practice.
- Lack of cooperation from outside service providers.

Some actions that can be taken to avoid or reduce these problems are:

- Implementation of a benefits management regime
- Careful selection of the PIR team to ensure independent review
- Formal agreements with providers to participate in the review process

Document Lessons Learned

The purpose of the lessons learned report is to bring together any lessons learned during the project that can be usefully applied to the conduct of other projects (as opposed to the PIR, which focuses on the business results of a specific project). At the close of the project, the lessons learned report is completed and prepared for dissemination. As a minimum, lessons learned should be captured at the end of each stage of the project; ideally a note should be made of any good or bad point that arises in the use of the management and specialist products and tools at the time.

The lessons learned report should describe for the project:

- What went well
- What worked
- What went badly
- What project management improvements can be made in the future
- A description of any abnormal events causing deviations from plans

- An assessment of technical methods and tools used
- Recommendations for future enhancement or modification of project management methods
- Useful measurements on how much effort was required to create the various products
- Notes on effective and ineffective quality reviews and other tests, including reasons why they worked well or badly

The lessons learned report should be viewed as information that can be shared (although, sometimes areas may have to be kept confidential), as well as what would be valuable for future projects in the form of recommendations on any enhancements or modifications. At the start of a new project, previous lessons learned reports should be reviewed to consider how lessons learned from previous projects could be applied to the project.

The data in the report should be used by a corporate group, such as quality assurance, who is responsible for the quality management system, in order to refine, change, and improve the standards. Measures of how much effort was needed for products can help improve future estimating.

Compare Value Measures Achieved to Planned Targets

With baseline, interim, and target measures established, actual value measurements are taken at the end of the project to monitor performance. Value measures are not static. Feedback and other information resulting from the analysis and use of the measures should be applied to revise value measures as the organization matures.

As the business case is a living document, actual implementation can still vary from planned or estimated. Financial targets may not have been met, objectives may not have been achieved, financial targets may have been exceeded, and objectives and performance measure targets may have been surpassed. The final business case should be modified accordingly but not before reasons for missing targets (either higher or lower) are explored.

For each objective, examine the figures of actual versus forecast, and investigate the reasons why targets were missed. It is not a witch hunt; it is an attempt to understand why the objectives were not achieved. Maybe the objectives were not achievable or realistic after all. Perhaps external factors changed. Perhaps other seemingly unrelated factors had an impact.

An understanding of why targets were missed must be reached before performance forecasts and new objectives can be put in place for the updated strategic plan for subsequent years.

Closing the Loop

Once the project has been completed, it still has to be monitored while other projects are being planned and executed. This is part of the constant cycle of strategic change. Each completed project provides a wealth of useful information and measurements that can, and should, be fed into the next investment planning cycle, thereby establishing new and better baselines. It is through this feedback that the strategic planning process continues to evolve and become more efficient.

If the project was successful, organizational performance measures have been moved closer to their target values. Performance in other areas is likely to become more important to address now that the area involving the project has been successfully addressed. If the project was unsuccessful, the organization will need to include the project area in its priorities and invest additional resources to improve performance in that area.

Organizations that can operate with a consistent strategic feedback loop in operation are operating at a high level of strategic maturity and will achieve the following benefits:

- The organization will be more effective than similar organizations at meeting strategic goals and spending resources efficiently. This will provide a competitive advantage in the private sector and help to better meet mission needs in the public sector.
- Strategic planning will have a longer-term, more linear focus based on benefits achieved from longer-term projects.
- Focus will be on the changes year-to-year versus a total revamp and investments are always in the pipeline—subject to changing priorities.
- Focus on changes will allow rapid construction of updated strategic plans, less scrambling at the last minute.
- Strategic decisions will be more quantitatively based.
- High-quality leaders will be attracted to the organization.

Considerations for U.S. Federal Agencies

With the federal budget deficit at record levels and agency budgets under tight fiscal scrutiny, it makes sense to ensure that IT projects are planned carefully and the money spent wisely. Federal IT projects are often larger and more complex than most IT projects in the world. The five-step process sets out a procedure for the successful integration of IT strategy and investment using proven investment management techniques and looking at the entire picture rather than focusing just on the IT project in hand. This macro approach ensures mission needs are achieved, business performance is enhanced, and budget constraints are met. It is the right process at the right time. It is a process that all federal and state agencies should strongly consider following.

Business Performance in the Federal and State Environment

A 2007–2008 Government Accountability Office (GAO) survey of 4,500 senior federal managers focused on their experience with performance information and their use of information in management decision making for the programs in which they were involved. The managers' reported use of performance information for program management activities "did not increase significantly between 1997 and 2007," according to Bernice Steinhardt, director of strategic issues at GAO. "Performance matters because it aids economic recovery and growth, assists long-term fiscal planning, and enables response to changing environment, demographics, technology, globalization, and security," she said.

Key practices to promoting the use of performance information in governmental management decision making are:

- Demonstrating and communicating leadership commitment to results-oriented management
- Creating a clear "line of sight" by aligning process and individual performance with organizational results
- Building organizational capacity to collect and use performance information and improve its usefulness

Federal managers are more likely to report using performance information in key management activities if senior leadership demonstrates a commitment to results-oriented management and their immediate supervisors pay attention to performance information. Leaders can demonstrate their support for results-oriented management by:

- Reviewing business performance information on a regular basis
- Communicating performance information frequently and effectively through different mediums, such as poster displays, performance scorecards, intranet sites, and so forth
- Using performance information to make resource allocation decisions

Strategic, business performance measurement-based management systems allow an organization to align its business activities to its strategy and to monitor performance toward strategic goals over time. How does an enterprise (agency, business) know how well it's doing? High-performing enterprises actively identify "key performance indicators" and measure their progress against established target values for those indicators, as a way of measuring their effectiveness. This is performance management, and the key indicators are the performance measures (or metrics) of the enterprise.

Performance management is used to track an organization's progress against its strategic plan and specific performance goals. While performance measures may be applied to individual projects to ensure that deadlines are met and costs are controlled, and so forth, it is essential for the project manager to understand how the project itself supports the organization's strategy, and how the project will impact or influence the organization's key performance measures.

The following diagram shows how the practices and uses of performance management can result in improved performance at federal agencies.

Investments should deliver results-oriented products and services to inform business decisions and increase the efficiency and effectiveness of IT investments, program management, and agency operations. Value measurement is a technique that federal agencies can use, and it applies a simple three-step process to define value measures, identify measurement data sources, and execute value measurement. The value-measurement process defines baseline and target measures and monitors actual results, allowing project managers and program staff to track progress on target values.

Identifying stakeholder communities is important because each community will have its own view of the value. A senior agency executive may be interested in identifying strategic consolidation initiatives to fulfill the mandate of recent legislation, while a programmer may be interested in understanding the technical standards of the agency for server platforms and identifying existing software components available for reuse. Examples of stakeholder communities include:

- Senior agency leadership
- Strategic planning team
- Chief information officer
- Budget and capital planning officials
- Program managers
- IT infrastructure managers
- Information assurance team members
- Project managers
- Software architects and developers

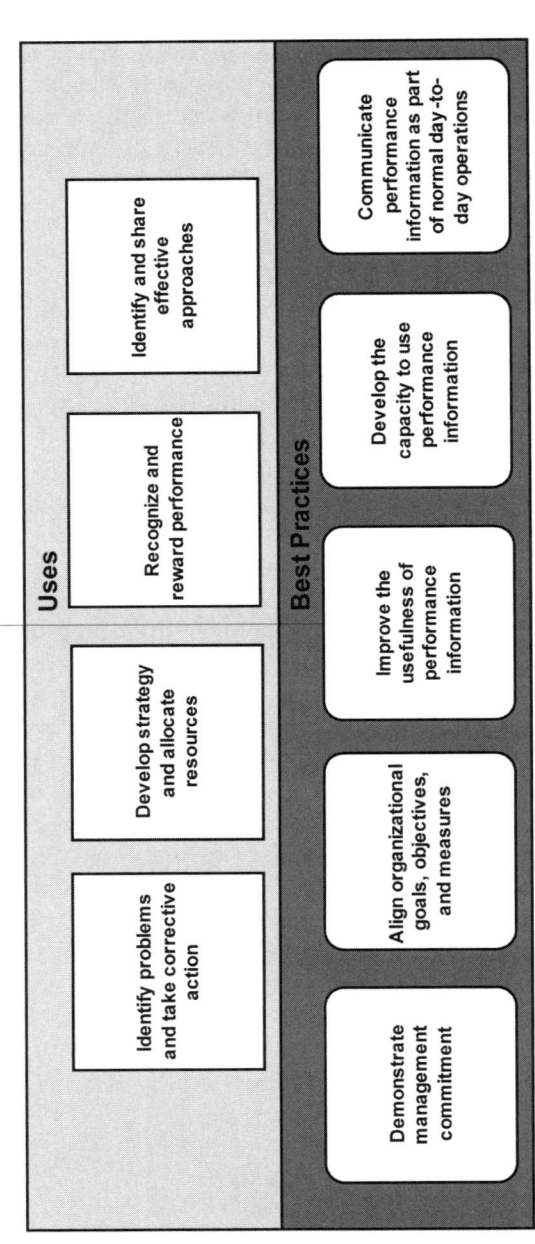

Improved Results

Uses

| Identify problems and take corrective action | Develop strategy and allocate resources | Recognize and reward performance | Identify and share effective approaches |

Best Practices

| Demonstrate management commitment | Align organizational goals, objectives, and measures | Improve the usefulness of performance information | Develop the capacity to use performance information | Communicate performance information as part of normal day-to-day operations |

FIGURE 5.2
Best Practices Yield Improved Results

Objective value measures are typically derived from agency statistics and documentation, such as agency budget exhibits, program assessment rating tool (PART) scores, external assessments of agency performance, IT inventories, and other sources. By contrast, subjective value measures are determined through discussion with stakeholders in the form of surveys, interviews, workshops, or other feedback mechanisms. Customer satisfaction surveys can be relatively simple; however, it is important to understand how the questions are worded, the target audience group, and the number of respondents necessary to be statistically valid. Wherever possible, agencies should reuse existing data sources for measurement rather than creating new instruments. This will minimize the effort of data collection and the associated burden on agency personnel.

The case study below is a good example of how one state organization realized the importance of performance measures while implementing a major project.

Case Study: New York State Workers' Compensation Board

While executing a large initiative to improve organizational business processes, the New York State Workers' Compensation Board recognized the need to measure performance within its organization. The project was expected to dramatically improve operational effectiveness, but how could that be proved? The volume of work performed was the only measurement being calculated, and this did not reflect other aspects of organizational performance. By identifying and implementing performance measures, the board would also be able to measure the effectiveness of its organizational business process improvements. Because the business process improvements being implemented were going to affect the entire organization, the board was challenged with identifying and developing performance measures that would be widely applicable. Appropriate metrics were needed for executive management, performing organization management, project management, and individual project team members. It became apparent that implementing performance measures to the level of detail required would become a project in and of itself! The board assembled a project team that was charged with:

- *Defining performance measures*: Team members quickly realized that while many ideas and methods for performance measurement already exist, it would require some effort to find the ones that would work best for them.
- *Formulating the project scope*: The team needed to identify business areas that would be involved in or affected by the project and obtain buy-in from the appropriate members of executive management.

- *Identifying the project approach*: Two teams were formed. The measures team was responsible for developing measurements, analyzing measurement results, recommending processes for improvement, and producing deliverables. The strategy team was the liaison between the measures team and executive management and ensured regular communication and contact among all involved parties.
- *Developing a plan*: The team assembled a plan that documented a phased approach to implementing performance measures within the organization. Earlier phases concentrated on measurements at a conceptual level. Detailed measures, measurement targets, data, and required reports were defined during subsequent phases. The outcome of the project was to be a set of detailed reports containing the information that would drive process improvements that would be consistent with the strategic vision of the organization. To enable the integration of performance measures into management programs within the organization, these reports would need to be readily produced and easily available to managers and staff.
- *Identifying risks*: Early in the project, the team identified and documented potential risk events that might be barriers to the success of the project and formulated plans to mitigate the risks should they occur. Some of the risk factors included:

  Organizational inertia
  Fear
  Availability of funding
  Availability of data
  Lack of skills necessary to implement process improvements

- *Evaluating best practices*: The team contacted state agencies and other public-sector entities to gather and evaluate existing best practices for performance measures. During the beginning stages of the Worker's Compensation Board project, however, very few successful implementations existed in the public sector.

Without a system of performance measures available "out of the box," the team formulated a methodology that drew heavily upon the concepts of the balanced scorecard. The team discovered that there are a number of factors affecting measuring performance in a public-sector enterprise that require a customized approach to implementing the balanced scorecard. Most public-sector organizations are in the business of policy, not profit, whereas for-profit organizations would supplement extensive and standard measures of financial performance with the other perspectives of the scorecard. In addition, it was difficult to reconcile the business process improvement notion to "measure the process, not the people" within a system of measuring performance that encourages the linkage between strategy, process, and individual performance. Also, the limited number of measures recommended by the methodology may not necessarily allow a public-sector organization to meet the public's demand for information on how the organization was performing.

Once the up-front planning was complete, the team categorized the business and functional areas that would be measured and developed a mission statement for each. Team members then agreed upon the criteria against which all proposed performance measures would be assessed. Depending upon the factors determining success of the business or functional areas being measured, potential measurement criteria were narrowed down to a key set. The team refined the key set of measures by defining and expressing them in terms of target goals, based on the long-term vision of executive management.

These were refined throughout the course of the project. The list of measures numbered only 50, but when the data were leveled, trended, sliced, and diced, it translated into 300 reports! It was then necessary for the team to define a way to deliver the information contained in the reports in a way that would be meaningful and could translate into process improvements. Data were grouped into reports appropriate to the selected audience: executive management, performing organization management, project management, and individual project team members. Standards were defined to report data in a valid, user-friendly way, displaying information as it related to defined target goals.

With the support of executive management, business process improvements based upon the data collected and reflected in the reports were introduced in the organization. Measurements translated into results! For example:

- As a result of reengineering, the average time required to index a case at the board dropped from 31.4 days to 16.5. After implementing performance measures for this process, the average days dropped again to 6.7, with the best-practices district achieving an average of only 3.4 days.
- The number of cases resolved through informal processes increased from 2,100 per month to 3,750 per month. Shortly after implementing performance measures, with fewer claims examiners, the number increased to 5,000. Despite a 300 percent increase in the volume of administrative determinations produced by workers' compensation claims examiners, the approval rate for administrative determinations remains above 95 percent.
- Every area of the board's operations related to handling claims for benefits saw improvement almost immediately after implementing performance measures.

Although the board's electronic case folder (the technological corner-stone of the OPTICS project) is nearly four years old, through continuous improvement activities and performance measures, the board continues to see improvement in its business processes. Areas not yet measured continue to provide opportunities for improvement. The following were noted by the Workers' Compensation Board as important lessons learned as a result of successfully implementing a performance measures system:

- Strong executive sponsorship is critical in order to resolve policy and strategy issues that arise when an organization attempts to implement a successful performance measures system. In fact, some propose that "leadership" should be added as a fifth perspective to the balanced scorecard for public-sector organizations.
- Measures should come in sets. Measures drive behavior, and therefore, balance must exist not only between the components of the framework but also within each component.
- It is easy to develop measures—the challenge is defining the right set of measures that tie directly to the strategic vision for the organization.
- Measures must be few in number, have quantifiable goals, and be derived from what drives operational success in the organization.
- Set targets! If you cannot establish a target for a proposed measure, you must ask the question, "why do we measure this?"
- If meeting the performance goals of the strategic vision is not possible at the outset, establish pragmatic targets for today. Review these targets periodically, and increase them over time until they meet the vision. If you do this, you will establish a culture of continuous improvement!
- Measures must be produced more frequently than an annual report.
- Reporting standards reduce the learning curve and ease the process of implementing performance measures in the field.
- Measures should, wherever possible, involve the individual performer, but supervisors and managers must not confuse a scorecard with a report card. Performance measures supplement the traditional performance evaluation process.

When implemented correctly, an organization should see improvements in every area measured.

The success of the efforts of the Workers' Compensation Board did not go unnoticed. The MIRROR Project (management information, research, references, and operational reports), which has been described as one-stop shopping for performance data and information about the performance measures project, has won many prestigious awards (New York State Office for Technology 2003).

The PDM approach directly supports the current administration's budgeting reporting and transparency requirements. The focus on performance measurement, the business case, and large IT project risk management directly tie to the goals of transparency (through the performance measures) and enhanced management of federal IT projects.

Critical Success Factors for Federal Investment Implementation

There are four recurrent themes that have evolved from "best-practices" assessment of federal agencies:

- Quality participation or "buy-in" by the highest-level agency managers in the IT capital planning process is necessary for successful agency implementation.
- Collaboration of senior executives is necessary to provide focus for the process.
- Decision making at the lowest appropriate level helps drive the process.
- IT investment selection processes are critical—agencies have made progress in this area.

Factors for senior management "buy-in" and involvement include:

- Recognize the need for top management involvement
- Use the budget process as a driver
- Involve functional-level IT executives
- Involve top management in the IT strategic planning board
- Develop partnerships between the CIO, CFO, and CEO
- Form a business planning council
- Have open communication among agency's top leadership
- Consider establishing working capital funds
- Have strong leadership at the senior leadership level

Factors for collaboration include:

- Include staff from program, IT, and financial offices in the IT capital planning review processes
- Have implemented, or are close to completing implementation of, formal systematic processes to handle proposed project submission requirements through decision making for funding
- Have adopted an integrated team approach in the composition of the review groups by including representatives from the different functional areas of program (operations), finance, and IT

- Provide staff analysis that informs decision making
- Have senior management review summaries on project costs, benefits, and risks of their IT investments
- Be prepared to stop a project when necessary
- Be prepared, also, to help in making changes

Factors for investment selection include:

- Define thresholds for investment planning and control
- Include agency infrastructure in the investment portfolio
- Develop a method for selecting investments
- Evaluate investments for support of goals
- Use a scorecard
- Develop portfolio management approaches
- Standardize reporting formats
- Develop criteria for applying decision criteria

Other factors include:

- Use the portfolio to manage costs and oversee implementation
- Control investments, independent of the selection process
- Ensure that problems are surfaced and discussed when they occur
- Monitor results or outcomes
- Manage high-risk projects
- Remain faithful to the scheduled project reviews
- Agree up front on what is to be evaluated
- Select the right staff to perform evaluations
- Tie proposed investments to program initiatives
- Develop an explicit relationship to the performance plan and report
- When measuring performance, keep your eye on the prize
- Incorporate lessons learned into the process
- Incorporate evaluation results into overall IT business practices

Implications

Challenges in Implementing the "It's All about Performance" Approach

The PDM approach would require that agencies manage strategically, measure business performance (outputs and outcomes), select investments based on sound, comprehensive analytical business cases, revalidate business cases as projects proceed, and conduct comprehensive benefits realization efforts. Also critical is the willingness of federal agency governance boards to cancel projects that are headed toward failure. These activities are new or infrequently practiced at many agencies and will require strong leadership, training, and cultural change to implement. However, the benefits of more effective projects and reduced risk of potentially colossal project failures should more than offset the investment.

The federal government must address and adapt to a range of major trends and challenges in the nation and the world—a long-term, structural fiscal imbalance; a transformation from an industrially based to a knowledge-based economy; revolutionary changes in technology that have altered how we communicate and do business globally; greater reliance on market forces and competition; and changing national security threats. To respond to these trends and challenges, government must have the institutional capacity to plan more strategically, identify and react more expediently, and focus on achieving results.

Yet, in many cases, the government is still trying to do business in ways that are based on conditions, priorities, and approaches that existed decades ago and are not well suited to addressing 21st-century challenges. For example, some agencies do not yet have all the necessary abilities, more flexible legal authorities, and leadership and management capabilities to transform their cultures and operations. Consequently, to successfully navigate transformations across the government, it must fundamentally reexamine not only its business processes but also its outmoded organizational structures, management approaches, and, in some cases, outdated missions.

Most major outcomes of federal activities are supported by multiple programs and tools that, in turn, are often sponsored by many different federal agencies. Although these individual programs address common or similar performance goals, they result in an overly fragmented delivery network and, at times, work at cross purposes. For example, federal food safety programs are carried out by 12 agencies with differing enforcement criteria and inspection practices. The fragmentation of federal programs reflects a policy-making process that is overly stove-piped by agency and program, with insufficient focus on how individual programs contribute to overarching, crosscutting goals and missions. As a result, the capacity to periodically reexamine the alignment and relevance of policy portfolios in a changing society is limited. The Government Performance and Results Act (GPRA) provided for a government-wide performance plan to address these issues, but this plan has not yet been developed by the executive branch. Furthermore, the federal government lacks a government-wide strategic plan to provide a framework for addressing crosscutting goals.

Increasingly, the government relies on new networks and partnerships to achieve critical results and develop public policy, often including multiple federal agencies, domestic and international non- or quasi-government organizations, for-profit and not-for-profit contractors, and state and local governments. The federal government uses an array of different tools and program designs to work in this environment, such as direct service delivery, loans and loan guarantees, tax preferences, insurance programs, grants, and regulations. Ranging from education to homeland security, a complex network of governmental and nongovernmental entities shape the actual outcomes achieved, whether it is through formal partnerships in grant programs or through independent actions of each acting locally to address common problems. Notwithstanding the increased linkages in our system, each level of government often makes decisions on these interrelated programs independently, with little interaction or intergovernmental dialogue. While the magnitude of the nation's challenges calls for a concerted effort across sectors, there are limited opportunities for leaders of those sectors to come together to reach consensus about the kinds of mutual commitments that are necessary.

More specifically, government has also begun to fundamentally change who does its business—recognizing that it could better partner with the private sector in new, more cost-effective ways. Agencies are assessing what functions and transactions the private sector could perform and asking their employees to compete with private entities for this business to improve quality and reduce costs. But the government does not yet know how this trend is affecting its workforce and its ability to refocus more on strategic needs or the extent to which it has delivered real cost savings. Collecting and evaluating data to ensure such transformations are implemented effectively and deliver the desired results will be critical.

Performance, mission, cost, schedule, and other risks are inherent in major federal programs and investments, such as weapons systems, homeland security, federal buildings and other infrastructure, transportation subsidies, environmental cleanup, and IT systems. Despite these risks, federal agencies often lack comprehensive risk management strategies that are well integrated with program, budget, and investment decisions. As one example among many, homeland security investments are designed to reduce risks to the nation's communities and assets, but the availability of a common set of analytical tools and procedures on how agency management should use them can be improved to better align the allocation of homeland security resources with risk-related measures, such as relative risk and risk reduction per dollar invested. Government-wide guidance generally does not fully integrate risk management into all aspects of decision making, such as policy making, program planning, implementation, and monitoring. More broadly, Congress and the executive branch face a series of difficult and contentious trade-offs as they reexamine, reprioritize, and restructure the base of federal programs in response to current budget demands and long-term fiscal challenges and the changing risk profiles faced by programs and agencies. Much of the base of the federal government structure was put in place in response to the wants, needs, and budgets of an earlier era. For example, some risks to farmers and to the aging population have changed over the decades, as have the tools for evaluating and communicating risk about costs and other outcomes. A more thorough and disciplined approach to identifying and managing risk across the federal government could help in structuring and informing the daunting decisions that need to be made.

A range of individual agencies needs to successfully complete their specific transformation initiatives. For example, the U.S. Postal Service is under increasing financial pressure as the Internet, electronic bill payment, and growing competition from private delivery companies are changing the nation's communication and delivery sectors and adversely affecting mail volume. Yet the Postal Service's ability to address these challenges has been hindered by an older business model that relies on mail volume growth to cover rising costs. The service is working to cut costs, improve productivity, reduce its workforce, and make other needed changes, but it will need attention and support as it adapts a new and more competitive business model.

The government has not transformed, in many cases, how it motivates and compensates its employees to achieve maximum results within available resources and existing authorities. Even though people are critical to any agency's successful transformation, define its culture, develop its knowledge, and are its most important asset, a number of agencies still try to manage this asset with a "one-size-fits-all" approach. For example, employees are compensated through a system that (1) rewards length of service as well as individual performance and contributions; (2) automatically provides across-the-board annual pay increases, even to poor performers; and (3) compensates employees living in various localities. To address these problems and provide the services the public expects, the federal civil service system will need to be reformed government-wide, and this reform must be guided by a set of consistent principles, criteria, and practices.

Performance and analytic tools may be as important as, or more important than, specific process reforms in facilitating reexamination. In this regard, the performance metrics and plans ushered in by the GPRA of 1993 have led to a growing supply of increasingly sophisticated measures and data on the results achieved by various federal programs. Agencies and the office of management and budget (OMB) have been working over the years to strengthen the links between this information and the budget. Under the PART, for example, the OMB rated the effectiveness of each program in the budget over a five-year period. While these initiatives provided a foundation for a baseline review of federal policies, programs, functions, and activities, several changes are in order to support the type of reexamination we have in mind. First, the PART focus on individual programs can provide important new assessments, but it needs to be supplemented by a more crosscutting assessment of the relative contribution of portfolios of programs and tools to broader outcomes. Most key performance goals of importance—ranging from low-income housing to food safety to counterterrorism—are addressed by a wide range of discretionary, entitlement, tax, and regulatory approaches that cut across a number of agencies. While the OMB moved to include some crosscutting assessments in the fiscal year 2006, PART, fully developing the government-wide performance plan provided for under GPRA, would provide a more systematic vehicle for addressing the performance of programs cutting across agencies to broader goals.

The current administration, recognizing the limitations of PART, is moving forward with additional performance focus but in a broader, more transparent approach. Whatever approach is taken, the focus of the federal government needs to remain on improving measurable agency performance and ensuring that large IT projects meet business case objectives.

Cost Estimating and Assessment

Cost estimates are necessary for government acquisition programs for many reasons: to support decisions about funding one program over another, to develop annual budget requests and acquisitions, to evaluate resource requirements at key decision points, and to develop performance measurement baselines. Moreover, having a realistic estimate of projected costs makes for effective resource allocation, and it increases the probability of a program's success. Developing reliable cost estimates has been difficult for agencies across the federal government. Too often, programs cost more than expected and deliver results that do not satisfy all requirements.

Developing a good cost estimate requires stable program requirements, access to detailed documentation and historical data, well-trained and experienced cost analysts, a risk-and-uncertainty analysis, the identification of a range of confidence levels, and adequate contingency and management reserves. Even with the best of these circumstances, cost estimating is difficult. It requires both science and judgment. And, since answers are seldom, if ever, precise, the goal is to find a "reasonable" range. However, the cost estimator typically faces many challenges.

These challenges often lead to bad estimates—that is, estimates that contain poorly defined assumptions, have no supporting documentation, are accompanied by no comparisons to similar programs, are characterized by inadequate data collection and inappropriate estimating methodologies, are sustained by irrelevant or out-of-date data, provide no basis or rationale for the estimate, and can show no defined process for generating the estimate.

Software and systems development experts agree that early project estimates are imprecise by definition and that their inherent precision increases during a project's life cycle as more information becomes known. The experts emphasize that to be useful, each cost estimate should indicate its degree of uncertainty, possibly as an estimated range or qualified by some factor of confidence.

The U.S. Customs Service did not reveal the degree of uncertainty of its cost estimate for the Automated Commercial Environment (ACE) program to managers involved in investment decisions. For example, Customs did not disclose that it made the estimate before fully defining ACE functionality. Instead, Customs presented its $1.05 billion ACE life-cycle cost estimate as an unqualified point estimate. This suggests an element of precision that cannot exist for such an undefined system, and it obscured the investment risk in the project.

Program proponents often postulate the availability of a new technology, only to discover that it is not ready when needed and that program costs have increased. Proponents also often make assumptions about the complexity or difficulty of new processes, such as first-time integration efforts, which may end up to be unrealistic. More time and effort lead directly to greater costs.

Managing Knowledge and Human Capital in a Business Performance-Driven Environment

A number of skill sets are required to effectively and successfully implement and manage under PDM. Skill requirements include:

- Financial analysis
- Risk analysis
- Business/IT analysis
- Performance management
- Measurement systems
- Interpersonal skills
- Consensus management
- Decision-making discipline
- Quantitative measurement
- Managing in uncertainty
- Adjusting to a transparency environment
- Willingness to be visible in terms of goals, progress, and success/failure in meeting agreed upon goals

The federal government is working at developing a structured approach using common processes and tools across the federal acquisition community focused on developing the characteristics of the workforce, which are important for meeting current and future needs. Workforce shaping includes developing and managing competencies, strategic human capital planning, collecting and managing appropriate workforce data, and recognizing skill and experience achievements through a standard certification. Strategic planning is essential for building and retaining a workforce capable of supporting an agency's mission. Successful planning is needed to ensure adequate personnel resources are in place, training is available, and organizational structures match agency needs.

To retain essential knowledge and skills necessary for successful management, an organized process is needed for attracting new employees at all levels through recruiting and retention strategies, education and diversity alliances, and incentives. To facilitate career planning and retention in the federal environment, professionals need a structure providing opportunities for interaction with other professionals and tools that allow management of one's career.

Overall Summary

PDM is a new approach to investment and project management, focused on IT projects but useful for business projects as well. PDM offers a way to mitigate project risk, avoid catastrophic project failures, and, most of all, more reliably deliver value to the organization or agency.

The federal government is well positioned to benefit from the PDM approach. Implementation of the approach will require strong agency leadership and commitment but can provide outstanding business value to the agencies.

Appendix A: Federal Legislation, Requirements, and Guidance for IT Initiative Management

CLINGER-COHEN ACT (CCA) OF 1996. The CCA was formerly known as the Information Technology Management Reform Act or ITMRA. It requires each agency to undertake capital planning and investment control by establishing a process for maximizing the value and assessing and managing risks of IT acquisitions of the executive agency.

Federal Acquisition Streamlining Act (FASA) of 1994. FASA requires agencies to define the cost, schedule, and performance goals for major acquisition programs and to monitor and report annually on the degree to which those goals are being met. Agencies must assess whether acquisition programs are achieving 90 percent of their cost, schedule, and performance goals.

Government Performance and Results Act (GPRA) of 1993. GPRA requires agencies to prepare updateable strategic plans and to prepare annual performance plans covering each program activity displayed in the budget. The performance plans are to establish performance goals in objective, quantifiable, and measurable form and performance indicators to be used in measuring relevant outputs, service levels, and outcomes.

Paperwork Reduction Act (PRA) of 1995. PRA intends to: minimize the paperwork burden resulting from collection of information by or for the federal government; coordinate, integrate, and make uniform federal information resources management policies and practices; improve the quality and use of federal information to minimize the cost to the government of the creation, collection, maintenance, use, dissemination, and disposition of information; and ensure that IT is acquired, used, and managed to improve efficiency and effectiveness of agency missions.

Chief Financial Officers' Act (CFOA) of 1990. CFOA establishes the foundation for effective financial management, including requiring agencies to develop and effectively operate and maintain financial management systems. The CFO Act focuses on the need to significantly improve the financial management and reporting practices of the federal government. Having accurate financial data is critical to understanding the costs and assessing the returns on IT investments. Under the CFO Act, CFO's are responsible for developing and maintaining integrated accounting and financial management systems that include systematic measurement information on agency performance.

OMB Circular A-11, Part 2, "Preparation and Submission of Strategic Plans." This section provides guidance for preparing and submitting overall agency strategic and performance plans required by GPRA.

OMB Circular A-11, Part 3, "Planning, Budgeting, and Acquisition of Fixed Assets." This section provides guidance on the planning, budgeting, and acquisition of fixed assets, which include IT capital assets, and requires agencies to provide information on these assets in budget submissions and provides guidance for planning. It also provides guidance for coordinating collection of agency information for OMB reports to Congress for FASA and the CCA. Under FASA, the OMB is required to report on the cost, schedule, and performance goals for asset acquisitions and how well agencies are meeting their goals. CCA requires that the OMB report on program performance in information systems and how benefits relate to accomplishing the goals of the agency.

OMB Circular A-130, Management of Federal Information Resources. A-130 provides information resource management policies on federal information management/information technology (IM/IT) resources required by the PRA of 1980 as amended.

OMB Memorandum M-97-02, Funding Information System Investments. This memorandum contains eight decision criteria commonly referred to as Raines Rules, which the OMB will use to evaluate major information system investments. Raines Rules are described below.

Executive Order no. 13011, Federal Information Technology. The executive order highlights the need for agencies to significantly improve the management of their information systems, including the acquisition of IT, by implementing the relevant provisions of PRA, CCA, and GPRA. Agencies are to refocus their IT management to directly support their strategic missions, implement an investment review process that drives budget formulation and execution for information systems, and rethink and restructure the way they perform their functions before investing in IT to support that work. Agency heads are to strengthen the quality and decisions of employing information resources to meet mission needs through integrated analysis, planning, budgeting, and evaluation processes.

OMB and IT Investment Management

The Office of Management and Budget (OMB) has developed some significant requirements for investing in IT. An early guideline provided to agencies is known as the "Three Pesky Questions." The OMB recommends each agency answer these questions when considering an IT initiative:

- Does the government need to do it?
- If so, can some other organization do it better than we can?
- If not, have we reengineered our process so we can spend less and use the technology most efficiently?

OMB director Frank Raines issued policy guidelines for funding IT investments. Although dated in 1996, these rules provide good quality guidance to the agencies. This policy is known as "Raines' Rules" and directs agencies to ensure IT investments:

- Support core or priority federal government missions
- Are impossible for another agency, company, or government to efficiently perform
- Support work already redesigned to cut costs, improve efficiency, and use off-the-shelf technology
- Show a return on investment equal to or better than other uses of available resources
- Are consistent with agency- and government-wide architectures that integrate work and information flows with strategic plans, incorporate standards allowing information exchange and resource sharing, and retain flexibility in the choice of suppliers
- Reduce risk by avoiding custom design, using pilot projects and prototypes, establishing clear measures of success, securing buy-in from users

- Are put into effect in phased, successive chunks that are short-term and narrow in scope and independently solve part of an overall mission problem
- Appropriately allocate risk between government and contractor, tie payments to accomplishments, and use commercial technology

Appendix B: PRINCE2

PRINCE2 IS A GENERIC, tailorable, simple to follow project management method developed by the U.K. government's Office of Government Commerce (OGC). It is included in this appendix because the PRINCE2 approach includes a strong focus on the business case and continued business justification—characteristics in common with the PDM approach.

PRINCE2 is often cited as the world's most widely used project management method. Its success is largely due to it being nonproprietary but also due to the ability of organizations to apply it to a variety of industries, environments, and project sizes.

It covers how to organize, manage, and control your projects. It is aimed at enabling an organization to successfully deliver the right products, on time and within budget. As a project manager, one can apply the principles of PRINCE2 and the associated training to any type of project. It will help a project manager to manage risk, control quality, and change effectively, as well as make the most of challenging situations and opportunities that arise within a project. A PRINCE2 project has the following characteristics:

- Continued business justification
- Learning from experience
- Defined roles and responsibilities
- Managed by stages
- Managed by exception
- Focuses on products and their quality
- Tailored to suit the particular product environment

PRINCE2 does not cover all aspects of project management. Areas such as leadership and people management skills and detailed coverage of project management tools and techniques are well covered by other existing and proven methods and are, therefore, excluded from PRINCE2.

There is also a rapidly growing international interest. PRINCE2 is designed to incorporate the requirements and experiences of existing users around the world.

The PRINCE2 method is documented in the OGC publication *Managing Successful Projects with PRINCE2*, readily available from the official publisher, TSO. This is aimed at those working in the project environment and the project manager in particular. *Directing Successful Projects with PRINCE2* covers the duties and behaviors expected of the project board. These core books are supported by a number of complementary publications.

The approaches to deliver these principles are outlined in the seven themes of:

- Business case
- Organization
- Quality
- Plans
- Risks
- Changes
- Progress

And they flow through to the underpinning processes of:

- Starting up a project
- Directing a project
- Initiating a project
- Controlling a stage
- Managing stage boundaries
- Closing a project

PRINCE2 acts as a common language between all of customers, users, and suppliers, bringing these parties together on the project board. And although PRINCE2 doesn't include contract management as such, it provides the necessary controls and boundaries needed for everybody to work together within the limits of any relevant contracts. In addition, the project board provides support to the project manager in making key decisions.

Most important of all, PRINCE2 allows businesses to focus on doing the right projects, at the right time, for the right reasons, by making the start of a project and its continued existence dependent on a valid, ongoing business case.

Using PRINCE2 provides greater control of resources and the ability to manage business and project risk more effectively, which provides benefits to:

- Project managers
- Directors/executives (senior responsible owners) of projects
- Organizations

Using PRINCE2 on projects will provide common systems, procedures, and language. This will enable the organization to make fewer mistakes, to learn from those that are made, and ultimately save money and effort. The PRINCE2 method is nonproprietary and easy to learn, and embodies established and proven best practice across the wide cross-section of organizations who have contributed to its evolution since the 1980s. By adopting PRINCE2 the organization will be benefiting from lessons learned by these other organizations.

In summary, PRINCE2's formal recognition of responsibilities within a project, together with its focus on what a project is to deliver (the why, when, and for whom) provides an organization's projects with:

- A common, consistent approach
- A controlled and organized start, middle, and end
- Regular reviews of progress against plan
- Assurance that the project continues to have a business justification
- Flexible decision points
- Management control of any deviations from the plan
- The involvement of management and stakeholders at the right time and place during the project
- Good communication channels between the project, project management, and the rest of the organization
- A means of capturing and sharing lessons learned
- A route to increasing the project management skills and competencies of the organization's staff at all levels

Appendix C: Risk Management Approaches

RISK IS THE NET NEGATIVE IMPACT of the exercise of a vulnerability, considering both the probability and the impact of occurrence. Risk management is the process of identifying risk, assessing risk, and taking steps to reduce risk to an acceptable level.

"Today's enterprise faces a daunting range of IT risks—from security, business malfeasance and insider threats to business-critical IT service availability, performance and integrity issues," according to Scott Crawford, research director at Enterprise Management Associates. "Regulatory requirements intended to curb these risks have also driven the pursuit of more effective IT governance. IT risk management has become the lynchpin of all these demands. Putting a strategic IT risk management program into place can provide substantial benefits for the enterprise, not only in controlling threats to critical IT services, but also in giving the business a stronger competitive edge through more effective technology discipline," he said.

"The concept of a 'strategic' approach brings coherence to the enterprise," said Crawford. "IT risk management is no longer limited to one technology or meant to meet a single regulatory mandate. It seeks to unify and integrate siloed approaches to managing security, business, technology and trust risks—aligning them with strategic business objectives to enable the enterprise to consistently manage and measure their control."

Every organization has a mission. In this digital era, as organizations use automated information technology (IT) systems to process their information for better support of their missions, risk management plays a critical role in protecting an organization's information assets, and, therefore, its mission, from IT-related risk.

An effective risk management process is an important component of a successful IT security program. The principal goal of an organization's risk management process should be to protect the organization and its ability to perform their mission, not just its IT assets. Therefore, the risk management process should not be treated primarily as a technical function carried out by the IT experts who operate and manage the IT system, but as an essential management function of the organization.

The objective of performing risk management is to enable the organization to accomplish its mission(s) (1) by better securing the IT systems that store, process, or transmit organizational information; (2) by enabling management to make well-informed risk management decisions to justify the expenditures that are part of an IT budget; and (3) by assisting management in authorizing (or accrediting) the IT systems on the basis of the supporting documentation resulting from the performance of risk management.

Personnel who support or use the risk management process include:

- Senior management, the mission owners, who make decisions about the IT security budget
- Federal chief information officers, who ensure the implementation of risk management for agency IT systems and the security provided for these IT systems
- The designated approving authority (DAA), who is responsible for the final decision on whether to allow operation of an IT system
- The IT security program manager, who implements the security program
- Information system security officers (ISSO), who are responsible for IT security
- IT system owners of system software and/or hardware used to support IT functions
- Information owners of data stored, processed, and transmitted by the IT systems
- Business or functional managers, who are responsible for the IT procurement process
- Technical support personnel (e.g., network, system, application, and database administrators; computer specialists; data security analysts), who manage and administer security for the IT systems
- IT system and application programmers, who develop and maintain code that could affect system and data integrity

Risk is a measure of the inability to achieve overall program objectives within defined cost, schedule, and technical constraints and has two components:

(1) the probability of failing to achieve a particular outcome, and (2) the consequences/impacts of failing to achieve that outcome. For processes, risk is a measure of the difference between actual performance of a process and the known best practice for performing that process.

Risk events are those events within the program that, if they go wrong, could result in problems in the development, production, and fielding of the system. Risk events should be defined to a level such that the risk and causes are understandable and can be accurately assessed in terms of probability/likelihood and consequence/impact to establish the level of risk. For processes, risk events are assessed in terms of process variance from known best practices and potential consequences/impacts of the variance.

Technical risk is the risk associated with the evolution of the design and the production of the XYZ system affecting the level of performance necessary to meet the operational requirements. The developer's design, test, and production processes (process risk) influence the technical risk and the nature of the product as depicted in the various levels of the work breakdown structure (product risk).

Cost risk is the risk associated with the ability of the program to achieve its life-cycle cost objectives. Two risk areas bearing on cost are (1) the risk that the cost estimates and objectives are accurate and reasonable, and (2) the risk that program execution will not meet the cost objectives as a result of a failure to handle cost, schedule, and performance risks.

Schedule risks are those associated with the adequacy of the time estimated and allocated for the development, production, and fielding of the system. Two risk areas bearing on schedule are (1) the risk that the schedule estimates and objectives are realistic and reasonable, and (2) the risk that program execution will fall short of the schedule objectives as a result of failure to handle cost, schedule, or performance risks.

Risk ratings is the value that is given to a risk event (or the program overall) based on the analysis of the probability/likelihood and consequences/impacts of the event. For the program, risk ratings of low, moderate, or high will be assigned based on the following criteria:

- Low risk: Has little or no potential for increase in cost, disruption of schedule, or degradation of performance. Actions within the scope of the planned program and normal management attention should result in controlling acceptable risk.
- Moderate risk: May cause some increase in cost, disruption of schedule, or degradation of performance. Special action and management attention may be required to handle risk.

- High risk: Likely to cause significant increase in cost, disruption of schedule, or degradation of performance. Significant additional action and high-priority management attention will be required to handle risk.

Independent risk assessor is a person who is not in the management chain or directly involved in performing the tasks being assessed. Use of independent risk assessors is a valid technique to ensure that all risk areas are identified and that the consequence/impact and probability/likelihood (or process variance) are properly understood. The technique can be used at different program levels (e.g., program office, service field activities, contractors, etc.). The program manager will approve the use of independent assessors, as needed.

Metrics are measures used to indicate progress or achievement.

Risk management encompasses three processes: risk assessment, risk mitigation, and evaluation and assessment. The risk assessment process includes identification and evaluation of risks and risk impacts. Risk mitigation refers to prioritizing, implementing, and maintaining the appropriate risk-reducing measures recommended from the risk assessment process. Continual evaluation and assessment is the key to a successful risk management program. The DAA or system authorizing official is responsible for determining whether the remaining risk is at an acceptable level or whether additional security controls should be implemented to further reduce or eliminate the residual risk before authorizing (or accrediting) the IT system for operation.

Risk management is the process that allows IT managers to balance the operational and economic costs of protective measures and achieve gains in mission capability by protecting the IT systems and data that support their organizations' missions. This process is not unique to the IT environment; indeed, it pervades decision making in all areas of our daily lives. Take the case of home security, for example. Many people decide to have home security systems installed and pay a monthly fee to a service provider to have these systems monitored for the better protection of their property. Presumably, the homeowners have weighed the cost of system installation and monitoring against the value of their household goods and their family's safety, a fundamental "mission" need.

The head of an organizational unit must ensure that the organization has the capabilities needed to accomplish its mission. These mission owners must determine the security capabilities that their IT systems must have to provide the desired level of mission support in the face of real-world threats. Most organizations have tight budgets for IT security; therefore, IT security spending must be reviewed as thoroughly as other management decisions. A well-structured risk management methodology, when used effectively, can help management identify appropriate controls for providing the mission-essential security capabilities.

Minimizing negative impact on an organization and need for sound basis in decision making are the fundamental reasons organizations implement a risk management process for their IT systems. Effective risk management must be totally integrated into the system development life cycle (SDLC). An IT system's SDLC has five high-level phases: initiation, development or acquisition, implementation, operation or maintenance, and disposal. In some

SDLC Phases	Phase Characteristics	Support from Risk Management Activities
Phase 1—Initiation	The need for an IT system is expressed and the purpose and scope of the IT system is documented	• Identified risks are used to support the development of the system requirements, including security requirements, and a security concept of operations (strategy)
Phase 2—Development or Acquisition	The IT system is designed, purchased, programmed, developed, or otherwise constructed	• The risks identified during this phase can be used to support the security analyses of the IT system that may lead to architecture and design trade-offs during system development
Phase 3—Implementation	The system security features should be configured, enabled, tested, and verified	• The risk management process supports the assessment of the system implementation against its requirements and within its modeled operational environment. Decisions regarding risks identified must be made prior to system operation
Phase 4—Operation or Maintenance	The system performs its functions. Typically the system is being modified on an ongoing basis through the addition of hardware and software and by changes to organizational processes, policies, and procedures	• Risk management activities are performed for periodic system reauthorization (or reaccreditation) or whenever major changes are made to an IT system in its operational, production environment (e.g., new system interfaces)
Phase 5—Disposal	This phase may involve the disposition of information, hardware, and software. Activities may include moving, archiving, discarding, or destroying information and sanitizing the hardware and software	• Risk management activities are performed for system components that will be disposed of or replaced to ensure that the hardware and software are properly disposed of, that residual data is appropriately handled, and that system migration is conducted in a secure and systematic manner

FIGURE C.1
SDLC and Risk Management

cases, an IT system may occupy several of these phases at the same time. However, the risk management methodology is the same regardless of the SDLC phase for which the assessment is being conducted. Risk management is an iterative process that can be performed during each major phase of the SDLC.

Risk management is a management responsibility. This section describes the key roles of the personnel who should support and participate in the risk management process.

- *Senior management.* Senior management, under the standard of due care and ultimate responsibility for mission accomplishment, must ensure that the necessary resources are effectively applied to develop the capabilities needed to accomplish the mission. They must also assess and incorporate results of the risk assessment activity into the decision-making process. An effective risk management program that assesses and mitigates IT-related mission risks requires the support and involvement of senior management.
- *Chief information officer (CIO).* The CIO is responsible for the agency's IT planning, budgeting, and performance, including its information security components. Decisions made in these areas should be based on an effective risk management program.
- *System and information owners.* The system and information owners are responsible for ensuring that proper controls are in place to address integrity, confidentiality, and availability of the IT systems and data they own. Typically, the system and information owners are responsible for changes to their IT systems. Thus, they usually have to approve and sign-off on changes to their IT systems (e.g., system enhancement, major changes to the software and hardware). The system and information owners must, therefore, understand their role in the risk management process and fully support this process.
- *Business and functional managers.* The managers responsible for business operations and IT procurement process must take an active role in the risk management process. These managers are the individuals with the authority and responsibility for making the trade-off decisions essential to mission accomplishment. Their involvement in the risk management process enables the achievement of proper security for the IT systems, which, if managed properly, will provide mission effectiveness with a minimal expenditure of resources.
- *Information system security officer (ISSO).* IT security program managers and computer security officers are responsible for their organizations' security programs, including risk management. Therefore, they play a leading role in introducing an appropriate, structured methodology to

help identify, evaluate, and minimize risks to the IT systems that support their organizations' missions. ISSOs also act as major consultants in support of senior management to ensure that this activity takes place on an ongoing basis.

- *IT security practitioners.* IT security practitioners (e.g., network, system, application, and database administrators; computer specialists; security analysts; security consultants) are responsible for proper implementation of security requirements in their IT systems. As changes occur in the existing IT system environment (e.g., expansion in network connectivity, changes to the existing infrastructure and organizational policies, introduction of new technologies), the IT security practitioners must support or use the risk management process to identify and assess new potential risks and implement new security controls as needed to safeguard their IT systems.
- *Security awareness trainers (security/subject matter professionals).* The organization's personnel are the users of the IT systems. Use of the IT systems and data according to an organization's policies, guidelines, and rules of behavior is critical to mitigating risk and protecting the organization's IT resources. To minimize risk to the IT systems, it is essential that system and application users be provided with security awareness training. Therefore, the IT security trainers or security/subject matter professionals must understand the risk management process so that they can develop appropriate training materials and incorporate risk assessment into training programs to educate the end users.

Risk Assessment

Risk assessment is the first process in the risk management methodology. Organizations use risk assessment to determine the extent of the potential threat and the risk associated with an IT system throughout its SDLC. The output of this process helps to identify appropriate controls for reducing or eliminating risk during the risk mitigation process.

Risk is a function of the likelihood of a given threat-source's exercising a particular potential vulnerability and the resulting impact of that adverse event on the organization. To determine the likelihood of a future adverse event, threats to an IT system must be analyzed in conjunction with the potential vulnerabilities and the controls in place for the IT system. Impact refers to the magnitude of harm that could be caused by a threat's exercise of a vulnerability. The level of impact is governed by the potential mission impacts and, in turn, produces a relative value for the IT assets and resources affected (e.g., the criticality and sensitivity of the IT system components and data). A risk assessment methodology encompasses nine primary steps:

- System characterization
- Threat identification
- Vulnerability identification
- Control analysis
- Likelihood determination
- Impact analysis
- Risk determination
- Control recommendations
- Results documentation

Glossary

acceptance management: A process to be used throughout the project to obtain approval from an authorized customer decision maker for work done on the project to date. This process is defined and included in the project plan. The approval at each stage means that the deliverable(s) for that stage are completed to the satisfaction of the customer. In order for a deliverable to be considered "complete" and "acceptable," it is measured against predetermined acceptance criteria.

accessibility: Access to information and data for customers with disabilities comparable to that accorded customers who do not have disabilities.

accountability: The security goal that generates the requirement for actions of an entity to be traced uniquely to that entity. This supports nonrepudiation, deterrence, fault isolation, intrusion detection and prevention, and after-action recovery and legal action.

activity: Is equivalent to a process and is a piece of work accomplished during a project. A process can be broken down into tasks.

alternatives analysis: Definition and comparison of viable alternatives to fulfill business and information management requirements and implement target architecture. For more information on alternative analysis for major IT investments, refer to OMB Circular A-11, Section 300.

assistance data from 2000 to 2006: Assistance data from 2000 to 2006 is from FAADS system operated by census.gov and may contain more types of assistance than FFATA data submitted directly to USASpending.gov from 2007 onward.

assistance data from 2007 to YTD: Assistance data from 2007 onward is from data submitted by agencies directly to USASpending.gov per FFATA legislation.

assurance: Grounds for confidence that the other four security goals (integrity, availability, confidentiality, and accountability) have been adequately met by a specific implementation. "Adequately met" includes (1) functionality that performs correctly, (2) sufficient protection against unintentional errors (by users or software), and (3) sufficient resistance to intentional penetration or bypass.

attribute: A data element that holds information about an object (entity).

audit. See **project audit**

availability: The security goal that generates the requirement for protection against intentional or accidental attempts to (1) perform unauthorized deletion of data, or (2) otherwise cause a denial of service or data or unauthorized use of system resources.

baseline: An initial measurement that can serve as the basis for future comparisons. Applies to the project schedule.

baseline architecture: Describes the current ("as is") state of the agency in terms of performance, business, data, services, and technology.

benchmark: A standard against which measurements or comparisons can be made.

best practices: Certain procedures recognized during the course of the project by the project manager, project sponsor, or project team, that, when exercised, improved the production of a deliverable, streamlined a process, or improved standardized templates, and so forth. These best practices must be documented and shared with other project managers so that they can be repeated.

brainstorming: A technique used to stimulate creative thinking and overcome impasses to problems. Team members gather in a room and offer ideas for solutions to a problem(s). No idea is rejected no matter how absurd or impractical. Often, a practical solution surfaces, and a decision is reached by group consensus.

business case: Provides the justification for an investment. For more information on business cases for major IT investments, refer to OMB Circular A-11, Section 300.

business continuity planning/disaster recovery (BCP/DR): The process of developing advance arrangements and procedures that would enable an organization to respond to a disaster and resume its critical business functions within a predetermined period of time, minimize the amount of loss, and repair or replace the damaged facilities as soon as possible.

business fund indicator: It represents the source of funding made available through a legislative action, such as the American Recovery and Reinvestment Act, to fund awards related to a specific purpose. USAspending.gov tracks award obligations using such business indicators separately for better transparency and accountability.

business process reengineering (BPR): A technique used to optimize organizational processes.

business rules: Practices associated with certain business processes that are required by regulation, law, accounting controls, or business practices. Rules should be defined in as much detail as possible using techniques such as structured English.

business services: Defined by the agency business model, business services include the foundational mechanisms and back-office services used to achieve the purpose of the agency (e.g., inspections and auditing, direct loans, program monitoring, and financial management).

capability maturity model (CMM): A description of the stages through which software organizations evolve as they define, implement, measure, control, and improve their software processes. This model provides a guide for selecting process improvement strategies by facilitating the identification of current process capabilities and the issues most critical to software quality and process improvement.

Catalog of Federal Domestic Assistance (CFDA): The Catalog of Federal Domestic Assistance (CFDA) program is a database maintained by the General Services Administration that classifies all federal programs that provide funding to local government agencies, private institutions, and individuals. Each program is assigned a number and name.

Central Contracting Register (CCR): Central Contractor Registration (CCR) is the primary registrant database for the U.S. federal government. CCR collects, validates, stores, and disseminates data in support of agency acquisition missions, including federal agency contract and assistance awards. Please note that the term "assistance awards" includes grants, cooperative agreements, and other forms of federal assistance. Whether applying for assistance awards, contracts, or other business opportunities, all entities are considered "registrants." Both current and potential federal government registrants are required to register in CCR in order to be awarded contracts by the federal government. Registrants are required to complete a one-time registration to provide basic information relevant to procurement and financial transactions. Registrants must update or renew their registration at least once per year to maintain an active status. In addition, entities (private nonprofits, educational organizations, state and regional agencies, etc.) that apply for assistance awards from the federal government through Grants.gov must now register with CCR as well. However, registration in no way guarantees that a contract or assistance award will be awarded.

change control: A plan for handling changes to a project aimed at minimizing the negative effect on a project's outcome. Change is defined as any adjustment to any aspect of the project plan or to any already approved deliverable(s).

change drivers: Strategic, policy, performance, and industry factors impacting on the design and implementation of business and information management solutions. A mature EA program monitors change drivers and applies relevant drivers to maintain the enterprise architecture.

charter. See **project charter**

client-server: A system architecture where a host computer or "server" provides data and services to requesting or "client" workstations.

competition category: There are five data fields in federal procurement data system (FPDS) that are useful for assessing the level of competition of a contract: the extent competed, reason not competed, number of offers received, statutory exception to fair opportunity, and type of set aside. USAspending.gov has combined information from all five of these fields into one overall summation of the amount of competition for each transaction, called the competition category.

Computer-Aided Software Engineering (CASE): A tool that automates and improves aspects of the system development life cycle (SDLC).

confidentiality: The security goal that generates the requirement for protection from intentional or accidental attempts to perform unauthorized data reads. Confidentiality covers data in storage, during processing, and in transit.

configuration management: A discipline applying technical and administrative direction to identify and document the functional and physical characteristics of a system component, control changes to those characteristics, record and report change processing and implementation status, and verify compliance with specified requirements.

constraint: Something that establishes boundaries, restricts, limits, or obstructs any aspect of the project.

contract: A federal contract is an agreement between the federal government and a private entity, for-profit or nonprofit, to execute mandated services for a fee for the federal government. Federal contracts data contained in USAspending.gov are based on the Federal Procurement Data System (FPDS) government database. FPDS includes procurement contract transactions reported by approximately 65 U.S. government or executive branch departments, bureaus, agencies, and commissions and summarizes who bought what, from whom, and where.

contractor: Entity that performs the service mandated by a contract with a federal agency. In some cases, the service will actually be performed by a subcontractor, subject to the approval of and conditions set by the contracting agency. In other cases, such subcontracting is not permitted under the contract. Contractors are usually for-profit companies, but they also include universities, independent nonprofits, hospitals, and other types of entities.

core mission areas: Unique service areas that define the mission or purpose of the agency. Core mission areas are defined by the agency business model (e.g., tactical defense, air transportation, energy supply, pollution prevention and control, and emergency response).

cost-benefit analysis: A comparison of the cost of the project to the benefits it would realize to determine whether the project or portion of the project should be undertaken.

critical success factor (CSF) interviewing: A process in which a series of strategic questions are asked to identify what objectives and goals need to be met in order for the project to demonstrate success.

cross-agency initiatives: OMB-sponsored initiatives, such as E-Gov initiatives, line-of-business (LOB) initiatives, and other government-wide initiatives, such as Internet Protocol Version 6 (IPv6) and Homeland Security Presidential Directive 12 (HSPD-12).

CRUD matrices: A tool used to cross reference the process model to the logical data model and to identify which business functions map to which data elements. CRUD is defined as follows: C (for *create*), R (for *replace*), U (for *update*), and D (for *delete*).

CSSQ: The interdependent quadruple constraints of the project (scope, cost, schedule, and quality), represented by project scope, project budget, project schedule, and quality management plan.

database: An integrated collection of data (entities and attributes) organized to avoid duplication of data and allow for easy retrieval.

database schema: A view of the physical database detailing the specifics of the tables, fields and their relationships, and identifying keys, indexes, and triggers.

data dictionary: Reference material that describes and defines each piece of data used in a system. This may include entity and attribute definitions, discuss relationship characteristics, and provide sizing information.

data flow diagram: A picture diagramming how data flows through a system. It depicts the external entities (which are sources or destinations of data), the processes that transform that data, and the places where the data are then stored.

Data Universal Numbering System (DUNS): The Data Universal Numbering System (DUNS) number is a unique nine-character identification number provided to entities interested in contracting with the federal government.

The numbers are distributed by the private company Dun and Bradstreet (D&B). Companies interested in contracting with the government must have a different nine-digit DUNS number for each physical location and different address in the company, as well as each legally distinct division that may be co-housed at the same address or location. Contact Dun and Bradstreet for more information.

decision trees: A branching chart showing the actions that occur from various combinations of conditions and decisions.

defect: A flaw in a system or system component that causes the system or component to fail to perform its required function.

defect tracking: The process of ensuring that all test cases have been executed successfully. If cases have not executed successfully and defects have been identified, a log is generated to track the defects so that the project team can correct them and perform a retest.

deliverable(s): A product or service satisfying one or more objectives of the project.

denial of service: The prevention of authorized access to resources or the delaying of time-critical operations.

differences between place of performance and contractor/recipient locations: The place-of-performance search shows the geographic area where the majority of the work was done under the award. The place-of-performance location is not necessarily the same as the address of the contractor/recipient. When you fill in a city, county, or state in the contractor/recipient search, you're searching for recipients whose address is located within that particular city, county, or state. When users fill in a city, county, or state in the place-of-performance search, USAspending.gov searches for work done in that geographic area. Therefore, searches by the same city, county, or state in both the place-of-performance search and contractor/recipient searches will yield two different results.

direct loans: Financial assistance provided through the lending of federal monies for a specific period of time, with a reasonable expectation of repayment. Such loans may or may not require the payment of interest.

direct payments: A classification of federal assistance spending in USAspending.gov. This classification of spending contains two types of payments—"specified use" and "unrestricted use."

Specified use: Financial assistance from the federal government provided directly to individuals, private firms, and other private institutions to encourage or subsidize a particular activity by conditioning the receipt of the assistance on a particular performance by the recipient. This does not include solicited contracts for the procurement of goods and services for the federal government.

Unrestricted use: Financial assistance from the federal government provided directly to beneficiaries who satisfy federal eligibility requirements with no restrictions being imposed on the recipient as to how the money is spent. Included are payments under retirement, pension, and compensatory programs.

due care: Managers and their organizations have a duty to provide for information security to ensure that the type of control, the cost of control, and the deployment of control are appropriate for the system being managed.

effort estimate: An estimate of the amount of effort necessary to perform each project task.

encryption: The coding of data either at its source or as part of a data stream to prevent unauthorized access to the data. For example, information transmitted over a telecommunications line is scrambled at one end and unscrambled at the other.

enterprise architecture (EA): A management practice for aligning resources to improve business performance and help agencies better execute their core missions. An EA describes the current and future state of the agency and lays out a plan for transitioning from the current state to the desired future state.

enterprise services: Common or shared IT services that support core mission areas and business services. Enterprise services are defined by the agency service component model and include the applications and service components used to achieve the purpose of the agency (e.g., knowledge management, records management, mapping/GIS, business intelligence, and reporting).

entity: A distinct object that is represented in the database containing source data or acting to collect data. An example would be a customer table.

entity relationship diagram (ERD): A pictorial representation of the relationships between entities. This diagram can be helpful in communicating information needs with business users and can also provide information to technical specialists for design of physical databases, foreign keys, business views, and so forth.

face value: Reflects the full amount of the loan award to the recipient.

federal assistance: Federal assistance represents a broad category of federal spending including direct payments to individuals (like Social Security), loans, insurance, and grants. A grant is a particular type of federal assistance spending. At times, USAspending.gov broadly refers to all federal assistance as simply "grants," mostly for display purposes (e.g., in the tabs at the top of the left-hand navigation bar).

Federal Assistance Award Data System (FAADS): One of the current databases maintained by the federal government to report information and data on all types of financial assistance awards made by federal agencies listed in the Catalog of Federal Domestic Assistance (see above). The data includes the type and amount of financial assistance, the type and location of the recipient, and the geographic place of performance. See the FAADS website for more information.

federal fiscal year: The federal government operates on a fiscal year that begins on October 1 and ends the following September 30. Fiscal years are notated with FYXXXX or FYXX. The year notates the calendar year when the fiscal year will end. For example, fiscal year 2007 (FY07) runs from October 1, 2006, through September 30, 2007.

Federal Procurement Data System (FPDS): The current database system the U.S. federal government uses to report information and data on all federal contracts. FPDS supplies the majority of the contracting data found in USAspending.gov. See www.fpds.gov for more information.

flowchart: A graphical representation of the flow and interaction of a process or system.

functional decomposition: The process of dividing higher-level functions into subfunctions and processes.

grant recipient: Any nonfederal entity, usually a state or local government, or a private, usually nonprofit organization, such as an educational or religious institution, a relief agency, or an individual.

grants: A classification of federal assistance spending in USAspending.gov. A federal grant is an authorized expenditure to a nonfederal entity for a defined public or private purpose in which services are not rendered to the federal government. This classification of spending comes in two types—"formula grants" and "project grants."

Formula grant: Allocations of money to states or their subdivisions in accordance with distribution formulas prescribed by law or administrative regulation, for activities of a continuing nature not confined to a specific project.

Project grants: The funding, for fixed or known periods, of specific projects. Project grants can include fellowships, scholarships, research grants, training grants, traineeships, experimental and demonstration grants, evaluation grants, planning grants, technical assistance grants, survey grants, and construction grants.

graphical user interface (GUI): The front-end of an application through which the user interacts with the system by utilizing buttons, the mouse, drop down menus, and so forth. The GUI is the face of the application where the user will see data displayed.

guaranteed loans: Programs in which the federal government makes an arrangement to indemnify a lender against part or all of any defaults by those responsible for repayment of loans.

hosting: A service in which a provider or organization may house an application and support the software and hardware needs required to run that application. This may also include the housing and management of a networking and or telecommunications infrastructure.

individual: One of the categories of recipient type in USAspending.gov for federal assistance (grants) is called "individuals." This designation comes from the government's FAADS database and refers to a person who receives federal assistance as an entity independent of any public or private institution. Examples of this type of spending would be Social Security retirement insurance payments to citizens, payments to individuals qualifying for food stamps, and other individual payments.

insurance: Financial assistance provided to assure reimbursement for losses sustained under specified conditions. Coverage may be provided directly by the federal government or through private carriers and may or may not involve the payment of premiums.

integrity: The security goal that generates the requirement for protection against either intentional or accidental attempts to violate data integrity (the property that data has when it has not been altered in an unauthorized manner) or system integrity (the quality that a system has when it performs its intended function in an unimpaired manner, free from unauthorized manipulation).

"invalid or blank": This usually means there are no data reported in the government database or there is an error in the data reported to the government.

issue management and escalation: A process for capturing, reporting, escalating, tracking, and resolving problems that occur as a project progresses.

IT-related risk: The net mission impact considering (1) the probability that a particular threat-source will exercise (accidentally trigger or intentionally exploit) a particular information system vulnerability, and (2) the resulting impact if this should occur. IT-related risks arise from legal liability or mission loss due to:

- Unauthorized (malicious or accidental) disclosure, modification, or destruction of information
- Unintentional errors and omissions
- IT disruptions due to natural or man-made disasters
- Failure to exercise due care and diligence in the implementation and operation of the IT system

IT security goal. See **security goals**

joint application design (JAD): A process that brings the project team, customers, and stakeholders together to clarify, define, and gain consensus on business requirements. JAD sessions are formal meetings involving a detailed agenda, visual aids, and a facilitator who moderates the session and an analyst who records the specifications. By utilizing JAD, customers become directly involved in the application design.

known versus unknown congressional districts: Each transaction is assigned to a congressional district (CD) (for federal assistance, the CD where the recipient is located, for federal contracts, both a CD where the contractor is located and one where the work takes place). Unfortunately, many records have either blank congressional districts or obviously incorrect ones (i.e., a bad state abbreviation or a district number that does not exist in that state). Since we don't have any way of knowing which CD these records apply to, they are grouped together as "unknown districts" within their state.

Many of the displays that show congressional districts on USAspending .gov do not display the unknown districts—for instance, the "Top 5 Known Congressional Districts" in the summary output does not. However, you should be aware that sometimes the amount which can't be assigned to any district and is, therefore, unknown is sometimes larger than that assigned to any known district.

loans: A classification of federal assistance spending in USAspending.gov. This classification of spending comes in two types—"direct loans" and "guaranteed loans."

local area network/wide area network (LAN/WAN): Local area networks provide a means to link multiple computers within a single location. LANs may be interconnected with one another or with wide area networks, using interface devices such as bridges, routers, and gateways. WANs provide a link for widely separated locations.

lessons learned: Information resulting from feedback on the project and based on the assessment of project performance that may benefit the project manager as well as managers and team members of similar projects.

matrix diagram: A format used to clarify or highlight the relationship between two factors. For example, the matrix diagram may be used during gap analysis to validate that all business requirements identified during JAD sessions have been accommodated in the process and logical data model deliverables. The matrix displays requirements down the left side of the grid, while processes or data elements are tracked across the top of the grid. A checkbox at the intersection of a requirement and a process or data element would indicate that the requirement has been successfully accounted for in a deliverable.

major agencies/other agencies: USAspending.gov has modified FAADS and FPDS data to streamline the display of federal government agencies. Rather than produce tables that include each subagency within the data, it is advantageous to be able to produce tables and output by "major" agency. These generally correspond to departments of the federal government, but some were also chosen because they have a large number of awards/contracts. See the "About the Data" section for more information.

mission: The mission of the organization drives the development of the business case. When the business case is developed, it will explain how the expected outcome of the project supports the organization's mission.

multi-tier/client-server (MT/CS): A client-server system architecture (see **Client-Server**), where a software application is decomposed into operational areas or layers (e.g., database, business objects, and presentation layers), which are then physically distributed across multiple computers.

negative numbers in USAspending.gov: Dollar amounts of awards in USAspending.gov are actually amounts of obligations and deobligations, which accounts for the appearance of negative dollar amounts in some parts of USAspending.gov. An obligation is a commitment to pay. A deobligation is "a downward adjustment of previously recorded obligations. This results from the cancellation of a project or contract, price revisions, or corrections of estimates previously recorded as obligations." When negative numbers appear in USAspending.gov, this means the amount of federal resources authorized to be spent has been reduced.

normalization: A process by which complex data relationships are simplified with the goal being to eliminate redundancies in the database design. This process simplifies data management and software development efforts while improving data consistency and optimizing system performance.

North American Industry Classification System (NAICS) Code: The NAICS codes are used as a categorization system within contracting data to give a higher level of detail about the type of economic or industrial output being done under a contract. These codes were created jointly by the United States, Canada, and Mexico and are assigned by the federal government according to the NAICS.

original subsidy cost: Reflects the net present value of expected cash flows to and from the government over the life of the guarantee, excluding administrative costs. Reestimates are preformed to update the subsidy cost for actual performance and future expectations as long as there are loans outstanding.

"other"—type of assistance: The Federal Assistance Award Data System (FAADS) classifies some federal assistance spending into an "other" category.

FAADS defines this category as other reimbursable, contingent, intangible, or indirect financial assistance.

outsourcing: The practice of contracting out a project, a portion of a business, or an IT operation.

parallel testing: The concurrent testing of both the current and new system with identical data to compare the outputs for consistency and accuracy.

partial year: In some cases, not all data for a given fiscal year is available on USASpending.gov. In such cases, the quarters for which data is available are indicated. This is always the case for the current fiscal year.

peer code reviews: A formal, repeatable review technique that gathers peers to examine a deliverable or work product for defects so they can be corrected early in the development cycle.

"percent of total": Some column headers are titled "percent of total" or "% of total." This column lists the percent of total dollars allotted to that entity out of the total amount of money in either the contracting system (contracts) or the financial assistance system (grants/other or loans), not the total in the entire database of USAspending.gov.

performance goals: Target performance measures and time frames. Goals should be outcome-oriented and targets should be ambitious. For more information on performance goals, refer to the Government Performance and Results Act (GPRA), OMB Circular A-11, and the PART.

performance improvement life cycle: A three-phase process agencies can use to close performance gaps and improve the overall performance of the agency. The life cycle is made up of these phases: architect, invest, and implement.

performance measurements: Actual results generated by the implementation of enhanced business and information management solutions. Results are monitored and measured to verify target benefits resulting from the implementation of business and information management solutions.

phase: A series of processes organized into a distinct stage of project development. The end of a project phase usually coincides with the approval of a major deliverable.

post-implementation report: A summary of information gathered as a result of conducting the post-implementation review. The report documents the successes and failures of the project and provides a historical record of the planned and actual budget and schedule. It also contains recommendations for improvement to be used by other projects of similar size and scope.

process: A series of tasks performed to bring about a result.

process flow diagram: A diagram used to analyze the flow of a process, find problems, create solutions, and measure efficiency. Symbols are used in a visual representation that can quickly point out delays, unnecessary events, and other problem areas.

program assessment rating tool (PART): A review of a program to help identify the program's strengths and weaknesses to inform funding and management decisions aimed at making the program more effective. A PART review looks at all factors that affect and reflect a program's performance, including its purpose and design; performance measurement, evaluations, and strategic planning; program management; and program results and accountability.

program management plan: Establishes the overall approach to managing the program. Describes the program, deliverables, related management plans and procedures, and methods used to plan, monitor, control, and improve the project development efforts.

project: A temporary endeavor undertaken to create a unique product or service.

project audit: A process designed to ensure that the quality assurance activities defined in project planning are being implemented and to determine whether quality standards are being met.

project life cycle: A collection of phases whose number and names are determined by the control needs of the performing organization.

project management: Direction and coordination of human and material resources for a project using management techniques to achieve cost, scope, schedule, quality, and customer satisfaction objectives.

project repository: A collection or archive of all information and documents from the project.

proof-of-concept: A technique used to confirm the feasibility of one or more components of the technical solution. A proof-of-concept approach helps to minimize cost by "testing the waters" first on an idea or a design.

prototyping: The process of building a small working version of a system design as a means of hedging risk and attaining customer buy-in. Prototyping can provide a better understanding of customer requirements, validate those requirements, and sometimes perform as a proof-of-concept tool.

pseudo-code: A tool for specifying program logic in English-like readable form, without conforming to the syntactical rules of any particular programming language.

quality assurance: Evaluation of project performance on a regular basis to ensure that the project will satisfy the established quality standards.

quality control: Monitoring of project results to ensure compliance with the appropriate established quality standards and to eliminate causes of noncompliance.

quality standards: Criteria established to ensure that each deliverable created meets a certain level of quality agreed to by the customer and project manager.

rapid application development (RAD): A technique that allows users to participate in an iterative design and development process. Conceptually, the project "loops" through the design, construction, and acceptance stages, followed by a redesign, revised construction, acceptance, and so on.

Recovery Act (ARRA) data: From 2009 onward, data submitted by agencies may include awards related to Recovery Act (ARRA) as well.

regression testing: The process of testing new software components in an environment where other existing modules (or the entire application) are also tested to ensure that the new components do not negatively impact any existing software. Prior to a release to production, the project team will execute test cases that have previously been successfully executed to determine that the new piece of software works within the context of the system.

release management: A process used to manage the release of software into different test environments. It is typical for projects to identify a release engineer or department to monitor versions of software and their release into the next environment. For example, if modifications to existing code are made and tested in the QA environment, the process to move that code to acceptance would be executed according to the procedure outlined in the release management process.

risk: An anticipated event with the potential to positively or negatively affect the project.

risk assessment: A process to identify which risks are likely to affect a project, documenting them, and determining which require a mitigation plan.

risk management: The total process of identifying, controlling, and mitigating information system–related risks. It includes risk assessment, cost-benefit analysis, and the selection, implementation, testing, and security evaluation of safeguards. This overall system security review considers both effectiveness and efficiency, including impact on the mission and constraints due to policy, regulations, and laws.

security: Information system security is a system characteristic and a set of mechanisms that span the system both logically and physically.

security goals: The five security goals are integrity, availability, confidentiality, accountability, and assurance.

segment: Segments are individual elements of the enterprise describing core mission areas and common or shared business services and enterprise services. Segments are defined by the enterprise architecture.

segment architecture: Detailed results-oriented architecture (baseline and target) and a transition strategy for a portion or segment of the enterprise.

segment architecture process: Multiple-phase methodology to develop segment architecture work products. Each phase provides an increasing level of architectural detail to support IT investment decision-making and solutions development and implementation. The *Concept of Operations for Cross-Agency Initiatives* provides an example of a multiple-phase architecture development methodology.

skills inventory: A record of the skills learned and used on the project by the project team.

Software Engineering Institute (SEI): The Software Engineering Institute (SEI) is a federally funded research and development center sponsored by the U.S. Department of Defense through the Office of the Under Secretary of Defense for Acquisition, Technology, and Logistics, or OUSD (AT&L). The SEI's core purpose is to help others make measured improvements in their software engineering capabilities. (See www.sei.cmu.edu.)

software quality assurance: This is (1) a planned and systematic pattern of all actions necessary to provide adequate confidence that a software work product conforms to established technical requirements, and (2) a set of activities designed to evaluate the process by which software work products are developed and/or maintained. (Derived from IEEE-STED-610.)

solution architecture: An architecture for an individual IT system that is part of a segment. A solution architecture is reconciled to the segment architecture above it.

storyboarding: A technique to use during a JAD session to aide in the brainstorming process. Ideas are written down on cards and posted immediately on a wall by the participants. Once all the ideas are posted, several passes of categorization take place. Some ideas may be dropped via group consensus; others may be enlarged or improved.

strategic plan: A formal document produced by the performing organization outlining organizational goals and direction over a designated period of time. The strategic plan drives the proposed solution developed during project origination.

structured English: A precise form of English that uses the logical structures of structured coding to represent policies and procedures.

subsidiary companies in USAspending.gov: Many large companies may control or incorporate other smaller companies, called subsidiaries. Subsidiaries may have a different name from the parent company for a variety of business and legal reasons.

USAspending.gov groups subsidiaries of larger companies under the "contractor names" list in each contractor profile page—available under the "medium (contractor profiles)" level of detail. Contracts for subsidiaries are grouped together under the parent company profile pages in USAspending.gov. It is possible to search for the names of subsidiaries in USAspending.gov and see all individual contracts for all subsidiaries by choosing increased levels of detail in the output.

system context diagram: A graphical representation of how the system fits into the current environment. It shows all interfaces to and from the system and allows the project team to visualize how the new system will interact with other systems, outside entities, and consumers.

system load analysis: A process to ensure that the application or system developed will operate under peak usage conditions. For example, if transaction levels are consistent every day and every month except during peak holiday hours, system load analysis will help identify the performance requirements necessary to avoid failure for those instances. It is important to consider these requirements during the requirements analysis and design phases of the SDLC.

target architecture: Describes the future ("to be") state of the agency in terms of performance, business, data, services, and technology.

task: A single piece of work itemized in the project schedule to which effort and resources must be applied.

test cases: Individual test scenarios that may be executed singularly or in combination to test modules or strings of modules. Test cases should be developed by the project team to test what is expected, as well as what should not be expected.

test plan: A series of test cases that, when compiled into a whole, constitute a testing plan for the project team to follow. A well-formulated test plan should ensure that all internal components and system interfaces operate as they should according to the functional and technical specifications.

test scripts: Pieces of code that when executed for a test case or a test plan are automatic. The advantage of developing test scripts are to help save time when testing components on a regular basis with large amounts of data or when planning to execute a test plan on a recurring basis, such as with regression testing.

threat: The potential for a threat-source to exercise (accidentally trigger or intentionally exploit) a specific vulnerability.

threat analysis: The examination of threat-sources against system vulnerabilities to determine the threats for a particular system in a particular operational environment.

threat-source: Either (1) intent and method targeted at the intentional exploitation of a vulnerability, or (2) a situation and method that may accidentally trigger a vulnerability.

total quality management (TQM): Both a philosophy and a set of guiding principles that represent the foundation of a continuously improving organization. The application of quantitative methods and human resources to improve the materials and services supplied to an organization, all the processes within an organization, and the degree to which the needs of the customer are met, now and in the future.

transactions: The issuance, renewal, or modification of a single contract between a contractor and the federal government for the performance of designated tasks. The number of transactions is not equal to the total number of contracts. One contract could have hundreds or thousands of transactions during the course of the contract.

transition strategy: A multiyear plan to implement target architecture for all or part of an enterprise. Defines logical dependencies between transition activities and helps to define the relative priority of each activity.

unified modeling language (UML): UML is a modeling language used to define a system prior to construction, much like a blueprint is used prior to building a house. It allows the project team to specify, visualize, and document an application, including its structure and design, in a way that meets all of the user business requirements. There are several tools on the market that utilize the UML methodology. For more information see www.uml.org.

use cases: A modeling technique within UML, used to define business requirements from the point of view of the user. Use cases help provide an understanding of the functionality of the system and interactions among objects and form the basis of both system construction and system testing. A use case is a sequence of actions that an actor (usually a person), but perhaps an external entity (such as another system), performs within a system to achieve a particular goal.

vision statement: Summary description of the target business and information management environment to fulfill requirements, address change drivers, and achieve performance improvements.

vulnerability: A flaw or weakness in system security procedures, design, implementation, or internal controls that could be exercised (accidentally triggered or intentionally exploited) and result in a security breach or a violation of the system's security policy.

walkthroughs: A technique for performing a formal review, which takes place at review and inspection points throughout the life cycle being utilized, to observe and verify what has been accomplished.

work breakdown structure (WBS): A grouping of project elements or components that defines the total project scope. A WBS is deliverable-oriented and each descending level represents an increasingly detailed definition of a component.

work flow diagram: A graphical representation of the organization's work-flow, which is helpful when documenting the current working model and when looking for opportunities to improve a process.

References

"Architectural Principles for the Federal Government." http://colab.cim3.net/file/work/BPC/2006-08-21/FedArchPrinciples2006_6_23_final.doc.

Concept of Operations for Cross-Agency Initiatives. www.whitehouse.gov/sites/default/files/omb/assets/egov_docs/LoB_ConOps_1_0.pdf.

Doran, George T. 1981. "There's a S.M.A.R.T. Way to Write Management's Goals and Objectives." *Management Review* 70 (11): 35–36.

Executive Guide: Measuring Performance and Demonstrating Results for Information Technology Investments. www.gao.gov/special.pubs/ai98089.pdf.

FEA Consolidated Reference Model, Version 2.0 (FY08 Budget Formulation). www.apdip.net/projects/gif/country/US-GIF.pdf.

Federal Enterprise Architecture Practice Guidance. www.whitehouse.gov/omb/e-gov/fea/.

Federal Enterprise Architecture Reference Models. www.whitehouse.gov/omb/e-gov/fea/.

Federal Transition Framework. www.egov.gov/ftf.

How to Use the Performance Reference Model, Version 1. www.whitehouse.gov/sites/default/files/omb/assets/fea_docs/FEA_CRM_v23_Final_Oct_2007_Revised.pdf.

National Institute of Standards and Technology Special Publication 800-14. *Generally Accepted Principles and Practices for Securing Information Technology Systems.*

National Institute of Standards and Technology Special Publication 800-27. *Engineering Principles for IT Security.*

New York State Office for Technology. 2003. *New York State Project Management Guidebook, Release 2.* New York: New York State Office for Technology. www.cio.ny.gov/pmmp/guidebook2/.

Office of Government Commerce (OGC), HM Treasury, U.K. Government. www.ogc.gov.uk.

OMB Circular A-11. www.whitehouse.gov/omb/circulars/a11/current_year/a11_toc .html.

OMB Enterprise Architecture Assessment Framework. www.whitehouse.gov/omb/ e-gov/eaaf/.

Practical Guide to Federal Enterprise Architecture. www.whitehouse.gov/omb/E-Gov/ pgfsoa.

Program Assessment Rating Tool (PART). www.whitehouse.gov/omb/expectmore/ part.html.

Wholey, Joseph S. 1998. "Performance Measurement and Performance-Based Management: An Interview with Joseph S. Wholey."

Index

About the Author

Ira S. Sachs has over 20 years of experience in enterprise architecture, information systems development, capital planning, strategic planning, business and software process analysis, reengineering, performance management, and program management. He currently leads enterprise architecture competency for High Performance Technologies, Inc.(HPTi), assisting clients in planning and integrating enterprise-wide IT. He is a recognized expert in this field, speaking at conferences nationally and internationally. Prior to joining HPTi, he was the chief architect for the U.S. Department of Education and assessed large, mission-critical information systems investments for the Government Accountability Office. He has assisted many federal agencies in preparing enterprise architecture and CPIC plans and has focused more recently on business performance management. Mr. Sachs was a key contributor to the development of IEEE-Std-1471-2000, Recommended Practice for Architectural Description of Software-Intensive Systems, IEE Std 1016-2009, Systems Design—Software Design Descriptions, and he provided technical review on the Federal Segment Architecture Methodology (FSAM). Additionally, he was a contributing author to *Capital Planning and Investment Control (CPIC) Overview—The Definitive Guide to Completing the OMB Exhibit 300*. Mr. Sachs has a B.S. in mechanical engineering from the University of Maryland and an M.B.A. in finance from Loyola University.